We are entering a new phase in the search for unity in the Church. For more than thirty years pioneering conversations have been going on between pairs of churches or communities, and multilaterally. These have put forward solutions to old disagreements which have shown a remarkable closeness, and which are beginning to make possible the building of a new 'ecumenical' theology. By exploring the methods used by ecumenists, G. R. Evans indicates which obstacles exist in the face of unity, and illustrates how these might be overcome successfully. By making judicious use of interdenominational archival material, and drawing apposite conclusions – from this, and from the appropriate secondary literature – the author provides a timely resource for all those interested in recent ecumenical progress.

When it comes to taking actual steps towards unity there is often a drawing-back from the final commitment. This study examines the way the methodology of ecumenical theology is being taken into the lives of the churches, from the point of view of the experience which has been reported so far. Dr Evans shows that finding the methodology as we go along, the discovery of the process, is part of what must happen now and that it is not enough to engage in common action but we must work steadily on a shared theology, as we move into the future.

Method in Ecumenical Theology is the third of a trilogy of Dr Evans's books addressing questions relating to ecumenical dialogue; the others are *Problems of Authority in the Reformation Debates* and *The Church and the Churches*.

METHOD IN ECUMENICAL THEOLOGY

METHOD IN ECUMENICAL THEOLOGY

The lessons so far

The lessons so far

G. R. EVANS

CAMBRIDGE
UNIVERSITY PRESS

Published by the Press Syndicate of the University of Cambridge
The Pitt Building, Trumpington Street, Cambridge CB2 1RP
40 West 20th Street, New York, NY 10011-4211, USA
10 Stamford Road, Oakleigh, Melbourne 3166, Australia

© Cambridge University Press

First published 1996

Printed in Great Britain at the University Press, Cambridge

A catalogue record for this book is available from the British Library

Library of Congress cataloguing in publication data
Evans, G. R. (Gillian Rosemary)
Method in ecumenical theology: the lessons so far / G. R. Evans.
p.   cm.
Includes bibliographical references and index.
ISBN 0 521 55304 0 (hardback)
1. Christian union.   2. Church – Unity.   3. Ecumenical movement.
4. Theology – Methodology.   I. Title.
BX8.2.E83   1996
262′001′1 – dc20
95–2048
CIP

ISBN 0 521 55304 0 hardback

Contents

This study was partly prompted by the conversation with J. M. R. Tillard from which there also grew the germ of the idea for the *Festschrift* in his honour published a few months before this book. I do not know whether he will approve of what I have written here, but I would like him to know how profoundly I, like all who write on ecumenical subjects, am in his debt.

Preface

At a recent small meeting of representatives from Eastern and Western Europe which was brought together as a forum for the exchange of ideas on European cultural identity I found myself the object of the profound concern of one of the delegates. It was obvious to him that I shared his faith. 'If you have seen the light why do you not join us?' he argued. I told him that I did indeed share his faith, but that I did so within the Anglican Church. I should feel equally at home in other churches too. But for me as an individual to become a Lutheran or Roman Catholic or Reformed or Orthodox would not help the cause of unity, because it would do nothing to bring the existing separated churches together. I argued that my job was to stay where I happened to be, and work for the mutual understanding without which there can be no meeting and no convergence. I could, as it were, come alone, or in company, and it seemed to me that Christ's intention is that Christians should meet in company.

From his point of view there was only one true Church and, although I saw it to be the true Church, I was refusing to belong to it. From mine, too, there is only one Church, and I am already in it just as he is. Ecumenists will recognise the encounter. It takes place, with variations, between Christians of all sorts of traditions when they first confront the ecumenical imperative.

It underlined how much there is still to do in the winning of minds to the patient processes of learning to listen on which all ecumenism is founded. But in its way it marked progress, because in that conversation I became, for one individual who had never thought ecumenically before, a fellow-Christian with my heart in the right place, even though one who puzzlingly saw the implications of what was required by that position differently. From such tiny beginnings ecumenical growth begins. The minute and intimate and perhaps at the time frustrating encounter is not to be despised. Ecumenical method may come to take a large and eventually quite systematic view of the way forward. But it is still experimental, and experiment is experience.

In this study I have tried to review the present position in ecumenical methodology from the point of view of the experience which has been reported so far. Behind the abstractions lies a wealth of trial and error in the lives of hundreds of individuals who have become caught up despite themselves in what must for any Christian be the great cause of fulfilling the Christ's stated intention that his Church should be one.

Abbreviations

A–O, Moscow	Anglican–Orthodox, *The Moscow Statement* (1976)
A–R	Anglican–Reformed
ARCIC I	The First Anglican–Roman Catholic International Commission
ARCIC II	The Second Anglican–Roman Catholic International Commission
ARCIC *AI*	ARCIC I, *Authority in the Church I*
ARCIC *E*	ARCIC I, *Eucharistic Doctrine*
ARCIC *M*	ARCIC I, *Ministry and Ordination*
BEM	*Baptism, Eucharist and Ministry*, the Lima Report of the World Council of Churches Commission on Faith and Order, 1982
B–R	Baptist–Reformed
Churches Respond to BEM	*World Council of Churches, Churches Respond to BEM*, (Geneva, 1986–), Vols 1– .
Congar, *Divided Christendom*	Y. Congar, *Chrétiens désunis* (Paris, 1937), published in English as *Divided Christendom* (London, 1939)
Congar, *Dialogue between Christians*	Y. Congar, *Chrétiens en dialogue* (Paris, 1966), tr. P. Loretz and published in English as *Dialogue between Christians* (London, 1966)
Frere, *Malines*	Walter Frere, *Recollections of Malines* (London, 1935)
Growth	*Growth in Agreement: Reports and Agreed Statements of Ecumenical Conversation on a World Level*, ed. H. Meyer, L. Vischer (London/Geneva, 1984)
Halifax, *Malines*	*The Conversations at Malines. Original Documents*, ed. Lord Halifax (London, 1930)

Lambeth	Conferences cited from the Lambeth Conference Reports
L–RC	Lutheran–Roman Catholic
M–RC	Methodist–Roman Catholic
Nichols, *Congar*	A. Nichols, *Yves Congar* (London,1989)
P–RC	Pentecostalist–Roman Catholic
Stacpoole	*Vatican II by those who were there*, ed. A. Stacpoole (London, 1986)
Stormon	*Towards the Healing of Schism: the Sees of Rome and Constantinople: Public Statements and Correspondence between the Holy See and the Ecumenical Patriarchate 1958–1984*, ed. E. J. Stormon (New York, 1987)
UR	Vatican II, *Unitatis Redintegratio*
Vatican II	*Documents of the Second Vatican Council*, ed. Flannery (revised edition, Dublin, 1988)

Introduction: the 'winter of ecumenism'?[1]

In the late 1960s it began to look as though it would be possible to achieve within our lifetimes a definitive coming together in unity between a number of the existing separated communions. After the Second Vatican Council

> rapid developments in the doctrinal dialogues initiated at the request of the protestant observers at Vatican II, and encouraged by Pope Paul VI, showed that substantial agreements could be reached in areas that had seemed to be insurmountable barriers . . . the progress of the bilateral doctrinal dialogues indicated that the Churches of the Reformation and the Roman Catholic Church could be reconciled at least to the extent that the reasons for the original division were resolvable . . . those involved in the dialogues began to hope that Christian unity might actually be achieved within a generation.[2]

But in many cases the churches which joined in this enterprise so eagerly at first are not proving able to make wholeheartedly their own the agreements arrived at through the dialogues; and consequently they cannot act out such agreements in actually moving towards union.[3] When it comes to turning the (real enough) experience of mutual affection into ecclesial union, everything stops short and the parties tend to retreat towards the familiar ground of their life in division.[4]

Parallels with recent experience in the European Union irresistibly suggest themselves. All is goodwill and convergence until a point is

---

[1] *The Tablet*, Leader, 13 January 1990.
[2] J. C. Murray, 'Ecumenism: the next steps', *One in Christ*, 25 (1989), 163–8, p. 163.
[3] Lukas Vischer suggests that 'one can speak with reason today of a growing discrepancy between the extensive agreement reached in the various dialogues and the actual situation of the Churches' . . . 'Consensus is not finding the open ears and hearts needed for reception.' L. Vischer, 'The reception of consensus in the ecumenical movement', *One in Christ*, 17 (1981), 294–305, pp. 294–5.
[4] 'Today the Churches are once more laying renewed emphasis on their own identity and tradition'. L. Vischer, 'The reception of consensus in the ecumenical movement', *One in Christ*, 17 (1981), 294–305, pp. 294–5.

reached (as with the Maastricht treaty of the early 1990s) where those
who had made a commitment to come together begin to see
themselves as perhaps having to sacrifice their identity and its
distinctiveness – and with it perhaps their autonomy – to a common
identity under a single administration. Then there is resistance and
withdrawal. We are, in other words, facing ecumenically a problem
with roots as deep as those which nourish entrenched nationalisms,
with all their potential for warfare. But there is the difference that the
Christian commitment to the search for unity is not prompted by
expediency, or by economic or political interest. It is an imperative
with the force of the very essence of Christianity behind it.

Vischer made the comments I began with in a footnote in 1981.
They can be made a decade and a half later, with even more force and
puzzlement. One author speaks of 'disillusionment', 'profound
scepticism', 'resignation'.[5] But he can also suggest that some of this is
in fact a sign of progress. 'The ecumenical journey is like travelling
along the road to Emmaus, sharing one another's disillusionments
and expectations. It is not insignificant where one is located on that
road.'[6] 'Every ecumenical advance will unavoidably create tension
and fermentation within the churches',[7] but that can be a useful
tension, and in its turn creative of advance. J. M. R. Tillard argues
that apparent failures are themselves a phenomenon of ecumenical
theology which ought to be taken into account in discussion of its
processes. 'Wave upon wave rolling endlessly toward the shore,
without ever producing the swell-tide that might break down the
dykes of division . . . this state of affairs, has not yet been taken
seriously enough in ecumenical theological discussions.'[8] Failure or
deferred success have their own dynamics. They not only change the
course along which past events seemed to be leading; they also alter
the direction of subsequent events.

But ecumenical problems solved create new ones.[9] They are also

[5] J. E. Vercruysse, 'Prospects for Christian unity', *One in Christ*, 26 (1990), 185–200, p. 185.
[6] J. E. Vercruysse, 'Prospects for Christian unity', *One in Christ*, 26 (1990), 185–200, p. 186.
[7] J. E. Vercruysse, 'Prospects for Christian unity', *One in Christ*, 26 (1990), 185–200, p. 188.
[8] In his view, this is a warning that 'organic, lasting unity cannot be effected simply by doctrinal consensus, no matter how profound this may be. It will not be realized by the declarations of official authority figures, no matter how representative these may be. Without what we may call "evangelical space", deriving from the life of grace, the most promising ecumenical dialogues will peter out. Frequently, they will only contribute to a rebirth of hardened reactions'. J. M. R. Tillard, 'Elements of unity in recent ecumenical discussion', *One in Christ*, 14 (1978), 94–105, pp. 94–5.
[9] 'Ecumenical progress becomes harder, not easier, because it cannot be a mere linear progress in the negotiating of differences'. M–RC, *The Denver Report* (1971),5; *Growth*, p. 308. See, too, John d'Arcy May, 'Integral ecumenism', *Journal of Ecumenical Studies*, 25 (1988), 573–91.

harder ones. At best the going will get more difficult. The easy-to-resolve and merely 'apparent' differences have already for the most part been got out of the way. An analogy can be drawn with learning languages. 'After the first painful steps, we are delighted to find ourselves being understood and understanding other people.'[10] Then we discover it is not so easy after all and that communication has run into difficulties. 'The ecumenical journey is sometimes compared to the ascent of a high and difficult mountain. In the early stages of such a climb, one makes rapid and relatively easy progress; then the going gets more difficult and in the final stages every move forward is the result of great effort combined with special technical skill.'[11]

The ecumenical dialogues between churches have on the whole been confronting the now increasingly recognised 'difficult' questions squarely.[12] This has by now had the result of making it possible to list topics which have become recurrent issues, or perhaps it would be more exact to call them stubborn. These topics sometimes seem to the participants in a given conversation to have been resolved; but they can be expected always to cause recalcitrant movements when the time comes to consider seriously any move forward into unity. Making an analysis of the Responses to the *Baptism, Eucharist and Ministry* (Lima) text of the World Council of Churches, Geoffrey Wainwright noticed such areas of repeated concern: about the meaning of 'the Word'; 'liturgical structures';[13] 'Word and Spirit'; sacraments;[14] signs and effects; symbols; *katabasis* and *anabasis*; the

[10] M. Richards, 'Twenty-five years of Anglican–Roman Catholic dialogue – where do we go from here?', *One in Christ*, 18 (1992), 126–35, p. 127.
[11] 'The early stage, in which we sought to know each other better and to rid ourselves of the prejudices that had bedevilled our relationships, proved to be relatively easy. We discovered just how much we had in common ... Our ascent of the ecumenical mountain has now entered a new stage and the going becomes more difficult, simply because the ground that we seek to conquer is all the more important for the successful outcome of our endeavours. Our journey is one of exploration ... We know the destination that we seek to reach, yet there is much about it that is still a mystery for us.' Edward Cassidy, 'The uphill ecumenical journey', *Catholic International* 2 (July 1991), p. 653.
[12] Hans Küng describes his time as director of the Institute of Ecumenical Research at Tübingen in terms of a working 'systematically for the convergence of divergent theologies without attempting to avoid questions hitherto regarded as taboo.' Hans Küng, 'Why I remain a Catholic', *Journal of Ecumenical Studies*, 17 (1980),141–7, p. 143.
[13] Here the problem concerns not the differences of rite, which have always tended to be relatively non-controversial, but the fact that 'most Protestant responses to *BEM* assert with some vigour the integrity of the preaching service. The Baptist Union of Scotland reports that "in many of our Churches the Lord's Supper is observed every Sunday as an additional service following *a full worship service*".' On variation in rites and ceremonies, see Thirty-Nine Articles, Article 34.
[14] Where he notes Protestants tend to say that *BEM* places too much emphasis and Roman Catholics not enough on 'sacramentality'.

presence of Christ in the Eucharist; ordination as a sacramental sign; episcopal succession as a sign; the mystery of the Church; the Kingdom of God.[15]

There is remarkable consistency of attitude in each community about these 'issues which will not lie down', because certain positions have come to be identified with its very ecclesial being. That is the most obvious reason why the old concerns often persist through dialogue to resurface again and again. In the Lima text *Baptism, Eucharist and Ministry* itself some implicitly contradictory points are left standing side by side in tacit recognition of the existence of these intractables. 'Many differences of theology, liturgy and practice are connected with the varying frequency with which the Holy Communion is celebrated', comments the Eucharist text (30). On the reservation of the consecrated bread and wine, *BEM* can ask only that 'each church should respect the practices and piety of the others' and suggest that 'the primary intention of reserving the elements is their distribution among the sick and those who are absent' and that 'the best way of showing respect for the elements served in the eucharistic celebration is by their consumption, without excluding their use for communion of the sick' (32).

As a result of lingering difficulties of this sort there will sometimes be a call to go 'back to the drawing board'. Thus it is possible to go back on, or to reopen for question, or to betray, what had seemed a firm agreement not only about content but about the very method by which it has been arrived at. When after a decade Rome gave its official response to *The Final Report* of ARCIC it expressed disquiet about methodological fundamentals to a point where one commentator remarked that 'the Vatican Response will seem to many Anglicans to challenge the hitherto agreed method established and agreed by Paul VI and Michael Ramsey.'[16] Again, this is not as discouraging as it might seem. It is now in fact impossible to go back to the situation of half a century ago precisely because the talking and the agreement have happened. But it is bound to create a sense of taking two steps forward and one back.

We are now entering a new phase. It is clear that we have to take a longer-term view and think again about methods of proceeding.

[15] G. Wainwright, 'Word and sacrament in the Churches' response to the Lima text', *One in Christ*, 24 (1988), 304–27.
[16] Which Christopher Hill identifies as 'founded upon the Gospels and on the ancient common traditions', *Catholic International*, 3 (1992).

Several straightforward reasons can be suggested why ecumenical effort is apparently not getting the results of union which its solid achievements of agreement seemed to promise when they were arrived at, beyond this perhaps primary and very human one of the need to cling to a familiar identity when the alternative seems a leap into the unknown. Loss or dimming of hope, and withdrawal from commitment are both associated with fear. These two negative reactions manifest themselves respectively in the committed ecumenist who sees what looked promising prove to be, for the moment at least, not promising at all; and in the Christians who have not been involved in the process up to now, and who fear that rapprochement must 'constitute a threat to all that is distinctive and true in their own traditions'.[17] There is an intimate relationship between these two negative responses, and it lies, paradoxically, in the very fact of the progress, which creates a changing and frightening scene, with a number of retreating figures upon it.

We might see all this in terms of barriers, standing between hope and fulfilment, which we have to identify and remove. Certainly such blockages are detectable from time to time.[18] But it is helpful, I think, to pose the question differently. We ought to ask 'Why is ecumenism subject to repeating patterns of hope dashed, to the point where dispirited professional ecumenists are commonly heard to speak of "ecumenical gloom"?' Since the same ecumenists are not moved by this experience to give up – I know of no one who has once become committed to the ecumenical cause who has abandoned it – there must be a positive and constructive way of reading these events.[19] Central here is the realisation, already referred to, that setbacks are still marks of progress, for they do not take us right back to the beginning. In fact, they reveal solid achievements still in place. Anyone who compares the ease of ecumenical intercourse today with the situation thirty years ago must be struck by that.

But a large part of the answer undoubtedly lies in taking our time and a long-term view. The ecumenical task is enormous and we have to adopt a timescale appropriate to the scale of the problems. On that

[17] Conclusion to *The Final Report* of ARCIC I.
[18] 'A point of view is not ecumenical because it naively believes that obstacles to unity are, after all, not a serious matter.' Elwyn A. Smith, Editorial, *Journal of Ecumenical Studies*, 4 (1967), p. 301.
[19] There can be no place for loss of hope or for complacency. 'Whoever thinks that the present state of ecumenical relations is either so bad that no decisive improvement is possible, or so good that no decisive improvement is necessary, is acting in opposition to hope.' L–RC, *Growth*, p. 220, para.28.

proper scale, the setbacks look like small interruptions and not major disasters. It is rather like the problem which confronted Augustine of Hippo in the fourth century, when educated non-Christians asked him how, if Christians were right in their faith, their God could allow a Christian Roman Empire to fall into barbarism at the hands of pagan invaders. He wrote *The City of God* to answer the question and it obliged him, too, to learn to look at things on a sufficiently grand plan to see God's long-term purposes at work even at a time of profound discouragement.

If that is the way we should look at it, we also need to ask what positive purposes a delay is serving. Congar was optimistic that 'active' patience is not just marking time. 'In all great things delay is necessary for their maturation.'[20] There are things we come to see only because we have to persevere in order to grasp them, because we ourselves have to mature in perception before we can see. At present delay is visibly forcing ecumenical stocktaking, adjustment, learning-processes of great subtlety; and harder effort, deeper commitment. 'Ecumenism is mostly struggle.'[21] 'We do not find cynicism. We find frustration and struggle, and we find commitment and faith, and we find profound insight and vision for what ought to be done.'[22]

But there are also dangers in being held up, and seeing expectation frustrated. Fashions in ecumenical priorities change as delay makes us restless to be doing something which will get results, with a visibly desirable purpose and where progress can be seen. That can involve abandoning, or pushing away out of sight, the hope of attaining a more perfect union. One form of such 'giving up' is to decide to stop worrying about 'unity across doctrinal and structural barriers' and concentrate solely upon common action about 'concerns that press on Christians from the wider human community'.[23] In other words, it is argued that finding a shared theology and a shared order is not as important as was thought; and that energies ought now simply to concentrate on common action. This has been a strong temptation. It is obviously true that Christians ought to be loving their neighbours

---

[20] Congar, *Dialogue between Christians*, p. 44.
[21] 'Ecumenism today. A survey by the RC/WCC Joint Working Group', *One in Christ*, 11 (1975), 30–87, p. 87.
[22] 'Ecumenism today. A survey by the RC/WCC Joint Working Group', *One in Christ*, 11 (1975), 30–87, p. 87.
[23] G. Gassmann, 'The relations between bilateral and multilateral dialogues', *Journal of Ecumenical Studies*, 23 (1986), 365–76, p. 380.

and caring actively for the needs of the world. And this often proves to be something they can relatively easily do together without old divisions seeming to matter. But this is a temptation which ought to be resisted, because it involves settling for something much less than a common life. 'The greatest scandal . . . is not the lack of generosity of the People of God in its service of humanity.'[24] Tillard is vigorous on this point. 'It is easier here and now to *work* together than to *be* together the one communion of faith that Christ wills . . . Bilateral dialogues force Christian communities to go directly to their most demanding task. The doctrinal agreements they are preparing tend to prevent the Churches from reducing the Church of God on earth to a purely caritative body. To deal with problems such as justification, baptism, eucharist, ministry, and authority, amounts to a recognition of the essential importance of the inner being of the Church of God.'[25] They implicitly refuse to see it as an organisation so totally oriented toward the service of humanity as to be deprived of any serious internal finality.[26] 'If, at the end of the process, the kind of unity the dialogues help to produce is not rooted in these most demanding issues but is made of easy political compromises, ecumenism itself will have worked against the truth of the gospel . . . it will have been an instrument of evil.'[27]

Method is linked to purpose. If we can see the end in view clearly, it becomes possible to begin to plan how to get there. A good deal is being written at present about the problem of the goal of unity. It is proving hard to agree what kind of 'one Church' there ought to be, whether visible or invisible, how structured, how served by its leadership, how embodying in its common life the life of Christ.[28] Any notion that 'one Church' must be a monolith of institutional uniformity to which all Christians must ultimately submit in obedience would now, and rightly, be unacceptable. The truth historically has been that a strong sense of the importance of unity has

[24] J. M. R. Tillard, 'The ecclesiological implications of bilateral dialogue', *Journal of Ecumenical Studies*, 23 (1986), 412–23, p. 416.
[25] J. M. R. Tillard, 'The ecclesiological implications of bilateral dialogue', *Journal of Ecumenical Studies*, 23 (1986), 412–23, p. 416.
[26] J. M. R. Tillard, 'The ecclesiological implications of bilateral dialogue', *Journal of Ecumenical Studies*, 23 (1986), 412–23, p. 416.
[27] J. M. R. Tillard, 'The ecclesiological implications of bilateral dialogue', *Journal of Ecumenical Studies*, 23 (1986), 412–23, p. 418.
[28] The visible signs and instruments we can already share can be seen as tokens of the reality of visible unity.

not been incompatible with the presence of faults in a system of church-government which look rather like this.[29] But that does not mean that the 'one Church' exists, or should exist, solely as a mystical, spiritual or invisible unity. The concept of 'one Church' as a communion of mutual commitment as well as commitment to Christ; in which there is room for diversity; and which is an arena of freedom as well as of order, is ecumenically normative today. But that is much harder to define than the old models, and consequently much harder to grasp and much harder to trust.

For trust entails risk, and we have been acknowledging that groups of Christians prove unwilling to risk what they have (and love) ecclesially when it comes to making real ecumenical commitment. Even if the end in view were to seem secure, the entrusting would be a great matter because it would mean setting aside the old securities, which have usually included a degree of self-definition over against one another. Each community is asked not only to risk itself in the future united Church, but also to put itself in trust in the hands of others in entering into communion with them, and especially if that is going to involve, as it must, the establishment of common structures.

The lack of a clear end in view affects the processes by which any end might be arrived at. But it does not necessarily impede progress. Ecumenists have commonly had a sense of finding themselves engaged in a process of discovery of something as yet hidden but somehow already there. Commenting on the work of ARCIC I, William Purdy said, 'We were not like men sitting down to make some machine or piece of furniture in accordance with some blue-print or long-mastered craft. The report, we may say, is as much an act of discovery as of manufacture. The commission was doing something not quite like anything that had been done before.'[30] ARCIC found that 'we learned as we progressed'.[31] This unexpectedness, this 'finding out as we go along' seems to me to be the most important experience of all in ecumenical theology, because it keeps before everyone's minds the dependency of the whole enterprise upon the guidance of the Holy Spirit. That does not mean that problems about structures go

[29] Döllinger's key point in *Kirche und Kirchen* 'is that the Churches which are without the Pope drift into many troubles, whereas the Church which energetically preserves the principle of unity has a vast superiority, which would prevail, but for its discrediting failure in civil government.' *The Church and the Churches*, tr. W. B. MacCabe (Hurst and Blackett, 1862). Cf. Alfred Plummer, *Conversations with Dr Döllinger* , *1870–90* , ed. R. Boudens (Louvain, 1985), p. 259.
[30] William Purdy, 'Dialogue with the Anglican Communion', *One in Christ*, 18 (1982), 211–23, p. 211.   [31] ARCIC I, *The Final Report*.

away.[32] But it does mean that problems about structures must not be allowed to dominate the enterprise.[33] The recognition that it is necessary to work to some degree 'blind' is beginning to encourage a healthy willingness to put the experience and discovery of the process in the forefront of things and to defer the making of plans.

This study is concerned with what we are beginning to learn, both from our successes and from our failures, about the methods by which ecumenists work within the process. I have tried not to beg the question where we are going, although I think a number of pointers become clear as we look at the methodological lessons. This has seemed an appropriate moment, when the early confidences of the ecumenical movement are now being so widely brought into question, to attempt this exercise of drawing the methodological threads together.

THEOLOGY AND PRACTICE

The methodological issues with which this book is directly concerned have to do with learning to think and believe together rather than with the implications for what Christians can do together. In the present climate of thought that needs defending. Prayer together, active work together in the world, the prophetic[34] aspect of both these as witnesses to the world, are all important, and vividly so for many to whom the verbal theological dialogue is less attractive and perhaps seems less urgent than crying human need. There is in some quarters an awareness that talk may be misused, and that can seem a reason for being wary of it.[35]

---

[32] 'We really have almost no idea of what model we should have in mind . . . What is needed is a new ecumenical creativity but . . . it seems to be particularly [difficult] in this field, despite all our talk of the Holy Spirit's guidance, when in the end so much depends upon reconciling the hard requirements of existing establishments and doing this through a lengthy series of formal committee meetings.' Adrian Hastings, 'Anglican–Roman Catholic relations today', *One in Christ*, 28 (1992), 24–34, p. 25.

[33] That was a lesson already being learned in the 1970s. 'In the 70s the *process* of union became more important than the *plan* of union; and this is a first reason for being hopeful. Plans of union did not prosper in the [1960s] because they were geared too much to the reconciliation of systems of belief and structures of government, too little to the reconciliation of communities of believers.' M. Hurley, 'Christian unity by 2000?' *One in Christ*, 19 (1983), 2–13.

[34] For an early testimony to the prophetic power, ecumenically, of the Week of Prayer for Christian Unity, see G. Tavard, 'Tentative approaches to a mystique of unity', *Journal of Ecumenical Studies*, 3 (1966), 503–18, p. 507, on Paul Couturier (1881-1953) as 'the prophetic person who did most to orientate the week of prayer for unity of January in a truly ecumenical direction'.

[35] 'The ecumenical problem . . . is a mystery, calling not for cleverness and strategy, but for contemplation, participation and obedience'. G. Tavard, Editorial, *Journal of Ecumenical Studies*, 1 (1964), p. 100.

Strong claims can be put forward for what might be called a 'non-theological' methodology, a methodology which tries above all to embrace the lived and practical realities of Christian life.[36] We have already touched on their presence in the debate, and noted the temptingness of the fact that 'doing together' is in some respects easier to achieve than 'thinking together', more direct, more immediately rewarding. Christ's commands to love one's neighbour, to care for the poor and afflicted are clear. To act on these orders for life together with other Christians can give a sense of gratifying ecumenical progress, where the more theoretical aspects of the theological endeavour may continue to frustrate.[37]

But the question whether the theology is more, equally, or less important than the aspects loosely grouped in this way is not the one we should be asking. The issue is how the formal theology, the practice and everything else fit together into the whole picture.[38] In this study I have largely limited myself to topics which hang together technically, and of which there is a widely expressed current need for us now to engage in a systematic review. But I have assumed them to be intimately interconnected with the non-verbal, the informal, but still in the deepest sense 'theological' branches of ecumenical endeavour. It is important never to lose sight of the fact that spiritual life, worship, practice, and everything else in the Christian life imply, depend on, and express a theology.[39]

Nevertheless, there have been calls for 'a reorientation of the ecumenical problematic as a whole',[40] in various directions which

---

[36] The idea of 'non theological factors' affecting both division and unification was mentioned in the WCC at Edinburgh, 1937 and debated at Lund in 1952. See John May, 'From ecumenical theology to fundamental ecumenics', *Journal of Ecumenical Studies*, 14 (1977), 304–12, p. 306.

[37] J. M. R. Tillard, 'The ecclesiological implications of bilateral dialogue', *Journal of Ecumenical Studies*, 23 (1986), 412–23 makes this point strongly.

[38] Stephanopoulos comments that 'deliberately to collapse the tension by . . . establishing communion where there is not real consensus or by busily attending to the affairs of the "world" without radically exposing the terms of real salvation through the existential understanding of the mystery of the Church is to compromise the entire ecumenical enterprise.' Robert G. Stephanopoulos, 'Denominational loyalties and ecumenical commitment: a personal view', *Journal of Ecumenical Studies*, 17 (1980), 636–46, p. 640.

[39] 'This change of heart and holiness of life, along with public and private prayer for the unity of Christians should be regarded as the soul of the whole ecumenical movement, and can rightly be called "spiritual ecumenism"', A. C. Outler, 'Strangers within the gates', in Stacpoole, p. 180, quoting *UR*,8.

[40] New Valamo Orthodox Conference, Statement, *The New Valamo Consultation: The Ecumenical Nature of the Orthodox Witness* (Geneva, 1977), p. 20. See too Robert G. Stephanopoulos, 'Denominational loyalties and ecumenical commitment: a personal view', *Journal of Ecumenical Studies*, 17 (1980), 636–46.

tend to have in common a rejection or subordination of the role of theological dialogue. Something has to be said about that before we go any further. Clearly, 'the unity which we seek in the Ecumenical Movement cannot be the product of theological agreements, such as a common signing of a *confessio fidei*'[41] if these are taken in isolation. But we have to be clear about the dangers of setting them aside as unimportant or irrelevant or even placing them at the ecumenical margins. Various antitheses have been set out in attempts to adjust the balance of theological and practical aspects of ecumenism in these loosely defined senses.

The most obvious of these is this central false antithesis between engaging together in the Christian life and wrestling with the problems about the theory.[42] A more integrative approach suggests that local and particular collaborative experiences ought themselves to be the subject of ecumenical theological reflection. 'It is neces-sary . . . according . . . to two assumptions, which might be called the principle of concreteness and the principle of complementarity, for Christians in an ecumenical age to focus theological reflection upon the way Christians in various traditions actually live, and upon the ways in which these various ways of living challenge each other and round one another out.'[43] This seems a much more satisfactory way of looking at it. Ecumenical conversations consistently show that an 'either . . . or' approach is likely to be wrong and a 'both . . . and' one likely to be fruitful.[44]

In fact, practicalities are quite inseparable from the theological topics of the more theoretical sort. This makes it inescapably plain that there can be no ultimate conflict of interest between ecumenical practice and the exploration of ecumenical theory. In the conversations held at Malines between Anglicans and Roman Catholics in the 1920s, that was obvious almost at once, even to what were then

---

[41] New Valamo Orthodox Conference, Statement, *The New Valamo Consultation: The Ecumenical Nature of the Orthodox Witness* (Geneva, 1977), p. 20. See too Robert G. Stephanopoulos, 'Denominational loyalties and ecumenical commitment: a personal view', *Journal of Ecumenical Studies*, 17 (1980), 636–46.

[42] 'Perhaps unity . . . will come about in the end as the first of various forms of collaboration . . . It may be that an empirical road to unity may prove the best.' John Coventry, 'Visible unity: an interview with Cardinal Suenens', *One in Christ*, 8 (1972),336–44, p. 337, quoting Suenens.

[43] M. Novak, 'Concreteness and complementarity: two principles of ecumenical theology', *Journal of Ecumenical Studies*, 4 (1967), 120–4, p. 120.

[44] See my *Problems of Authority in the Reformation Debates* (Cambridge, 1992), Conclusion.

'beginners' in ecumenical dialogue.[45] The second of the Malines conversations set out to 'leave aside dogmatic controversy in order to consider possible methods of a practical kind by which, supposing a reasonable measure of agreement on doctrinal matters were reached, the Anglican Communion as a whole might be brought into union . . . with the Holy See'.[46] The president of the conversations, Cardinal Mercier, read to the assembled group an anonymous *Memorandum* on the theme 'united not absorbed', to try to work out how union might be possible without destruction of Anglican ecclesial being or identity. This proved to require extensive historical and theological analysis before it was possible to assert that 'il existe donc une formule catholique d'union des Eglises qui n'est pas une absorption mais qui sauvegarde et respecte l'organisation intérieure autonome des grandes Eglises historiques, tout en maintenant leur parfaite dépendance vis-à-vis l'Eglise romaine, principle d'unité de l'Eglise universelle'.[47] One would have to ask how matters of jurisdiction would be settled and what Rome would make of such a plan, it was pointed out.[48] In other words, the attempt to be practical itself required a theology as soon as it began to be worked out.

A different antithesis is often pointed to between official (sometimes 'academic') and 'grass-roots' theology. These, it is noticeable, 'often tend to level accusations at each other'. The result can be 'two parallel tracks which never meet'.[49] But again, 'the main problem . . . is to forge a link between these two categories of experience which are in a way complementary. The feeling is that the "top" must really recognize the daily life of Christians as a theological situation.'[50] To that we might add the equally important need for those engaged in theology at the grass-roots to recognise the value of the work done by those who produce the formal texts. The use of the expression 'the top' hints at an underlying agenda of buried resentment here. The problem is that the 'official' conversations can easily be seen as taking

---

[45] On the inception of these conversations, see Halifax, *Malines*, p. 83, where Cardinal Mercier describes how Lord Halifax came to see him with the proposal in the autumn of 1921. See further, Chapter 6.   [46] Halifax, *Malines*, pp. 79–80.   [47] Halifax, *Malines*, p. 254.
[48] Halifax, *Malines*, p. 259.
[49] Official ecumenists 'think that those at the "grass-roots" do not practise real ecumenism, that they have insufficient ecumenical education and that their work is frequently marked by ambivalence, indifference and confusion. The others say that those at the "top" are engaged in a doctrinal discussion which is either abstract or concerned with past divisions which have nothing to say to the realities of present-day life.' On the 'grass-roots' see further, Chapter 7.
[50] 'Ecumenism today: a survey by the RC/WCC Joint Working Group', *One in Christ*, 11 (1975), 30–87, p. 44.

place among an élite, and at a remove from what concerns the majority of the people of God. There is also the problem of 'the gap between theological convergence and the actual life of our congregations', which can seem enormous.[51]

Then there is the exploration of the antithesis, also already touched on, between the search for visible unity and the confidence that an invisible unity already exists, and that is all we need. Some would argue strongly that because the Church is already and eternally invisibly one, the attempt to give visible embodiment to its unity is misconceived and must result in the imposition of an institutional straitjacket. To hold that unity is essentially mystical or spiritual in this way is clearly right. But order has been important in the Church from New Testament times, and the intricacies of the theologians' struggle to construct a visible common order proves itself necessary every time a scheme for unity founders over a difference of order. Indeed such differences almost always lie at the root of such failures.[52]

Another false antithesis is between the 'world-wide and the local'. This tends to argue from the danger that a world-wide ecumenism will fail to take account of the reality of the differentiation of local or even denominational or confessional church life. The importance of preserving that diversity is correspondingly emphasised. The anxiety on behalf of the local warns that 'the ecumenical movement is suffering from a kind of uniformity which does not correspond to reality'.[53] It asserts that 'the local church is the most important place for ecumenism', that local ecumenism is not simply a matter of applying at local level universal concepts worked out in advance elsewhere. It is, on the contrary, 'an independent aspect of the ecumenical problem ... an original form of ecumenism and a starting-point independent of theological discoveries'.[54] This is not necessarily to create a conflict of interest between the theological and the 'practical' approaches; but there can certainly be a tendency to

---

[51] Michael Kinnamon, 'Bilaterals and the uniting and united churches', *Journal of Ecumenical Studies*, 23 (1986), 377–85, p. 377.

[52] The Anglican–Methodist unity scheme and the Covenant scheme in recent Church of England experience are cases in point. The idea of being joined to the Church *voto*, by desire, has relevance here. Pius XII in Encyclical *Mystici Corporis* and see Francis Sullivan, Christopher Hill, Günther Gassmann, 'The Decree on Ecumenism: 25 years', *One in Christ*, 26 (1990), p. 7.

[53] 'Ecumenism today: a survey by the RC/WCC Joint Working Group', *One in Christ*, 11 (1975), 30–87, p. 47.

[54] 'Ecumenism today: a survey by the RC/WCC Joint Working Group', *One in Christ*, 11 (1975), 30–87, p. 47. See further on the grass-roots, Chapter 7.

identify the local with the practical and direct; and the world-wide with the theoretical. And when that happens the dangerous contrasting of 'either' with 'or' is compounded.

A further antithesis is commonly perceived between issues of faith and order on the one hand; and concerns about fairness and responsibility in relation to the whole of creation on the other (grouping, to put it loosely, justice and peace for human beings, with ecology.) A recently urgent issue of ecumenical attitude is created in this context by the rising pressure, especially in the Third-World Churches and within the World Council of Churches, towards 'the wholesale abandonment of a "churchly" ecumenism for a more radically world-oriented ecumenism'.[55] 'We were reminded', said the Anglican–Reformed Commission in the 1980s, by members from Africa and Latin America, 'that the divisions and differences that stemmed from the Reformation are not felt to be as important in many regions of the world as the divisions between rich and poor, black and white, men and women'.[56] This definite shift in emphasis (if not in the very nature of the ecumenical enterprise), from the concern for Christian unity and the profoundly ecclesiological basis for ecumenical co-operation, to social activism and a secularised, 'post-ecumenical' involvement was noticeable two decades ago, and has grown more pronounced.[57] But, as in the case of the other 'antitheses', we have to be careful not to create an opposition where there need not be one. The challenge is squarely put by Albert Outler: 'The new generation of theologians profess to be more deeply scandalized by injustice than by disunity (as if they had been forced to such a choice!). There is, of course, a sense in which "liberation theologies", "feminist theologies", "pacificist theologies", are "ecumenical"; their stake in denominational particularities is typically minimal. There is, however, another sense in which they undermine the ecumenical cause in its traditional forms. They ignore the fact that Christians united for justice while separated from each other at their Lord's Table send the wrong message out to a skeptical world'.[58] Albert Outler here reflects on the change, within a generation, which has altered a theological climate dominated

---

[55] R. G. Stephanopoulos, 'Reflections on Orthodox ecumenical directions after Uppsala', *Journal of Ecumenical Studies*, 9 (1972), p. 303.
[56] A–R, *God's Reign and our Unity*, Preface, q. v.
[57] R. G. Stephanopoulos, 'Reflections on Orthodox ecumenical directions after Uppsala', *Journal of Ecumenical Studies*, 9 (1972), p. 303.
[58] A. C. Outler, 'Strangers within the gates', Stacpoole, p. 180.

more by a sense of the classical Christian heritage, to new doctrinal weather patterns. It is hard to see yet where this will lead.

The ecumenical enterprise has in its first decades focussed chiefly on the doctrinal barriers which have historically divided Christians from one another, and on the possibilities of a consensus which might surmount them. In discussing the issue whether ecumenism ought[59] to include not only issues of social justice and peace and even ecology, but also perhaps the belief-systems of the whole of humanity, and thus other faiths, two things need to be distinguished quite sharply. The first is the question of God's purpose for all humanity and the whole created world. Here Christians will be bound to hold that man's responsibility for the planet (which embraces duty to his neighbour) ought certainly to be global in scale. The second is the issue of the internal economy of the call to Christian unity. It was Christ's stated intention that his people should be one.[60] Christian ecclesiology has understood the mysterious union of Christ with his people, Head and body, as constitutive for being the Church. Harmony with peoples of other faiths is governed by the imperative to love, but it cannot by definition be the same union which Christians ought to enjoy with one another or their Lord. It does not make 'Church'. This study will limit itself to the problems of methodology which arise in connection with the search for the unity of Christians because of the special internal coherence these have, without thereby implying that the wider scene is not also the concern of Christians.

I have been suggesting that these antitheses share a tendency to be anti-intellectual, and thus to value the reports and agreed statements rather modestly as ecumenical contributions. I have also argued that they have in common a tendency to polarisation, to stress either one or the other of the two options in each pair which probably ought to be regarded as at least potentially complementary[61] ('as if they had been forced to such a choice'). There is a further danger of giving a disproportionate prominence to one aspect or area. Ecumenists, like other theologians, develop a fondness for a particular area of work and naturally come to consider it of prime importance. So a kind of exclusiveness easily develops in such 'sectors' of work. Examples from the experience of the World Council of Churches are the Life and Work Movement (with a concentration on social questions), Faith

---

[59] A. B. Crabtree, 'What ought the North American Academy of Ecumenists to be?', *Journal of Ecumenical Studies*, 22 (1985), p. 120 addresses some of these issues as they looked in the mid-1980s.
[60] John 17.11,21,22.   [61] Cf. ARCIC I, *The Final Report*; Malta Report,6.

and Order (doctrinal and structural), the World Council of Christian Education, the Universal Week of Prayer (spiritual ecumenism).[62] This too is a seductive danger which needs to be watched.

So here I propose to concentrate on the theological methods of the conversations which have produced the reports and agreed statements, because they raise a more or less coherent set of problems peculiar to themselves and in urgent need of solution, and because it is important to be clear about their place in the ecumenical scheme of things.

A NOTE ON SOURCES

In this study of contemporary ecumenical method I have concentrated mainly, though not exclusively, on two kinds of material. The first is the discussion in the published reports and agreed statements themselves of the methods used by the participants in the ecumenical conversations. The second is the debate carried on in the background, in lectures and books and articles in journals, which have been written while these reports have been produced, and in response to their publication. I have included a mosaic of quotations from these, to make accessible material not easily within everyone's reach. That is not to suggest that their authors are to be read as 'authorities'. They are not 'Fathers' like an Irenaeus or Augustine who have been tested by the *consensus fidelium* over time and carry a certain weight accordingly. Our ecumenical writers await that test. But their work is pioneering and it is important to use it, to keep it in play and accessible so as to help the testing go on.

I have confined myself chiefly to the period since about 1960, so as to concentrate upon the change of perspective brought about by the Second Vatican Council, without which we should certainly not have got as far as we have. But of course these questions of method are much older, and I have tried to give something of that longer perspective.

The need to keep close to the texts in the analysis has thrown up a difficulty. The Malines conversations of the 1920s 'were confidential and surrounded by an atmosphere of secrecy. Naturally, information leaked out and naturally much of it was garbled and inaccurate.'[63]

[62] 'Ecumenism today: a survey by the RC/WCC Joint Working Group', *One in Christ*, 11 (1975), 30–87, pp. 42–3.
[63] Henry St John, 'The Malines Conversations: a pioneer effort in ecumenism', *One in Christ*, 2 (1966), 377–84, p. 383.

There is always a problem about keeping a balance between the need to give the conversations quiet space in which to take their course, and the need for them to be open and accountable to the Christian communities their participants represent. ARCIC I began with a policy of openness, but became more private. The working texts of the 1970 meeting on eucharist, ministry and authority were published in three journals in 1971.[64] This was done with the express purpose of inviting discussion. 'It is vital that the work done and the progress made should be shared by a wider public, especially by other theologians. Hence the commission cannot wait to utter until it has reached finality. The present documents simply indicate what has so far emerged . . . They express work done in hard and serious collaboration and discussion. . . . Members of the commission would each feel free to participate in the further, wider discussion which it is hoped the publication of the drafts will promote.'[65] It did not prove possible to continue in that way.

It has not been easy to get access to the archive material which records the detailed development of the conversations of our own time. It is partly that it is too soon. There is also the problem of the unfinished and unpolished character of such material at stages before the publication of the resulting report. It is of course quite proper that these texts should be guarded. In them are contained evidences of a sometimes very personal sort. They display the vulnerabilities as well as the triumphs. They include discarded drafts and false starts, infelicities and even misunderstandings which do not represent the ultimate intention of the participants. Many of them are not verbatim records but paraphrases and minutes, which can notoriously misrepresent fine points. Anyone who has taken part in this sort of exercise knows that it would be a mistake to treat such records as texts for analysis on the same basis as the finished texts. Ecumenical progress is fragile, and it would be wrong to put it at risk by mistaking the character of the evidence such papers can constitute. I have, however, been able to find examples in published material which has taken that risk, some of which are discussed in Chapter 6.

It may not be out of place here to suggest that there is a need to begin to work out a common policy about the preservation of such archives and access to them by scholars. There is a good deal to be

---

[64] *The Clergy Review, Theology* and *One in Christ.*
[65] *The Clergy Review,* 56 (1971),126–45, pp. 126–7.

learned from them for ecumenical good. Above all, it is important that all should be seen to be done in full view of the Church and that what has been achieved is open for inspection in the future.

CHAPTER I

What is ecumenical theology?

THE RULES

Ecumenical theology has both to look towards and maintain unity; and to counter division. It has in these respects the traditional responsibilities of the theological exercises of earlier ages, when these 'positive' and 'negative' aspects of the theologian's task were already clear.[1] It also has a third task unique to, and novel in, ecumenical theology. It has to make what appear to be parallel lines meet. It has to make theology done in confessional and ecclesial separation a common theological exercise. This new role will be a principal theme of this study.

It is as controversial in its different way as the two older and more traditional tasks. Ecumenism gets two apparently mutually paradoxical kinds of negative response. The first is really no response at all. It is apathy. Those in the separated churches say 'We are very well as we are. We have all we need in our church to be Christians together.' This is of course true. The Church can be fully the Church wherever it is.[2] But it is also obviously the case that something is missing in a Church which cannot feel itself fully at one with other Christians in their communities. The other response is to acknowledge a sense of the threat posed to separate Christian identity by ecumenism.

I shall be arguing that theology done ecumenically is a discipline in its own right, and one whose methods and principles we now need urgently to develop.[3] If we want to go so far as to say that all theology ought in future to be done ecumenically, the implications are huge.[4]

---

[1] Theology as a whole has long been understood to be both a 'positive' and a 'negative' science, concerned both with describing the true faith and with disproving errors, see my *Alan of Lille* (Cambridge, 1983).
[2] Cf. the 'Church in each place' theme strong in Anglican–Orthodox Conversations.
[3] On what is a discipline see Chapter 5.
[4] See *Istina*, 10(1964), p. 393 on the concept of ecumenical formation, and the study of theology in an ecumenical perspective.

But that is what is now being suggested. The Decree on Ecumenism of the Second Vatican Council stresses that theology[5] needs to be studied *sub aspectu oecumenico*.[6] 'Ecumenism is not a speciality . . . it presupposes a movement of conversion and reform coextensive with the whole life of all communions,'[7] says Congar. 'To discover what unites us is the permanent task of theology.'[8] Yet the conscious recognition of this 'permanence' of the universality of ecumenical theology in terms such as these; and indeed the very framing of theology as an ecumenical task, are something comparatively new.[9]

Its 'newness' consists in part of the recognition of an imperative of 'communion'. 'Communion' ecclesiology has developed rapidly in the last few years,[10] and has reached a point where the technical loading of the term is delicately balanced between exactness and a comprehensiveness which may in due course make it less useful. But most importantly, it stresses the eschatological dimension, the grandness of vision which transforms the old debates and lifts eyes from old divisive preoccupations.

It is possible to speak of a 'pre-ecumenical' theology, and that is an obvious place to begin.[11] Yves Congar was able to look back at the writing of several of his own papers later collected in *Dialogue between Christians,* and see them as 'pre- or para-ecumenical'.[12] At an early stage of the development of modern ecumenical theology, an Orthodox pioneer of ecumenism, George Florovsky, said that 'there cannot be an ecumenical theology, there can only be theologies of ecumenism'. He meant by this that 'an understanding of the ecumenical movement' was at that time within reach, insofar as it confined itself to analysis of 'the principles and methodologies of a particular Christian Church'; but there was not yet an 'ecumenical theology', for that would have to be elaborated jointly by representatives from several churches.[13] This

---

[5] Especially historical theology, see Chapter 5.   [6] *UR*, 10.
[7] Congar, *Dialogue between Christians*, p. 21.
[8] G. Biemer, *Journal of Ecumenical Studies*, 1 (1964), 213–42, p. 227.
[9] 'The discipline of ecumenism is only now taking shape. Without it we will have little but memories of prospects that did not mature.' Elwyn A. Smith, Editorial, 'A question of agenda', *Journal of Ecumenical Studies*, 3 (1966), p. 354.
[10] For a recent survey, see my *The Church and the Churches* (Cambridge, 1994).
[11] 'There exists a kind of "pre-ecumenical" dialogue whose character is derived from and dominated by the full ecumenism towards which it looks.' Elwyn A. Smith, Editorial, *Journal of Ecumenical Studies*, 4 (1967), p. 303.
[12] Congar, *Dialogue between Christians*, p. 48.
[13] Quoted without reference by George Tavard, 'Ecumenical theology and the Catholic Church', *One in Christ*, 25 (1989),103–13. 'To pursue theology on the basis of scholarship rather than confession', is to seek to construct a method which can be serviceable everywhere,

same insistence that ecumenical theology has to be done by churches together is strongly expressed by J. M. R. Tillard. 'As soon as there is a question of visible unity, it is clear that the confession of faith means something other than a limping compromise, paring away divergences: credal confession must indicate the possibility of *proclaiming anew together the same* [my italics] Jesus Christ.'[14] The emphasis here is on proclaiming *together*, and while that is not going on, theology remains pre-ecumenical.

Yves Congar set out three stages, culminating in this same togetherness of working which I shall be arguing is constitutive of ecumenical theology. The first is the stage of explaining the [in his case Roman Catholic account of the] faith to others; the second of wishing to learn *from* others; the third of wishing to learn *with* others.[15] Both Florovsky and Congar would hold, then, that ecumenical theology can really begin only at a point where it becomes possible for divided Christians to do it together. But clearly the stages by which that possibility is arrived at have to be gone through, and because they look to ecumenical theology as their end they are very much to the point here. Indeed, the 'doing together' always proves to contain within it, in practice, elements of the learning-processes of the preliminary stages. As we shall see, these are taken into, and continue to be necessary to, the ecumenical theological task.

We can be more optimistic than Florovsky was about what is theologically possible, now that we can see something of this joint elaboration in the already considerable body of published reports and agreed statements. 'Ecumenical theology' in Florovsky's higher sense is what I have as the end in view in exploring method in this study. This ecumenical theology is producing a new kind of theological literature in the form of these texts, and that is a testimony to its viability.[16] But it is still necessary to distinguish conceptually between

in all ecclesial frameworks, because it is respected for its detachment from the concerns of any one church. That is a different principle from that of churches seeking to work together, but it has an important place in making an ecumenical theology intellectually respectable. John Pinnington, 'Symposium: Ecumenism and the Modern World', *Journal of Ecumenical Studies*, 2 (1965), p. 257. With the caveat that being systematic has obvious dangers of over-ordering of complex material.

[14] J. M. R. Tillard, 'Elements of unity in recent ecumenical discussion', *One in Christ*, 14 (1978), 94–105, p. 99.   [15] G. Tavard, Editorial, *Journal of Ecumenical Studies*, 1 (1964), p. 99.

[16] G. Tavard, 'For a theology of dialogue', *One in Christ*, 15 (1975), 11–20, p. 12 suggests that 'they challenge classical theologies, traditional methods of theologizing and defining doctrines, the interpretation of official dogmatic positions, and perhaps even the formulations of dogmatic or doctrinal positions'.

theologies of ecumenism and ecumenical theology. We are still only precariously at the point where we can begin to do the real thing, because we are still only barely and intermittently beginning to recognise that we must get back into the habit of expecting to 'believe together' as Christians if we are Christians at all, and to the acceptance, fundamental to the first Christian centuries, that only on that basis can we hope to live and worship and talk and act as one Church in one Christ.

Ecumenical theology is concerned with unravelling mutual misunderstandings among Christians which have occurred in the past; these, as we have seen and shall see again, constantly threaten to occur or recur in present and future. It seeks not only to make but also to maintain peace; and the latter is perhaps a harder task than the first. Some of the solutions will lie in finding a better understanding of the internal economy of the ecumenical theological process. The habit of doing theology separately remains strong. Many German universities still have separate Faculties of Theology for Protestants and Roman Catholics. United States ministerial and theological education is also strongly denominational in its organisation. So a sense of the fragility of the 'doing together' is never far away. The consciousness of the nodal points and fenced-in areas of old division still tends to shape a nascent ecumenical theology as it shaped theology in division.

That asks a lot of 'our ability to use the tools of theological criticism constructively, to distinguish between critical appraisal and anathema',[17] because the sharpest tools for getting at the truth are also sharp to wound those seen as opponents of the truth. But getting at the truth cannot be done without rigour, and sometimes sharp criticism. Congar comments that 'zeal for truth' requires frank seeking 'for the grounds, often arising from faulty reasoning, wrong categories, excessive haste or bias, which had caused the other to be deflected from his own aim to arrive at the truth'.[18]

Aristotle argued at the beginning of the *Posterior Analytics* that the distinguishing mark of a discipline is the possession of its own special first principles. That must prompt us to ask what are the first principles of ecumenical theology. By Aristotle's definition, these must be principles self-evident to anyone who understands them or acceptable on the basis of such self-evident principles, and forming a

---

[17] G. Tavard, Editorial, *Journal of Ecumenical Studies*, 1 (1964), p. 105.
[18] Congar, *Dialogue between Christians*, p. 61.

body of ground-rules distinctive to that discipline. If we can identify such laws or ground-rules in today's ecumenical theology, we are on the way to establishing the intellectual respectability of the study and to being able to give it the rigour without which no discipline endures.

For it must endure. Ecumenical theology cannot be a study whose usefulness will come to a natural end in a future united Church. Experience does not suggest that harmony established in human relations stays that way without being worked at; that is likely to be no less true of human relations within the human-and-divine community of a united Church. Ecumenical theology will be more necessary then ever if it achieves its purpose, because that achievement will need to be sustained under great and continuing pressures.[19]

Ecumenical theology is at present as various as the frameworks in which it goes on. Yet it already has common elements which arise out of its ecumenical character.[20] These we can begin to list.

1   The ecumenical theology we are striving for is done collaboratively, by representatives of churches which have no authority over one another. So the collaboration has to be willing, and it has to find its own way, under the Holy Spirit, for no higher human or ecclesial authority exists which can direct it as a whole. This process is like nothing which has happened before in the history of theology, [21] for in earlier attempts to achieve unitive agreement (such as the Council of Florence in the fourteenth century), each side sought first and foremost to ensure authoritativeness within its own tradition, and there was little if any sense that they might work together freely within a restored common tradition, which would in time bring with it common authority.[22]

---

[19]   That is why we must include the *story* of the movement in the discipline of ecumenical theology as well as method and content.

[20]   For 'ecumenism is an activity tending to develop ecumenicity', G. Tavard, Editorial, *Journal of Ecumenical Studies*, 1 (1964), p. 104.

[21]   'Such a theology will be new in relation to all the past theologies of the Churches engaged in dialogue', G. Tavard, 'For a theology of dialogue', *One in Christ*, 15 (1975), 11–20, p. 15.

[22]   The Lambeth 1920 Appeal 'pointed to an external unity which was not to be a mere federation, but a re-incorporation of the severed parts into one united body. the second suggested a policy, not of surrender, but of revision and reunion founded on the acceptance of what was held to be *de fide* by the Universal Church from the beginning. Further, that all controversies of the past should be reconsidered in this spirit, as was exemplified by the fact that the Anglican Bishops assembled at Lambeth had stated for themselves and their clergy that they were ready to accept from the authorities of other Churches whatever form might be considered necessary in order that the Anglican ministry could be fully recognised by them, providing an agreement has already been reached upon all the points which had hitherto divided them ... setting a conspicuous example of humility and mankind a great

2 Ecumenical theology makes an absolute requirement of respect for the ecclesial being of other communities. 'There must be no ecumenism by absorption.'[23] It is possible in this spirit of mutual respect to place a positive value even on what has had many negative results, to see that 'each of the great schisms which have become great Christian communities represents, in its positive aspect, certain genuine values, even if it is tragically astray in those aspects in which it is negative, exclusive and peculiar to itself'.[24] In a broadcast the day after the death of Pope John XXIII, M. D. Chenu spoke of 'dialogue in the fullest and richest meaning of the term: the recognition of the other as another, to love him as he is , and not as someone to be conquered, to accept the fact that he is different from oneself, and not to trespass on the integrity of his conscience and his inner quest, or allow motives of reserve to take precedence over trust'.[25]

3 Ecumenical method seeks to be non-adversarial and that again is something largely new; and is perhaps more than any other single factor constitutive of good ecumenical method. Moreover, it allows no place for the hostility of polemic which distorts thinking as well as destroying mutual respect.

In the Middle Ages from the mid eleventh century there was need to address theological differences on two main fronts: (i) with Jews, Moslems, and dissident and heretical Christians who were held to be (or had consciously set themselves) apart from the Church; and (ii) within the Church, especially in the schools, when masters arose whose teaching was not in accord with the wishes of the ecclesiastical authorities. In both cases the approach was adversarial, the working assumption that one side was in error. On this basis, Peter Abelard

---

sacrifice for the sake of unity.' (Halifax, *Malines*, p.8.) It thus foresaw to some degree the cost of the mutuality which requires humility and sacrifice but which also commands respect for things as they are in each community. Christopher Hill notes the same point in a recent article. He points to the tension between the unity signified by the Eucharist and the grace of unity given through the Eucharist. To meet in one celebration of the Eucharist is a sign that unity has been achieved. To celebrate the Eucharist together is to be open together to the work of grace. This 'will continue to be prominent in Anglican–Roman Catholic discussion for the future'. C. Hill, 'The Decree on Ecumenism: an Anglican view', *One in Christ* 26 (1990), 20–31, p. 26.

[23] G. Tavard, Editorial, *Journal of Ecumenical Studies*, 1(1964), p. 104. Ecumenical theology cannot be done at all where there is no goodwill. But goodwill alone is not enough. 'No amount of goodwill, for instance, was going to make it possible to conceive of "a little bit of infallibility".' John Pinnington, 'Symposium: Ecumenism and the Modern World' [held at Duchesne University, Pittsburgh], *Journal of Ecumenical Studies*, 2 (1965), p. 256.

[24] Nichols, *Congar*, pp. 96–7.   [25] Quoted by Congar, *Dialogue between Christians*, p. 54.

and Gilbert of Poitiers were tried and condemned for their opinions in the first half of the twelfth century (Peter Abelard twice). In the thirteenth century several series of propositions thought by the ecclesiastical authorities to be tainted by the study of ancient Greek pagan science and philosophy were condemned, and their study in the universities banned. The *contra* motif was everywhere.[26]

The thinkers of the periods when an adversarial approach was thought appropriate tended to see themselves as seeking a truth which could in some measure be proved.[27] Their task was therefore to demonstrate that truth to others, so that the others would be forced to concede that their own view had been wrong and to embrace the right one. The opinions of the other person or community in dialogue therefore had to be outweighed or overwhelmed and brought within the fold of orthodoxy. There was almost no conception or practice of common discovery of the truth by methods which treated both parties equally, with respect, and tried to win minds by shared effort.[28]

Even the internal economy of argumentation was adversarial. Questions, the staple of high-mediaeval theological methodology, are, as Boethius had pointed out in the sixth century, 'doubtful propositions', for every question is made up of contradictions. To ask a question is to be unsure which of two possibilities is right. 'Is this so (or not)?' So settling disputed questions involved marshalling the case for and against the contradictory views and showing in that way which stood up better to reason. In the *summa* as it had taken shape by the time of Aquinas in the thirteenth century, the arguments on one side are listed and then demolished in favour of a resolution on the other side. Later in the Middle Ages the focus shifted to the *conclusio*. The teacher would put forward the end result of a sequence of argumentation for and against, and then show how it had been arrived at. In the sixteenth century there was a move, in Roman Catholic and Protestant circles alike, to the *thesis* or 'article' or 'commonplace' *(locus communis)*. The Lutheran Augsburg Confession of 1530 and the Church of England's Thirty-Nine Articles later in the century are examples of the use of these in 'official' texts.[29] Individual authors on all sides (for example, Luther and Melanchthon and Eck

---

[26] In Alan of Lille's treatise *Contra haereticos* and Aquinas' *Summa contra Gentiles*, for example.

[27] Though not always by 'necessary' and therefore irrefutable 'reasons'. See my article, 'Probabilis and proving', *Archivum Latinitatis Medii Aevi*, 42 (1979–80).

[28] An exception perhaps is Anselm's community at Bec. See R. W. Southern, *Anselm: A Portrait in a Landscape* (Cambridge, 1991).

[29] See Chapter 6 on the use of the thesis in modern ecumenical texts.

and Bucer), employed them in argumentation, too. At base, these still served the purpose the *quaestio* had served. They all presented a view which must be argued, for and against, until it triumphed or was rejected. They allowed almost no possibility of the rapprochement of apparently contradictory ideas in the expectation that they might turn out to be fundamentally in harmony.

So there was virtually no room for the reconciliation of positions in the use of these various forms of adversarial hypothesis or proposition, and, accordingly, almost no sense that that might in some instances be the desirable end.[30] In the university context of the formal determination, even in Luther's disputations[31] the whole debate was conducted under the presidency of a person whose judgement was deemed to settle the issue authoritatively in favour of one side. Again, there was no scope here for the opposing sides to come together and agree a common position. This, the staple theological method of the West from the eleventh to the sixteenth centuries, remained so in the training of Roman Catholic scholars (and to a surprising degree of Protestant ones too) well after that. It left a heritage of scholarly habit in the doing of theology which has perhaps only been decisively broken in the last few decades, and partly by the transforming effect of ecumenical conversation.[32]

There is, however, one legacy of the adversarial method which can be of use ecumenically. 'Mathematicians are wont to say, "Let us suppose this problem solved". We applied this method at Stockholm,' comments Monod, speaking of the meeting of 1925.[33] 'We had recourse to the method advocated in psychology and spirituality, "Act as if . . . ". Go forward as if the Church of Christ here on earth were actually a united front.'[34] In a not dissimilar way, the mode of argument proper to ecumenical theology requires a shared effort which Christians cannot fully make before they are united, but must

---

[30] A possible exception is the Harmony of the Gospels literature, of which Augustine's *De Consensu Evangelistarum* is perhaps the most-used mediaeval example, where reconciliation was imperative because nothing in any Gospel could be 'wrong', and the divine inspiration could not be thought to have contradicted itself.

[31] See my *Problems of Authority in the Reformation Debates* (Cambridge, 1992) on these disputations.

[32] A useful recent compilation and study is *Veritá in Questione. Il problema del metodo in diritto e teologia nel xii secolo*, ed. P. Feltrini and M. Rossini (Bergamo, 1992).

[33] W. Monod, 'Que signifie le Message à la Chrétienté', in *La Conférence universelle de Stockholm*(1925), p. 47, quoted by Congar, *Divided Christendom*, p. 115.

[34] This 'as if' method of proving was seen in the Middle Ages by Anselm of Canterbury as a helpful way of approaching the problem of evil. Like Augustine, he held that evil is 'nothing'. But this nothing has to be treated as though it were something for purposes of discussion or we cannot get a grip on it.

deem themselves to be making in order to become united. They must think 'as if' they were one in order to be one. This is the working principle of all contemporary talk of 'degrees of communion.'[35] It says that we are profoundly and essentially united although it may not always look like it. That must be so, or it would not be possible to do theology ecumenically at all. Congar comments, in this connection, that 'it is assumed that there is in Christianity an essential reality in which we are already united, and which only needs to be discovered'. He had reservations about the assumptions which then underlay this position.[36] It would certainly need to be seen resolutely in an eschatological context, with the background and framework of eternity strengthening it and guarding it from becoming a recipe for settling for less than the real thing. But stated as it now can be, it seems methodologically of the first importance. This has to do with the helpfulness of approaching the problem in the twofold confidence that God has already provided a solution which we do not yet see, and that the opposition of positions is apparent not real.

We ought not to leave this area without noting one pioneering line of patristic and mediaeval exploration of the reconciling of apparent contradictions. There is a good deal in Scripture which seems contradictory.[37] The Gospel narratives notoriously disagree in points of detail. A substantial 'harmony of the Gospels' literature (in which Augustine's work was prominent) came into being from an early period, and was still a natural theme for Calvin. The essential for this work of reconciliation to be attempted was the confidence on all sides that the Bible is in fact consistent, because God its author cannot contradict himself. The task was to understand how. The reason for this exception to the pervasive adversariality was that the unique position of Scripture made it imperative to find it harmonious. Too much hung on that for anything else to be acceptable. We are now faced with a particular instance of a Scriptural imperative in Christ's instruction to his people to be 'one'. The whole future life of the Church hangs upon it. And once more, in that context, the adversarial approach has proved too limited.

It has been worth labouring the discussion about adversariality

---

[35] On 'degrees of communion' see the Report of the Eames Commission set up by the Archbishop of Canterbury following Resolution 1 of the Lambeth Conference of 1988.
[36] Congar, *Divided Christendom*, p. 119.
[37] See my *The Logic and Language of the Bible*, I (Cambridge, 1984), on mediaeval ways of dealing with contradiction.

somewhat in order to point up as sharply as possible the contrast with the ecumenical imperative to work together theologically as well as practically. I shall have more to say along this line in the next chapter.

It is sometimes suggested that there is a natural path for ecumenical discussion to take, arising out of the fact that it begins between separated parties. It has been argued that ecumenical theology:

involves as methodological steps the synchronic and diachronic description of dogmatic differences between denominations, the systematic logical reconstruction of these differences, and their metatheoretical reconstruction at a level of abstraction which reveals their presuppositions, both rational and irrational, theological and non-theological.[38]

These are proposed not as a chronological but as a logical series of steps. Nevertheless, they do have a natural sequence. Once the possibility of real conversation is established between communions which are treating each other with respect and not as enemies, talking will always begin with the making of comparisons. Separated communities can compare their faith and life now, and they can trace their common and respective histories separately and together. Once the differences are identified and clarified in this way, it becomes possible to study them systematically and to begin to see how they arose, by processes which may be strictly theological, or may be partly external to the intellectual theological process and involving spiritual and emotional as well as rational elements. Then it becomes possible to begin to stand away and take stock. But in practice progress is never as orderly. In reality these conceptually distinct 'stages' often take place simultaneously, or piecemeal or simply in a muddle. Or, and perhaps more importantly, they may take place in a climate of self-deception. 'Many Protestant theories do not deal adequately', M. Novak suggests, 'with the procedures, pressures, and compromises which actually characterize the life of their own institutions.' He points to the existence of prejudices in favour of one's own system of self-government and against those of others which may blind one to the political realities. 'Whether a Baptist convention is any more, or less, free and open than the Second Vatican Council is a fact to be

---

[38] John May, 'From ecumenical theology to fundamental ecumenics', *Journal of Ecumenical Studies*, 14 (1977), 304–12, p. 310, citing H. G. Stobbe.

discerned not by reading apologetics books but by observing events.'[39] So a first factor which makes it difficult for a discipline of truly scholarly and detached, as for truly 'done together', ecumenical theology to emerge is the high level of vested interest and feeling which stands in the way.

Making comparisons in ecumenical theology has a preparatory role. It is valuable at the beginning of the process during which the partners in dialogue get to know one another. The participants come to a better understanding of the background and particular tradition of other churches by comparing notes.[40] That makes it often primarily an exercise in comparative history,[41] in that it involves setting accounts of earlier events side by side and comparing the differences of view which have led the divided churches to see them, and their implications, differently. It may sometimes also be instructive to compare interpretations from different eras. A. Ganoczy, for example, conducted an experimental exercise across centuries in an article of 1965 in which he set out Calvin's ideas on collegiality alongside those of Vatican II's new constitution on the Church. He wanted to point up the problem of hypertrophy of the hierarchical and monarchical aspects of the constitution of the Roman Catholic Church by making the contrast sharp.[42] But the method is likely to prove most useful when it is able to demonstrate the traditional differences of interpretation of what are in fact the same events as they have been perceived in two or more churches' histories.

As well as being historical, the comparative method can be analogical, a search for a similarity of structure or pattern in the things compared. M.-J. de Guillou, for example, draws a series of parallels between the episcopal college and the 'college' of the Apostles. Christ communicated his powers to the Apostles. The Apostles chose their own successors. Christ constituted a college of Apostles in the sense that he entrusted to them not individual ministries but 'ministry', in a bond of faith and love which made it a

---

[39] M. Novak, Editorial, 'Authority in ecumenical perspective', *Journal of Ecumenical Studies*, 3 (1966), p. 362.

[40] It has been suggested that it 'corresponds fairly well to the purpose and method of Faith and order before the Lund meeting of 1952. This has been called the method of comparative ecclesiology, which enabled the participants to make headway in mutual understanding.' G. Tavard, 'The bi-lateral dialogues: speaking together', *One in Christ*, 16 (1980), 30–43, p. 37.

[41] Nothing is more fruitful than comparative history, comments L.-E. Halkin, 'Le Concile de Trente vu de Vatican II', *Irénikon*, 38 (1965), 195–202, p. 195.

[42] A. Ganoczy, 'La structure collégiale de l'Eglise chez Calvin et au IIe Concile du Vatican', *Irénikon*, 38 (1965), 6–32, pp. 7 ff.

single shared trust and responsibility. Peter and the Apostles may be compared analogously with the Pope and the bishops today.[43] This kind of approach seeks to build upon resemblance a platform of shared thinking between communions. There is a classic issue here, concerning the cogency of proofs by analogy.[44] They can have the force of what Anselm of Canterbury would call 'fittingness',[45] and that is a very considerable force to the mediaeval mind. To the modern theologian, the absence of comparability is perhaps stronger as a negative argument than its presence is of positive use. A lack of comparability or perceived equivalence may be a barrier to mutual acceptance.

It is necessary to try to move beyond a comparative methodology. The comparative method empties itself naturally but not inevitably[46] into dialogue as the participants talk the differences through. This happens because to find likeness is to discover common ground to build on. To discover difference is to be obliged to ask further questions, such as whether a particular difference matters; or whether it is 'resolvable', and so that too leads to dialogue.

The method of correlation

The 'method of correlation' described by Paul Tillich is relevant here, because it, too, involves the making of comparisons. As he describes it, this 'tries to correlate the questions implied in the situation with the answers implied in the message'. This he conceives as 'a theological method in which message and situation are related in such a way that neither of them is obliterated'.[47] There is, however, a significant difference in that the historical or analogical comparative methods are chiefly of use at an early stage of ecumenical conversation and this 'method of correlation' would seem to require a continual keeping in mind of the balance of requirements of historical and contextual reality on the one hand, and, on the other, of theological interpretation which is being brought to bear.

[43] M.-J. de Guillou, 'Le parallélisme entre le Collège apostolique et le Collège épiscopal', *Istina*, 10 (1964), 103–110.
[44] J. Butler, *Analogy* (London,1736) and ed. J. H. Bernard (London,1900).
[45] Anselm of Canterbury, *Opera Omnia* (6 vols.), ed. F. S. Schmitt (Rome/Edinburgh, 1938–68), *Monologion*, 19, Vol. I, p. 34.
[46] 'One can compare without dialoguing', G. Tavard, 'The bi-lateral dialogues: speaking together', *One in Christ*, 16 (1980), 30–43, p. 37.
[47] Paul Tillich, *Systematic Theology*, I, p. 8, discussed in A. Crabtree, 'Methodological consensus? A Protestant perspective', *Journal of Ecumenical Studies*, 17 (1980), 75–80.

Complementarity

'As we look at differences between Roman Catholics and Disciples we often discover in them elements of complementarity.'[48] To find the views of churches in conversation complementary is to discover in them a diversity which is essentially cohesive and centripetal, and which recognises that wholeness in the Church needs the contributions of the present divided churches to make it up. Here, too, is a form of comparative method which continues to be valuable as work goes on.

Consonance

The search for 'consonance in faith' has proved an important aspect of comparative methodology as it is employed at a more advanced stage of dialogue. The finding of likenesses becomes in this way, as ARCIC found, a shared apperception of a common faith.[49] In Lutheran–Roman Catholic dialogue in the USA, too, 'the basic search has been for consonance with apostolic teaching and practice'.[50] Yet even where 'the avowed purpose has ... been to discover convergences', not just 'any kind of similarity' will do. There has to be a focus to the consonance.[51] In the ARCIC case this is understood in terms of 'consonance with apostolic faith'. In the Lutheran–Roman Catholic case it is also deemed to be important that it is a jointly perceived faith which is consonant with the faith of each Church.[52]

So there is a loose group of 'comparative methodologies', of value at different stages of the ecumenical process. Of these undoubtedly the most important, both for its ramifications and for the weight of its

---

[48] Disciples–Roman Catholic; *Growth*, p. 164.   [49] See *The Final Report*.

[50] 'In the march of this dialogue, the consonance in question has been determined by extensive biblical and historical investigations. Next, fundamental teaching and practice have been compared with Reformation theology ... and with Catholic teaching ... and with more recent developments in both Lutheran and Catholic theology and practice. The conclusion, that the two Churches and traditions express basically identical doctrines in varying theological and ecclesial shapes, is finally the result of an effort at joint discernment.' G. Tavard, 'Ecumenical theology in the Catholic Church', *One in Christ*, 25 (1989), 101–113, pp. 107–8.

[51] 'The convergences in question are such as bring the theological mind back ... to the ... centre.' G. Tavard, 'Ecumenical theology in the Catholic Church', *One in Christ*, 25 (1989), 101–113, p. 108.

[52] 'Both Catholic and Lutheran theology must be at the heart [of what is agreed] though perhaps not in the forms and languages that they have inherited from the past.' G. Tavard, 'Ecumenical theology in the Catholic Church', *One in Christ*, 25 (1989), 101–113, p. 109.

relevance to the conversations in bilateral after bilateral, is the comparison of histories.[53]

A SETTLED DISCIPLINE? THE PROBLEM OF THE MULTIPLICITY OF TASKS

In a number of areas we are at the very beginning of thinking about the methodological questions. Should they vary with the *subject-matter* under discussion? Or with the *purpose* of the talks? Or between *bilateral* pairs? Or in different *multilateral* combinations of participants?

Differences in *purpose* may certainly affect methodology. Some dialogues have been designed to solve problems or to arrive at agreement where there was formerly disagreement. ARCIC I's agreements on Eucharistic doctrine, Ministry and Authority, and ARCIC II's *Salvation and the Church* were like that. In other instances, such as ARCIC II's *Church as Communion* there is an attempt to say something together on a matter about which the two sides have never quarrelled.[54] These are clearly different kinds of task and, arguably, they require, at least to some degree, different methodologies.[55]

There are different kinds of separation. In some cases the partners in dialogue have never gone through the actual process of separation, and these, too, may affect the choice of an appropriate method for mending the breach. Methodists and Roman Catholics, for example, were never united. Their separation was secondary to that of the already-separated Rome and Church of England, on which historically the separation of the Methodists and Rome followed. No healing of memory of mutual hurt[56] is directly involved here. In other cases sharp division occurred very soon after the beginning of disagreement

---

[53] Multilaterals have not gone in much yet for history because the shared history may not extend to all those involved.

[54] M. Richards, 'Twenty-five years of Anglican–Roman Catholic dialogue – where do we go from here?' *One in Christ*, 18 (1992), 126–135, p. 128. There is a danger of blandness and lack of tightness and economy in the writing of some statements where there is no hard knot to untie. No hostilities have to be got out of the way and consequently the natural edge to the proceedings, with its power to focus the mind, is lacking. Francis Sullivan sees *Church as Communion* as a 'modest' achievement. 'I would not characterise it as a major breakthrough', he says.

[55] The degree of difficulty of the problem-solving attempted seems to have an effect on quality. In a criticism of ARCIC II's text *Church as Communion*, F. A. Sullivan suggests that it 'could have made a more incisive contribution had it made a more realistic attempt to achieve a consensus between Anglicans and Catholics as to the conditions that would have to be met for the achievement of "full communion" between their churches', *Catholic International* 2 (1991), p. 31.

[56] See Chapter 5 on healing of memory.

and the painfulness of the event is part of the separation. In still other instances there was long-drawn-out mistrust, building up to separation over many generations. Orthodox–Roman Catholic division in 1054 was preceded by centuries of bad feeling and followed by centuries more. Prolonged estrangement can have the paradoxical effect of breeding a bond of its own. 'Catholicism has at least always known Orthodoxy as an alienated brother and has the familiarity with it that comes from quarrelling over matters of consequence.'[57]

Division may have taken place in anger or it may not, and if there is anger, that has to be purged. If two communities have tried and failed to unite before, there is a history of failure to be overcome. In each of these contexts, the method of ecumenical theology will need to be adapted to meet the situation.

There is, too, the issue of difference of priority between partners attempting dialogue. 'Just what are the subjects that must be discussed if truly serious conversation is to be held between parties too long alienated from one another?' asks one commentator. He notes that 'what is important to one may seem curious or captious to the other' yet all refusal to care about another's concerns is a grave obstacle to dialogue.[58] There will be a difference between trying to unite Anglicans and Roman Catholics, with their considerable degree of essential likeness and common history up to the sixteenth century; Orthodox and Roman Catholics with their profoundly different worlds of thought but largely common order; Reformed and Roman Catholics with their substantially different ecclesiologies.

All these factors make it impossible to look to a monolithic (or even moderately tidy single) ecumenical method which will do for all purposes and occasions. Flexibility is essential, with a sensitivity to the requirements of each situation.

BILATERAL AND MULTILATERAL METHODS

The principles we have been outlining are tested by a number of factors which arise in bilateral and multilateral contexts.[59] Talk of the adversarial has tended to focus on the conflict of two opposing views. But we are often dealing with a multiplicity of positions on any given point of difference. For such mathematical reasons alone, 'it is less

[57] Elwyn A. Smith, Editorial, 'A question of agenda', *Journal of Ecumenical Studies*, 3 (1966), p. 354.
[58] Elwyn A. Smith, Editorial, 'A question of agenda', *Journal of Ecumenical Studies*, 3 (1966), p. 354.
[59] The *Journal of Ecumenical Studies* devotes volume 23 (1986) to the bilateral–multilateral issue.

easy to prepare a text in which all Christian confessions are supposed to discover the essential elements of their convictions'[60] than to achieve a bilateral agreement. Most of the interchurch conversations so far attempted have been bilateral, with one or two 'three-sided' examples.[61] In its Lima text *Baptism, Eucharist and Ministry*, the World Council of Churches essayed the only truly multilateral enterprise so far which has also been large-scale in the issues it has addressed.

Even though experience with bilaterals is much more extensive than with multilaterals, a number of points and provisos can already be made. Bilaterals 'posit a challenge to the classical methods of confessional theology done in the isolation of one particular Church tradition'.[62] But they can create new bilateral 'islands'. There is a danger of bilaterals forming closed systems in which the partners' chief concern is to be reconciled with one another. Barriers to wider unity can inadvertently be set up in that way. Most notably, a pair engaged in bilateral dialogue become mutually trusting and can arrive at a shared view which cannot be immediately recognised by others.[63] It is tempting for a bilateral rapprochement such as this, which is going well, to seek to move ahead even at the risk of leaving others behind. This is not a new difficulty. The Anglicans 'emphasise the fact that the unity contemplated in the *Appeal*' of the Lambeth Conference of 1920, 'included both the Oriental Churches and the various Protestant groups throughout the world' . . . 'it was urged . . . in reply that some of those who were separated from the Roman Communion would be far from willing to make any approach, and that it would not do to wait for them. Perhaps the good of the Church might require that the Anglicans should set the example without waiting for the Orientals and the Nonconformists.'[64] A comparison of the ecumenical Resolutions of the Lambeth Conference of 1988 shows a wide diversity in the stages the bilateral dialogues are seen to have

[60] J. M. R. Tillard, 'Elements of unity in recent ecumenical discussion', *One in Christ*, 14 (1978), 94–105.

[61] For example, the Lutheran–Reformed–Roman Catholic conversations of 1976 on mixed marriages.

[62] G. Tavard, 'For a theology of dialogue', *One in Christ*, 15 (1979), 11–20, p. 15.

[63] That can apply in matters of order, too. The local united churches of the Indian sub-continent could not for some time regard themselves as still in communion with the Anglicans from whom some of their members were drawn, although they now take part in the decennial Lambeth Conferences.

[64] *The Conversations at Malines: Report Presented to the Archbishop of Canterbury by the Anglican Members* (Oxford, 1927), Supplement, p. 12.

reached and the possibility of going forward to practical steps towards unity. The Anglican–Lutheran conversations, for example, already saw stronger grounds for doing so than others.

If a method is found to work bilaterally it has been tempting to use it again in similar circumstances. In the 1930s the Lutheran Church in Finland was able to reach an agreement with the Church of England, and a similar line was taken with the Churches of Latvia and Estonia. 'The Report which we present follows very closely the lines of the Report of the Conferences with the Church of Finland, which has already been accepted, and the situation is somewhat similar to that in Finland. The theological and ecclesiastical problems are, for the most part, the same,'[65] it was suggested. In a similar spirit the Anglican–Orthodox conversations held soon after the successful conclusion of the agreement of Anglicans with the Old Catholics in the same period encouraged the attempt to build upon a success with method by trying it again. This has the important advantage, if it can be achieved, of preventing the difficulty that a bilateral agreement may exclude or hinder relations with other churches for one or both of the partners. But it requires sensitivity to shades of difference in the problems involved.

With that proviso, it may open the way so that a bilateral can grow into a multilateral. At a meeting of Anglican and Old Catholic bishops, in July 1930, the Archbishop of Utrecht 'spoke of friendly negotiations which had taken place . . . At the next International Old Catholic Congress in Vienna in 1931 he hoped the three Churches (Anglican, Old Catholic and Orthodox) would come together and discuss how they could be reunited. The Orthodox Church had proposed that they should come.'[66] There were Anglican–Orthodox conversations in the 1930s and they have continued since, with the Old Catholic 'third partner' now in communion with Anglicans. But this particular impetus did not last. The governing idea seems to have been that Old Catholic and Orthodox were close kin ecclesially and that what was proposed would be a natural extension of success

[65] Evangelical Lutheran Churches of Latvia and Estonia in conversation with the Church of England, 1936–8, *Lambeth Occasional Reports, 1931–8* (London, 1948), p. 211.

[66] The representatives of the Anglican Communion laid before the Commission the Report of the Conference that was held between representatives of the Anglican Communion and the Old Catholic Churches and the Resolutions therein agreed upon. The representatives of the Eastern Orthodox Church agreed to lay this Report and these Resolutions for the consideration of the Synod of the Eastern Orthodox Church.' *Lambeth Occasional Reports, 1931–8* (London, 1948), p. 35.

already achieved. Something similar may be said to have happened, this time successfully, in the case of the United Reformed Church in England, which has united with the former Disciples of Christ.

It must be ecumenically positive to proceed in this way from bilateral to multilateral if the results are unitive. But there is a drawback if what results is a series of enlarged kin-groups, because the problems of reconciling different systems of church-government and different leading ideas and different ecclesial styles remain; indeed, they may be enhanced by this bloc-creating process. There has proved too, to be limited hope of a 'local' union success extending to take in others. The united churches of the Indian sub-continent adopted differing solutions to the problem of reconciliation of ministry, and it has not been possible to build comprehensively upon their achievement.

In a number of ways, bilaterals are as various as the pairings they involve. For example, there are important differences between bilateral conversations in their style, tone and pace. Some hasten towards unity, others are very cautious.[67] Different communions have different priorities and requirements and therefore different methods are needed in their pairings with others bilaterally. The following example will illustrate graphically the need for even 'bilateral' methodology to be infinitely flexible:

The Orthodox said in effect: '. . . The Tradition is a concrete fact. Here it is, in its totality. Do you Anglicans accept it, or do you reject it?' The Tradition is for the Orthodox one indivisible whole: the entire life of the Church in its fullness of belief and custom down the ages . . . Faced with this challenge, the typically Anglican reply is: 'We would not regard veneration of icons or Mariology as inadmissible, provided that in determining what is necessary to salvation, we confine ourselves to Holy Scripture.' But this reply only throws into relief the contrast between the Anglican appeal to what is deemed necessary to salvation and the Orthodox appeal to the one indivisible organism of Tradition, to tamper with any part of which is to spoil the whole, in the sort of way that a single splodge on a picture can mar its beauty.[68]

This text underlines the contrast between the Orthodox approach and that of many Western communions. The Orthodox have tended to want to bear in mind throughout the conversations in which they

---

[67] The dialogues in which the Lutherans have been involved, for instance, have tended to be optimistic about the speed with which union can be achieved.
[68] Michael Ramsey in a comment on the 1956 Moscow Conferece, quoted by Kallistos Ware in A–O, Moscow, pp. 58–9.

have been involved the interdependence of all theological themes. Orthodox discussion 'tries to embrace the whole of theology, Christology, Pneumatology, Mysteriology, and all that relates to them'. One commentator suggests that 'this results in a confusion of themes and ideas, and too much identification . . . on the pattern of Christ is the Spirit, the Spirit is Christ, Christ is the Church, the Church is the Eucharist'.[69] Other dialogues have on the whole sought to take one problem at a time and to resolve differences step by step. Both approaches have drawbacks. The Orthodox way makes progress slow, and the organisation of discussion a nightmare. The other way can give a sometimes false sense of the amount of headway made.

It is possible for a communion to come to see itself as having a special vocation as a partner in many different bilateral dialogues, even as a natural intermediary. It has sometimes been suggested that the Anglicans have a natural role as mediators,[70] with their consciousness of being 'catholic and reformed' and with their awareness of the provisionality of their communion.[71] From the early sixties Anglicanism has been conscious of its own patterns of unity in diversity, and that, together with widespread experience in dialogue with other communions, has encouraged a concern for catholicity and universality.[72] Here again we see the experience of doing theology ecumenically developing out of a capacity to see things from many points of view, even within the confines of bilateral encounters, where a given communion has a number of bilateral partners. But there can be problems with this.[73]

Just as some of the tensions between the promising features and the difficulties of bilateral dialogue are beginning to emerge, so we can also see already some of the natural properties of multilateral dialogue. The whole dynamic of multilateral conversations is different, and the main danger here would seem to be that each participant

---

[69] Colin Davey, 'Orthodox–Roman Catholic Dialogue', *One in Christ*, 20 (1984), 346–64, p. 360.
[70] E. Lamirande, 'Solidarité interne et Oecuménisme: Le Congrès Anglican de Toronto, 1963', *Irénikon*, 36 (1963), 476–506, p. 494.
[71] 'The Anglican Communion has never claimed immortality. Unlike many other groups in the Christian world, it is quite prepared to reckon the possibility of its own disappearance.' S. Neill, 'The Anglican Communion looking ahead', *Pan-Anglican*, 12 (1963), 43.
[72] E. Lamirande, 'Solidarité interne et Oecuménisme: Le Congrès Anglican de Toronto, 1963', *Irénikon*, 36 (1963), 476–506, pp. 491, 494.
[73] 'Since most Churches are engaged in varying degrees in dialogues with other churches, are united parties automatically to be bound by agreements in which they had no vote?' asks one commentator. S. A. Quitslund, ' "United not absorbed", does it still make sense?', *Journal of Ecumenical Studies*, 8 (1971), 255–85, p. 284.

community may interpret the documents from its own perspective without really entering into the agreement with others.[74] It is a feature of multilaterals that it is harder to get resolutions of contradictions. It is significant here that on a number of points *BEM* contains a list of alternatives, not always fully resolved into a synthesis.

So we have to ask what is the relation of bilateral to multilateral. It can be agreed that bilateral dialogues are natural though not necessary precursors of multilateral ones. Bilateral dialogues were possible even before the notion of an 'ecumenical movement' had been formulated.[75] Yet the bilateral does not cease to be of value when the multilateral becomes possible. 'The two main types of interchurch conversations, the bilateral and the multilateral, have proved to be complementary and mutually beneficial.'[76] This mutual benefit has a great deal to do with borrowing from and building upon the work of others. 'The Faith and Order Commission in its own multilateral consideration of the three themes has tried to build as much as possible on the specific findings of the bilateral conversations.'[77]

One of the most promising and rewarding discoveries of recent decades has been the degree to which the findings of the bilateral conversations cohere. They thus move together informally towards a multilateral status. Max Thurian noted that 'the initial drafts which I was asked to produce from 1967 onwards as a basis for this quest for consensus consisted almost entirely of quotations from official reports, arranged in an intelligible theological pattern'.[78] This is something much more than a general hanging together; it involves a profound perception of coherence. It can be and is read as a sign that a rediscovery of one faith together is a real possibility.[79]

There are times when it is necessary to carry on in ecumenical *accidie*. Apathy may be a serious problem. It is, at the other end of the scale, equally important to be able to carry on where there is 'uphill

---

[74] Cf. *Churches Respond to BEM*, I, Anglican Church of the Southern Cone, p. 54.
[75] But 'multilateral dialogue is a natural child of that new historical fact called the ecumenical movement, because that movement is by definition multilateral'. G. Gassman, 'The relation between bilateral and multilateral dialogues', *Journal of Ecumenical Studies*, 23 (1986), 365–76, p. 370.
[76] *BEM*, Preface; *Growth*, p. 467. So far we 'at best consider their complementarity, interrelation, and interaction'. G. Gassmann, 'The relation between bilateral and multilateral dialogues', *Journal of Ecumenical Studies*, 23 (1986), pp. 365–76, p. 366.
[77] *BEM*, Preface; *Growth*, p. 467.
[78] *Churches respond to BEM*, I, p. 3, Preface by Max Thurian.
[79] The great rule would seem to be there should be consistency with the rest of the Christian faith. Ross McKenzie, 'Reformed and Roman Catholic understandings of the Eucharist', *Journal of Ecumenical Studies*, 13 (1976), 260–6, p. 260.

work' against a sense of threat to separate Christian identity, which stimulates active resistance. Then those engaged in the enterprise need the support of habits of work and practices of proven effectiveness simply to keep going. The machinery of ecumenical method, which has been developed largely by trial and error, is becoming sufficiently well-tested to sustain effort at such times as the present.

CHAPTER 2

Changing attitudes and stages in ecumenism

OTHERS AND OURSELVES

'The thing that separates us most radically from our . . . brethren is their attitude of mind and ours.'[1] Ecumenism cannot begin until there can be a shifting of the stances which have made Christians adversaries, and joined them in warfare instead of love. This has to take place both at a personal and at an ecclesial level. The two are intimately interconnected as we shall see in the next chapter. For our purposes in this one, the important thing is to stress the way the divided come to see others as 'Christians like themselves'. 'Ecumenism is basically personal relationships . . . the unity of the Church is . . . speeded by wider and deeper personal understanding.'[2] Cardinal Mercier had already thought of the possibility of Anglican–Roman Catholic talks before receiving the Lambeth Appeal and before Portal or Halifax had approached him with the suggestion which led to the Malines Conversations. In 1919 he went to the USA where he discovered a sense of brotherhood with other Christians, and *un vif désir d'unité*[3], and that transformed his view and his priorities.[4]

It is of the first importance to the dynamics that communities seem somehow collectively to feel a rivalry which echoes the personal adversariality and interacts with it in complex ways. Inter-Christian rivalry and competition tempts to proselytising, for example, with implications we shall come to in a moment.

To be successful in an adversarial debate it is necessary to see the opponent as 'the other', and to shut one's mind to any elements in his thinking which might be congenial or win one's assent. One

[1] Congar, *Dialogue between Christians*, p. 294.
[2] J. Coventry, 'British Church Leaders' Conference', *One in Christ*, 9 (1973), 75–8.
[3] R. Aubert, 'L'histoire des conversations de Malines', *Collectanea Mechliniensia*, 52 (1967), 43–54.
[4] See, too, the examples in *Encounters for unity*, ed. G. R. Evans, Lorelei Fuchs and Diane C. Kessler (Norwich, 1995).

cannot afford to agree with him. This blocking of channels of communication is of course the reverse of the valuing of another for the other's uniqueness, and for the different gifts he may have (in which difference as variety is duly respected). In a divisive understanding of 'otherness', there will be a place for understanding why the other thinks as he does, but only so as to see better how to refute him. This is depersonalising for both sides. What is true in dispute between persons is true for disagreement between churches. But what is depersonalising in the first case tends to 'unchurching' in the second.

The adversarial approach is also inimical to the refinement of intellectual sensibility through that interplay of reasoning and insight, analysis and sympathy which many of today's theologians especially want to emphasise.[5] A complex of such partly submerged factors is to be glimpsed – to take one example – even in an eirenic document such as the Anglican–Orthodox Llandaff Statement of 1980. There a hint of anti-Roman feeling seems to bind the participants in a common cause by permitting adversarial feeling against another communion to become a shared factor. There is talk of 'the abuses of the mediaeval West' coupled with the assertion that 'such a term as "the treasury of merits" is foreign to both our traditions'.[6] Failure to notice such things is likely to make for negativity.

The recentness of the changes which have made it possible to avoid approaching 'other' Christians in this negatively charged way is apparent within the span of the work of Yves Congar. In the 1930s he published *Chrétiens désunis*,[7] a pioneering study of 'divided Christendom' written from a Roman Catholic standpoint. He had discovered from an early age a sense of vocation to the cause of Christian unity[8] and that led him into friendships and shared experiences and sympathies with Christians of other communions which were relatively uncommon in the experience of Roman Catholics at that time. He tried in his book to take stock of the general situation, and to examine, communion

---

[5] 'Empathetic evaluation' is certainly needed when approaching the teaching of other churches, or we shall not understand them at all. This is inseparable from 'responsive listening'. *ARC-DOC II, Documents on Anglican–Roman Catholic Relations* (Washington, 1973), p. 51. 'As practical difficulties I would consider also questions of psychological and historical heritage in relationships, lack of knowledge, or understanding, attitudes of mistrust, fear of the unknown future.' John Coventry, 'Cardinal Willebrands interviewed', *One in Christ*, 8 (1972), 16.

[6] *Growth*, pp. 56–8, paras. 5,9.

[7] Congar, *Divided Christendom* (London, 1939), cited here from the English translation.

[8] Congar, *Dialogue between Christians*, Autobiographical preface. For a recent biography of Y. Congar, see Nichols, *Congar* .

by communion, what the major obstacles in the way of reunion then appeared to be.

It is in some respects now a dated book, as Congar himself saw and acknowledged in later reflections. It is the more instructive for that reason that there are many points at which his ecumenical instinct was already true, where he was already able to set out insights which have proved to be of enduring value. He saw clearly that division is self-perpetuating and, in the end, self-justifying. 'The worst thing is that the separations have lasted, that their very persistence has become not only a matter of habit and fact but a new motive for separate life. We have got into the way of living without each other, and in opposition to each other, as parallel lines of Christianity which never meet . . . The mere fact of not being on terms has been a fresh motive, and often the most prominent one, for remaining apart . . . Severed relationship . . . presently enters in as a factor in itself, and becomes the real cause of the established rupture, over and above the original misunderstanding.'[9] 'Controversies, prejudices and passions have piled up and have become a historic tradition and inheritance.'[10] That could not have been said by a writer who did not already perceive separated Christians *in their communities*, as truly members of the body of Christ, and who was able to perceive them in some measure as not 'other'.

This new perception prompted two pioneering attempts in Congar's book. The first was to look at the difference between the separation of the individual from the Roman Catholic Church; and the separation from it of various communities which all believe themselves to be churches. Congar's position remained as he wrote that the Roman Catholic Church is the Church. But he is clear that 'although for us the one and only Church is the visible Catholic Church, we know that outside her visible membership there are souls who belong to Jesus Christ'.[11] 'Directly a soul is in any degree united to Christ it belongs by that very fact to the Church.'[12] He is able to say that these individuals are not heretics. 'The majority of dissidents are in completely good faith.'[13]

Nevertheless, because a Christian body is not an individual but a *societas*, Congar could not then hold it to be possible for the Roman Catholic Church to have relations with the visible communities such souls belonged to, for a community severed, as he then saw it, from the

[9] Congar, *Divided Christendom*, p. 24.   [10] Congar, *Divided Christendom*, p. 25.
[11] Congar, *Divided Christendom*, p. 222.   [12] Congar, *Divided Christendom*, p. 226.
[13] Congar, *Divided Christendom*, p. 234.

true body of Christ, could not stand in quite this 'belonging' relationship which might be possible, by grace, for a person.[14] Something of the sense of 'otherness' as separation remains in his thinking here. This duality of all ecumenical encounter, which is at the same time of persons and of communities, will be a continuing theme of this study.'[15] Although it is true that 'ecumenism must be understood as directed towards the reconciliation of communions or churches rather than of individuals',[16] that is in the sense that individual conversions are usually not ecumenically helpful.[17] The communions are made up of persons and it is their individual souls, hearts and minds which have to be won.

To the attitudinal *minima* of requiring commitment to unity and honesty of purpose, the Second Vatican Council added two further criteria of ecumenism which are pertinent here and which take things further than Congar could before the Council towards eliminating divisive thinking about 'otherness'. The first[18] was that [those who take part] 'join in not merely as individuals but also as members of the corporate groups in which they have heard the Gospel and which each regards as his Church, and, indeed, God's'.[19] So participants speak out of their group identity as members of 'corporate persons',[20] and not simply as individual persons.

The second attempt made by Congar in this book was to explore the paradox that there has been a 'particular development of the [Roman] Catholic Church apart from other Christian Communions', alongside the separate developments of those other communions. (We shall come back to this in the final chapter on 'ecumenical reception'.)

[14] Congar, *Divided Christendom*, p. 242.
[15] The Vatican II Decree on ecumenism speaks 'primarily of individual Christian conversion' ... 'Conversion on the corporate level, i.e. on the part of any Church, can come to be seen as a change in perspective so that the Church in question comes in this conversion to a richer understanding of its own identity, by ceasing to view all other Churches only from the point of view of its own ecclesial life.' D. M. Schlitt, 'Ecumenism from a renewed Catholic perspective', *One in Christ*, 20 (1984), 48–61, p. 49.
[16] Report of the Ecumenical Observers to the Synod, Rome, 1985, delivered by Henry Chadwick, *One in Christ*, 20 (1984), 98–101, p. 99. Individual conversions from one Communion to another do not commonly take place for two main reasons, one ecumenically positive, the other ecumenically negative. The person believes he is already in the 'real Church' which is already united in God's eyes, and that he ought to stay where he is and work for the visible unity of the existing ecclesial bodies; or he thinks his own Church is the only true one. [17] See Preface.
[18] The second is that ecumenism should be Trinitarian. That is, that the question of inter-faith relations is fundamentally distinct from that of Christian unity. Cf. Elwyn A. Smith, Editorial, *Journal of Ecumenical Studies*, 4 (1967), p. 300. [19] *UR*, 1.
[20] See *Episcopal Ministry*, The Report of the Archbishops' Group on the Episcopate (London, 1991), Appendix on this concept.

He was able to see that this must imply some incompleteness in Roman Catholic development because that process had not been shared with the whole Christian community as it took place. It still seemed to him to be incontrovertible that the Roman Catholic Church itself 'is the Church'.[21] So it is striking that he can think that what he believes to be *the* Church may still suffer from the effects of the lack or loss of those who become separated 'others', so that its faith and life become somehow 'particular'.[22] That must imply a mutual need of one another in churches which have for a time become separated. What is needed for completeness cannot be 'other' in any sense which makes it 'alien'.[23]

On this principle rests the ecumenical rule that where a sense of 'otherness' persists, theology cannot be done in wholeness, and the Church cannot be fully herself. This acknowledgement takes a long step towards the acceptance that something of what is missing may be held or preserved in other communities, and that completeness requires the reunion, not only of the broken fragments of the single great community of the Church, but of the diminished actual communities formed over time by the separated. To say that is to allow the 'other' communities a true ecclesiality.

The shift in perception achieved by the Second Vatican Council makes all the difference to the task in hand because it radically altered the conception of what ecclesial communities not in union with Rome actually are. It became possible for the Council to say, after much discussion,[24] not that the Church 'is' the Roman Catholic Church, which had been the first and of course the most natural way for the drafters to put it, but that the Church 'subsists in' (*subsistit in*) the Roman Catholic Church. (A crucial term which has borne a variety of interpretations.)

Congar would not have faced the need to wrestle with his paradox of 'belonging and not belonging' in quite the form he presents it, if that could already have been said in the 1930s. He would, however, have confronted another, which now lies at the core of ecumenical ecclesiology. Today we frequently need to ask the secondary key

---

[21] Congar, *Divided Christendom*, p. 26.   [22] On 'separated reception', see Chapter 7.
[23] See Chapter 7 on separated reception.
[24] The ecclesiological base was malleable enough to receive a variety of forms and impressions in the period of the framing of the texts of Vatican II. See Camillus Hay, 'Comparative ecclesiology of the documents behind the Decree on Ecumenism', *One in Christ*, 3 (1967), 399–416, compares a series of texts drawn up at the same time by the Secretariat for Christian Unity, the preparatory Commission on the Oriental Churches and other bodies, embodying different ecclesiologies.

question he poses: how churches which have 'acquiesced in the setting up in separation' are to be 'related as varied units in the undivided whole'.[25] How, that is, if we get rid of any sense of 'otherness' which would stand in the way of believing and acting together and with mutual sensitivity, can we retain the differences which make for variety and richness and which satisfy 'different [God-given] Christian temperaments'?[26] To treat the other as an equal is to let the other be himself. Crucial here is the principle that 'each one must accept the other in the ecclesial reality in which he finds him'.[27]

This is the nub of the current debate about the place of diversity, with all its tail of rivalry and fear of loss of things precious to a given communion. For an insistence out of mutual respect that the existing differences of the other side must be *preserved*, for the sake of the richness they furnish, is not easy to reconcile with acceptance of the need for each side to be willing to change, to go some way to meet the other.[28] Fear of change is a mark of the uncertainty of the commitment to one another in a single Church. Confident risk-taking is, paradoxically, likely to be the best guarantee of preserving what is precious in our pluriformity.[29] 'A fragile unity does not allow a broad register of diversity, while a strong unity gives the freedom for a rich range of pluralism,'[30] argues Tillard.[31] There is a very

---

[25] Congar, *Divided Christendom*, p. 46.   [26] Congar, *Divided Christendom*, p. 46.

[27] In making this comment, Michalan adds the important rider, 'Of course there is no question here of what I should call an "objective" equality, which is the attitude which says: every position is as good as another.' P. Michalan, 'On ecumenical dialogue', *One in Christ*, 1 (1965), 357–60, p. 358.

[28] J. M. R. Tillard contributed this key memorandum at a Windsor meeting of ARCIC I:

This commission will have to work according to the Spirit of Vatican II and especially of *Dei verbum*. This means first that we shall have to discover, under our diverse and polemical expressions, the common 'tradition' from which we came. Our divergences are grounded in something that we shared in common, and probably continue to share even under our own polemical words. Some of these words are used to save it! - it will, thus, be necessary to discover what we were saying *together* before the division. Perhaps, we shall be surprised to see that we are united precisely in the matters that we consider as 'doctrinal divergences'! To demonstrate that *to* our two Churches, it will be necessary to use the common vocabulary we were using before the shift (if we discover that our faith was the same), and to express our agreements in using these words, no longer the words from polemical disputes. See, too, p. 178.

[29] 'If we go deeply enough into the notion of unity and what it demands, if we are firmly grounded in what is essential to unity, we will find wide room for diversity,' comments Pierre Duprey. Cf. P. Duprey, 'The unity we seek', *Journal of Ecumenical Studies*, 16 (1979), 303–10, p. 308.

[30] J. M. R. Tillard, 'The ecclesiological implications of bilateral dialogue', *Journal of Ecumenical Studies*, 23 (1986), 412–23, p. 417.

[31] But he stresses the proviso that 'the concept of reconciled diversity is inadequate if it is not implicitly agreed that this diversity is reconciled precisely by common reference to the most demanding truths of the apostolic faith.' J. M. R. Tillard, 'The ecclesiological implications of bilateral dialogue', *Journal of Ecumenical Studies*, 23 (1986), 412–23, p. 418.

hard core indeed of what *cannot* be different among Christians.[32] There has to be a meeting by moving together to the centre which is Christ, and that means, paradoxically, that there must be both change and preservation of the *status quo*. Congar offers a helpful image here of a rotation about a secure point or axis of common origin, in relation to which ecclesial communities can come together. 'Our business was to rotate the Catholic Church through a few degrees on its own axis in the direction of convergence towards others and a possible unanimity with them, in accordance with a deeper and closer fidelity to our unique source or our common sources.'[33]

To equip ourselves for the enterprise of a common or shared theological endeavour we have to be frank about the perennial and paradoxical tension between the once-and-for-all revelation of himself by God; and its theological expression in human ecclesial communities age by age. The first is by definition 'given' by God and is of its essence changeless (though not necessarily invariable in the language in which it is expressed). The second has to adapt itself to times and places, so as to meet the needs of particular Christians and their churches. This is a tension not only between sameness and difference, but also between the fixed and the contingent, theology and history,[34] and we shall meet it again and again as we go on. This sort of pluriformity is seen to be needed because nothing less can respect the richness and the ultimate incomprehensibility of the divine Mystery. Or it can be seen as accommodating human limitations by allowing different facets to be prominent in different communities. Either way, it is impossible to proceed ecumenically without taking account of it. Again and again we find the claim to be faithful to the 'original' Gospel challenging the view that what matters is that the Church should speak directly to people now, and vice versa.

That leads us conveniently to the question whether, where elements of the true Church are found in bodies not recognised as churches, these bodies are constituted as themselves by what differentiates them, or by what exists in them all in common despite their

---

[32] 'The goal of an authentic dialogue is not the mere acceptance of the other as it is; nor is it the pure decision, henceforth, to let it do as it wishes according to its own criteria.' J. M. R. Tillard, 'The ecclesiological implications of bilateral dialogue', *Journal of Ecumenical Studies*, 23 (1986), 412–23, p. 413. [33] Congar, *Dialogue between Christians*, p. 21.
[34] See especially Chapter 5 on this.

differentiation?³⁵ If the former, that identity may depend on separation being maintained; if the latter, it ultimately depends on union. The determinative breakthrough of Vatican II meant, again paradoxically, that now that it was possible to speak of 'churches' (*ecclesiae*) it would at last be possible to speak of 'one Church' in an ecumenical way which included them as they were, and would become, *together*.³⁶ There is an acknowledgement that bodies of separated Christians need not be 'other' in a separative sense because they are in some respects 'different'. They may be 'ecclesial' and therefore Church even if not identical with one another.³⁷ That could already be clearly seen soon after Vatican II, in 1967, on the grounds that 'ecumenism presupposes an acknowledgement that the other party may not be crucially deficient in his relationship to God, even if honesty requires us to admit that we believe him partially so; and that if we cannot believe ourselves crucially deficient, we may also be importantly so'.³⁸

Another crucial stage is acceptance of certain concomitants. The first is that recognition of the ecclesial equality of churches means that individual Christians ought as a rule to stay where they are and work for unity from there. In a number of cases, Christians have grown weary of the time it takes and have become in conscience, and after painful struggle, unable to wait. The Lutheran R. J. Neuhaus became a Roman Catholic after years of ecumenical work. In the end he had concluded that Lutherans were not going to unite with Rome. 'I know well the claim of some Lutherans that separated ecclesial existence is necessary for the sake of the Gospel.' 'I have repeatedly and publicly urged that the separated ecclesial existence, if it was once necessary, is no longer necessary; and if no longer necessary, such separated existence is no longer justified.'³⁹ His despair was ecclesiological. Lutheran preference for a 'reconciled diversity' seemed on his analysis at the time when he made the decision, to amount to a

---

³⁵ E. Lamirande, 'La signification ecclésiologique des communautés dissidentes de la doctrine des *Vestigia Ecclesiae*: panorama théologique des vingt-cinq dernières années', *Istina*, 10 (1964), p. 49.
³⁶ And mean the free coming together of ecclesial bodies without any absorption or takeover.
³⁷ The realisation took time to have its effect, within the Roman Catholic Church and outside it. The Archbishop of Canterbury, Michael Ramsey, writing on the meeting of the Pope and himself in March 1966 in the Vatican, pointed part of the way but not the crucial last mile when he suggested that 'Roman Catholics and Anglicans will continue to cherish their distinct doctrines', while learning 'to treat one another not as enemies and rivals but as allies in Christendom'. Michael Ramsey, 'Rome and Canterbury', *One in Christ*, 3 (1967), p. 398.
³⁸ Elwyn A. Smith, Editorial, *Journal of Ecumenical Studies*, 4 (1967), p. 301.
³⁹ R. J. Neuhaus, 'I can do no other', *Catholic International*, 2 (January 1991), 40–1, p. 40.

determination to sustain a claim to be the Church in a way no other can quite be. That is inimical to the mutual acceptance of true equality between partners in dialogue.

There is of course the question of the ecclesiological implications of then making a personal move.[40] In general individual conversions from one church to another are not ecumenically helpful. But one man speaking as an individual person can make a difference for ecumenical good not by changing churches but by acknowledging a change of heart which alters his stance in relation to another church. An important example here is the dawning recognition in Karl Barth's mind as he came to know Roman Catholic faith at first hand. Barth wrote a preface to Hans Küng's discussion of the Roman Catholic doctrine of justification:

> I freely acknowledge that you have omitted nothing from the ten volumes of my recently published *Dogmatik* which has any bearing on justification and that you have presented it correctly in accordance with my thought . . . If what you develop in the second part of your book as the doctrine of the Roman Catholic Church is in fact its doctrine then I must certainly agree that my doctrine of justification coincides with it . . . If what you borrow from Holy Scripture, from old and from recent Roman Catholic theology, and even from Denzinger and the texts of the Council of Trent, is really the doctrine of your Church and perhaps confirmed as such, then I, who have already twice visited the place to enter into dialogue with its *genius loci*, must once more hurry to Santa Maria Maggiore at Trent to confess sincerely and contritely: *Patres peccavi*.[41]

To make a personal decision to convert to another church at present separated from one's own is in a sense the obverse of proselytism, if that is to be defined as the attempted winning of converts from one communion to another. The issue of proselytism in ecumenical agreements has barely been touched on so far, although those in which Lutherans have been participants have been sensitive to the point. The Roman Catholic–Lutheran *Ways to Community* (1980) says that it is important to 'renounce every form of proselytism'.[42] Anglican–Lutheran conversations have argued that 'the development of Churches within foreign populations by proselytization should be

---

[40] See too, ibid., p. 41, response by way of an official statement by the Lutheran Bishop William H. Nazareth, 'Ecumenical gridlock results whenever imperative church consensus is replaced by precipitous personal conversions in either direction.'
[41] Preface to H. Küng, *Rechtfertigung. Die Lehre Karl Barths und eine katholische Besinnung* (Einsiedeln, 1957), pp. 11–12, quoted in Congar, *Dialogue between Christians*, pp. 123–4.
[42] 90; *Growth*, p. 235.

discouraged'.[43] This issue arose acutely in Eastern Europe in the early 1990s, with the collapse of communist régimes and the open revival of a Christianity which had largely gone underground.[44] When local churches are truly open to one another as equals[45] there will also be a trust and mutual respect which prevents 'poaching'. Proselytism can happen only in division. It is anti-ecumenical. It is a sign that the sense of sharing a common mind has broken down, and with it Christian friendship among equals. Treatment of the other as though ecclesially equal makes the 'as though' a significant proviso. 'As though' speaks of reservations. It is inimical to real 'openness'.[46] A respect for the other's liberty makes it a requirement that nothing shall be *imposed* on any party in ecumenism.[47]

If I think you are already in Christ in his Church where you are, I shall not want to win you for my church. Indeed I shall regard you as already a member of it. I may see a need to help with renewal, if the Church in your place has been damaged by events or has grown apathetic. That is mission. But its purpose will be to renew the Church in your place as itself, not to turn it into a daughter or offshoot or extension of the Church in my place.[48]

A sense of being victims, or of betrayal, or of a rivalry with other communities, are all signs that Christians are thinking of other Christians as being in some important ways not like themselves.[49]

---

[43] *The Pullach Report* (1972), 102; *Growth*, p. 28.

[44] See my article, 'Mission renews; proselytizing poaches', *The Church Times*, 12 June 1992.

[45] Cf. P. Duprey, 'The unity we seek', *Journal of Ecumenical Studies*, 16 (1979), 303–10, p. 308.

[46] In which one is 'genuinely willing, able, and determined to hear and understand' the other 'precisely as he is'. That is 'not to talk to him with an intention that must remain concealed and therefore under the surveillance of rules unilaterally imposed'. Elwyn A. Smith, Editorial, *Journal of Ecumenical Studies*, 4 (1967), p. 301.

[47] Text, translation and commentary on Vatican II's Decree on Ecumenism, *Istina*, 10 (1964), p. 381.

[48] See my article, 'Mission renews; proselytizing poaches', *The Church Times* 12 June 1992. The term 'mission' is sometimes incorrectly used as though interchangeable with proselytism. ' "Mission" [has] traditionally denoted an intention to convert: in effect a rejection of what the other holds: his manner of life and his familiar community in favour of our own belief, style of life and community . . . There is an unmistakable tension between ecumenical dialogue and all such communication . . . An intention to convert has to be at least suspended while conversation is in progress, and perhaps renounced . . . It must be bravely faced that ["conversionism"] is fundamentally inimical to ecumenism.' Elwyn A. Smith, Editorial, *Journal of Ecumenical Studies*, 4 (1967), p. 301.

[49] 'American denominations . . . have transmitted and preserved . . . aspects of the traditions from which they sprang; in that very act of conservation undertaken by uprooted persons utilizing their traditions for new purposes, in a new land, and under new conditions of religious pluralism, freedom, and voluntarism, the traditions were betrayed'. Russell E. Richey, ' "Catholic" Protestantism and American Denominationalism', *Journal of Ecumenical Studies*, 16 (1979), 213–231, p. 213.

That sense of 'otherness' can still be present even where there is growing closeness, but it is transformed. It can become a focus of loving interest instead of hostility.[50] In that way, it can be found ecumenically valuable to be 'intensely loyal to our own position', suggests Congar.[51] Such 'mutual emulation' involves taking into one's own system what is coming to be seen as good and right in the traditions of the others. That means that what is eventually brought together can be envisaged as a united Church made up of the existing churches in full agreement as equal participants, but at the same time transformed into one another.

Not yet par cum pari

So a fundamental rule of ecumenical theology would seem to be that there must be mutual acceptance, by churches engaging in dialogue, that each is truly body of Christ,[52] and at the same time that each has imperfections and faults for which repentance is needed. Without it the conversation cannot be between equals.[53] 'Meeting with a brother' is Congar's description.[54] He speaks of 'the cultivation of an attitude which is evangelical, fraternal and friendly'.[55] Certainly, anything less than a conversation between equals will not be a real conversation. That is the distinctive ecclesiological stance of ecumenism. There will be a good deal more to say about this in the next chapter when we come to look at dialogue. But we may take it as a starting-point here.

All this points to the law that accepting other Christian communities as ecclesially equal partners in dialogue is the indispensable methodological starting-point for ecumenical rapprochement. But it is not

---

[50] 'Now we are beginning to discover . . . how many admirable elements of the Christian tradition are represented more fully in others than in ourselves. We begin to feel the pressures of mutual emulation.' M. Novak, 'Concreteness and complementarity', *Journal of Ecumenical Studies*, 4 (1967), p. 120.

[51] Congar, *Divided Christendom*, p. 263. See, too, *Encounters for Unity*, ed. G. R. Evans, Lorelei Fuchs, Diane C. Kessler (Norwich, 1995), pp. 1–2.

[52] 'Catholics and Disciples along with many other Christians are discovering that, in essence, their commitment to Christ and their fellowship in the Gospel are the same'. Disciples–Roman Catholic Conversations, *Growth*, p. 164.

[53] 'If dialogue is the preferred instrument for arriving at an ever deeper and better understanding and expression of the truth about reality and our Christian faith, it must also be recognised that authentic dialogue can take place only between equals, *par cum pari*, as the Decree on Ecumenism puts it.' L. Swidler, 'Demo-Kratia or Consensus Fidelium', *Journal of Ecumenical Studies*, 19 (1982).   [54] Congar, *Divided Christendom*, p. 265.

[55] Congar, *Divided Christendom*, p. 264.

yet possible to do it perfectly.[56] There are still a great many lingering reservations. Vatican II's phrase for 'separated brethren', *fratres seiuncti*, would seem to hold within it an inherent anomaly. It accepts that individual Christians outside the Roman Catholic Church may be truly Christ's, but it does not in itself deem their communities to be sister-churches.[57] *Fratres* and *seiuncti* are in balance if not in tension, and it is ecumenically important that *fratres* be, as it were, underlined.[58]

Reciprocity is still hard to be sure of. Some Protestant communities continue to see Rome as Antichrist. That attitude has lingered well beyond the sixteenth century. In 1845 Philip Schaff (1819-93) published *The Principles of Protestantism*. In it he suggested that 'the Reformation is the greatest act of the Catholic Church itself, the full ripe fruit of all its better tendencies'. This startling insight into the presence of not only a common heritage but a single *ecclesia* behind[59] both Roman Catholic and Protestant traditions got him tried by a Reformed Synod in the USA which took the view that the papacy was guilty of apostasy and had ceased to be the Church at all.[60] Writing in the 1930s, Y. Congar was still able to recount of Protestants that:

one hears it said among them that our sacraments are nothing but 'magic' which automatically save their beneficiaries and that we rely exclusively on our own 'merits' and those of the saints. When such expressions have been used, everything has been said, for they are sufficient in themselves to convey the effect of a passionate aversion. Do they really believe that we worship idols, or that, for us, the Christian life is simply a profit-making enterprise which excludes the grace of God?[61]

---

[56] Carl E. Braaten, 'The reunited Church of the future', *Journal of Ecumenical Studies*, 4 (1967), 611–28, pp. 615–16. 'Can a Catholic give any acceptable meaning to the fundamental demand of the ecumenical attitude that he should recognize in Christian communities, such as the Eastern churches or Anglicanism, a positive role in connection with the development of Christianity in the world and the achievement of what the Catholic Church could be if reunion one day became a reality?' asks Congar. Congar, *Dialogue between Christians*, p. 114.

[57] A point made extensively in Y. Congar's *Divided Christendom*. The question of the status of other churches is addressed elsewhere in the documents of the Council.

[58] A point in Karl Barth's mind on his visit to the Vatican in 1966 where he spoke to Pope Paul VI. See Barth's *Ad Limina Apostolorum* and E. Busch, *Karl Barth* (London, 1976), p. 484.

[59] On 'getting behind', cf. Chapter 5.

[60] R. T. Handy, 'Freedom and authority in doctrinal matters', *Journal of Ecumenical Studies*, 12 (1975), 335–47.

[61] 'We desire our Protestant brethren to desist from this almost universal practice because it concerns a truth greater than ourselves, and we humbly beg them to do so in the full knowledge of our own unworthiness as the bearers of that truth.' Congar, *Dialogue between Christians*, p. 293, first published as 'La Protestantisme française', in *La vie intellectuelle* 10 February 1935.

He adds a plea for mutual understanding on the basis of the high call to unity. These old reservations of the Western churches about each other can go very deep, and linger in surprising places. There is a similar problem between East and West. The Orthodox churches have not yet been able to make together any definitive statement to parallel that of the Second Vatican Council, and thus acknowledge the ecclesiality of other communions. The Old Catholic–Orthodox conversations on Ecclesiology (1977-81) say, 'our Mixed Commission gives heresy and schism the appropriate significance and regards communities which continue in heresy and schism as in no sense workshops of salvation parallel to the true visible Church'. That seems to be saying that separated ecclesial bodies of Christians cannot be regarded as equally, equivalently or inter-changeably *in via*.

But there are other ways of achieving a working supposition of equality within Orthodoxy as elsewhere. The ancient tradition of economy in Orthodoxy is helpful here. It makes it possible to apply the 'as if' method in another way. It is, by the intervention of grace, as if the 'other' church were not 'other'.

Since it is impossible to set limits to God's power whose will it is that all should find salvation and come to know the truth, and since further the Gospel clearly speaks of salvation by faith in the unique Son of God . . . [John 3.36] . . . it can be considered as not excluded that the divine omnipotence and grace are present and operative wherever the departure from the fulness of truth in the one Church is not complete and does not go to the lengths of a complete estrangement from the truth.'[62]

Even where the principle of equality seems to be accepted, it is not without its shadings, and problems of commensurability. At one level this is a matter of having a sense of standing on level ground. If one side comes humbly asking help, does that mean that it is not claiming equality? To take an example: 'The church in their country had had no smooth path in late years,' admitted the Archbishop of Latvia in the discussions of the 1930s with Anglicans . . . 'They were glad to come into contact with other Christians who were prepared to assist them.'[63]

---

[62] 30; *Growth*, p. 407 .
[63] 'They had had hard struggles against godlessness and indifference' . . . 'They hoped and believed and prayed that the unity which had been realised among other Churches might be achieved between them and the Anglican Communion also.' Evangelical Lutheran Churches of Latvia and Estonia in conversation with the Church of England, 1936-8, *Lambeth Occasional Reports, 1931–8* (London, 1948), p. 216. Cf. Chapter 7 on the church which feels itself too junior to join in as an equal.

At another level commensurability has to fight with difference of emphasis. Even where other churches are in practice being accepted as equal partners in dialogue both at 'official' and at 'grass-roots' level there still remains the possibility of a difference of emphasis which can make ecclesiologies seem incommensurable. To press for commensurability may then look like pressing for a sameness which will not fully respect the identity and integrity of the 'Church in each place' or each distinct community. 'The Orthodox Church cannot recognise itself in other Christian groups', said Thomas Hopko at a conference of 1972.[64] Something of a crisis presented itself in Orthodox ecumenism at the time of the New Delhi meeting of the World Council of Churches in 1961. The WCC had made (and makes) no claims to be a church in its own right.[65] But there seemed a possibility that it might be entering a new phase of self-understanding where it might come to be seen as a means through which the *una sancta* might manifest itself.[66] Here the Orthodox (and others) would have had difficulties because their ecclesiological structures could not readily embrace that possibility. Some would hold that there is no visible Church but the local congregation and that therefore it is meaningless to speak of 'the Roman Catholic' or for that matter 'the Methodist' or 'the Anglican' Church. 'The problem is primordially a matter of the orientation of interior life,'[67] argues the view that 'the problem of Christian unity is not so much to reunite the visible Churches, as progressively to bring into one the visible Church and the invisible community of all those who are united to Christ'.[68] This in itself is an ecclesiological stance, but one which avoids the confrontational aspects of the problems of uniting visible churches.

It might be said, for example, that the search for a basic consensus looks, in Orthodox eyes, to an existing unity which is, 'in the last analysis, the criterion for the truth of faith and witness. Whereas, for the Protestant theologians, reformation means returning to the truth, the only possibility from the Orthodox standpoint seems to be a return to unity in the unbroken historical continuity and existing fellowship of the Church.'[69]

[64] G. C. Papademetriou, 'The Second International Theological Conference of USA Orthodox, 1972', *Journal of Ecumenical Studies*, 10 (1973), 209–13, p. 211. See, too, the Pan-Orthodox Conference of 1961 at Rhodes, reported in *Istina*, 9 (1963), p. 44.
[65] But see Chapter 7 on the objection of one respondent to *BEM* that it was doing so.
[66] New Delhi Assembly, 1961, *Istina*, 9 (1963), p. 338, and cf. *Journal of Ecumenical Studies*, 9 (1972).
[67] Paul Couturier, in *Oecuménisme spirituel*, ed. M. Villain (Paris, 1963), p. 148.
[68] G. H. Tavard, describing this view, *Journal of Ecumenical Studies*, 3 (1966), p. 510.
[69] WCC Faith and Order paper, 76, pp. 77–8. From a practical point of view it can be a further methodological difficulty in this area of 'commensurability' that the Orthodox tend to

As long as it remains the case that we are trying to treat as equally churches ecclesial bodies with very different kinds of self-understanding, or of understanding of what it is to be 'church', it remains hard to say whether we are trying to reunite one Church or to unite many churches.[70] And we have not really begun to address the problem of the fringe communities at the edges where sect blurs into cult, or Christianity becomes so 'inculturated' as to drift towards the syncretism the first generations of Christians so successfully resisted.

The provisionality of a state of separation

A key stage in the shift of ecclesiological stance ecumenism makes necessary is the acceptance that the divided state is abnormal. That is a very hard lesson to learn. Many churches have defined themselves over against others and thus built into their very sense of identity an acceptance of the normality of separation. 'Protestantism has yet to recognise clearly its interim mission, the extreme abnormality of its separate existence. Exiles know that they live in a crisis situation and they hope it is only temporary; they know that all is lost if they lose sight of the goal of ultimate reintegration of those who belong together.'[71] A key episode in the process of coming to understand the questionableness of a separated state was the nineteenth General Assembly of the World Reformed Alliance in 1964, when it was found possible actually to discuss whether confessionalism is a sin.[72] Parallels

---

'favour extensive study programmes embracing the whole universe of the faith' in bilateral conversations, 'and to attach little, if any, ecclesial value to an isolated agreement on a specific topic . . . unless it forms part of a cohesive and comprehensive convergence'. 'For example, the Tradition of the Church seems to the Orthodox an invisible totality, and it is impossible to conceive of tradition being set over against Scripture.' Protestants can and do work piece by piece. They ' . . . tend to assume that advance can be achieved more rapidly and surely by isolating the problems, probing forward as far as possible in well-defined areas, viewing the interim results as possessing a truth value in their own right, and then transposing them analogically to other problem areas in order to elicit further advancement of knowledge'. WCC Faith and Order Paper, 76, pp. 32–3.

[70] Y. Congar, 'Les ruptures de l'unité', *Istina*, 10 (1964), 133–78 explores changing implications of this question from the patristic period when schism is seen as a rupture of a single altar fellowship.

[71] Carl E. Braaten, 'The reunited Church of the future', *Journal of Ecumenical Studies*, 4 (1967), 611–28, p. 612.

[72] R.-C. Gerest, 'La XIX Assemblé générale de l'Alliance Réformé Mondiale' (August, 1964), *Istina*, 19 (1964), p. 224. Some would hold that there is no visible Church but the local congregation and that therefore it is meaningless to speak of 'the Roman Catholic' or for that matter 'the Methodist' or 'the Anglican' Church. 'The problem is primordially a matter of the orientation of interior life,' argues the view that 'the problem of Christian unity is not so much to reunite the visible Churches, as progressively to bring into one the visible Church

can be found in other communions. 'There is a temptation on the part of most Orthodox Christians to make "Orthodoxy" an object toward which all allegiance, devotion and veneration is focused ... it appears to be a phenomenon parallel to the ultramontanism of the Roman Catholic Church in the early nineteenth century and fundamentalist protestant bibliolatry in the same period,'[73] notes one observer.[74] Similar devotions to one or two key aspects of their own ecclesiology or ecclesiality can be found in many churches. A church may change its mind about what counts,[75] but it will tend to find its 'role' definitive for its being and to cling to it. While that remains so generally the case, it presents a methodological stumbling-block, because it is a barrier to the change of attitude which must precede reciprocal movement together.

The phenomenon of role-reversal

An ecclesiological stance which learns to see things as others see them, and indeed to cease to see the other as 'other' at all, can, by contrast, lead to patterns of role-reversal in conversations. This is familiar to anyone who has been involved in such dialogue. It means that each team is never a 'monolith'.[76] It always turns out that someone on each

and the invisible community of all those who are united to Christ.' This in itself is an ecclesiological stance, but one which avoids the confrontational aspects of the problems of uniting visible churches. It is possible to take a positive view of this: Y. Congar suggested in *Chrétiens désunis* (Paris, 1937), that separated communities might comprise souls sanctified not despite their confession but in and by their confession. See E. Lamirande, 'La signification ecclésiologique des communautés dissidentes et la doctrine des "vestigia ecclesiae" ', *Istina*, 10 (1964), 25–8, p. 26.

[73] R. G. Stephanopoulos, 'Reflections on Orthodox ecumenical directions after Uppsala', *Journal of Ecumenical Studies*, 9 (1972), pp. 301–17, p. 305.

[74] R. Stephanopoulos also made the point that it is a 'temptation of. . . Orthodox theologians to make the Church an "object of worship" which leads to "idolatry of the institution". "Orthodox" should,' he suggests, 'be as it has been in the patristic writings, an "adjective" which objectifies the content of faith, the reality of the life of the Church and the experience of the Holy Spirit'. G. C. Papademetriou, 'The Second International Theological Conference of USA Orthodox , 1972', *Journal of Ecumenical Studies*, 10 (1973), 209–13, p. 211. See, too, the Pan-Orthodox Conference of 1961 at Rhodes, reported in *Istina*, 9 (1963), p. 44.

[75] P. M. Harrison, *Authority and Power in the Free Church Tradition: A Social Case Study of the American Baptist Convention* (Princeton, 1959).

[76] This is vividly described by Tillard. 'One of the most misleading assumptions of ecumenical enquiry is that practice follows theology. According to their assumption, those who hold to the theology of justification by faith do, in practice, rely upon grace, while those who hold to a theology of works do, in practice, rely upon their own efforts.' J. M. R. Tillard, 'Anglican–Roman Catholic Dialogue', *One in Christ*, 8 (1972), 242–63, p. 255. Cf. M. Novak, 'Concreteness and complementarity: two principles of ecumenical theology', *Journal of Ecumenical Studies*, 4 (1967), 120–4, p. 120.

side is arguing in favour of points which might have been expected to be pressed by the other.[77]

This has its negative as well as its positive aspects.[78] Those whose personal experience of 'role-reversal' has taken them from membership of one communion to membership of another often resist rapprochement with it. 'Persons coming from Catholic or Orthodox backgrounds often bring with them the hostility converts usually have to their former faiths and oppose any ecumenical contacts with these groups,' notes one commentator.[79] But this is not always so.[80] So getting to know the other side can be a complex and unsettling experience. Whether or not the roles remain in place there can be unbalancing swings both ways.[81]

Yet in the process there can be a clearing of what has been blurred thinking and self-deception. This is frankly admitted by the partners in one Lutheran–Roman Catholic dialogue, for example.[82] And there can be fresh insights into where a church belongs.[83] In one sociologically

---

[77] 'The experience of dialogue, inspired by a desire to be honest and to search for the truth, compels Roman Catholics to realize very quickly that there are to be found within their own fold as well the same lines of division which in the Anglican tradition constitute officially-accepted movements ... Hence the debating of questions leads often to a confrontation *not* of the two Churches so much as of two ways of reading the data of the faith or of two ecclesial mentalities present in *both* groups.' J. M. R. Tillard, 'Anglican–Roman Catholic dialogue', *One in Christ*, 8 (1972), 242–63, p. 255.   [78] 'Ecumenism today', *One in Christ*, 11 (1975), 30–87, p. 45.

[79] On the phenomenon of role-reversal leading to an actual changing of 'sides' by joining another Church. Glenn A. Igleheart, 'Ecumenical Concern among Southern Baptists', *Journal of Ecumenical Studies*, 17 (1980), 49–61, p. 57.

[80] 'On the other hand the presence of so many former members of other protestant churches in the Southern Baptist Convention membership predisposes a lessening of denominational distinctiveness and an opening to interdenominational relations.' Glenn A. Igleheart, 'Ecumenical concern among Southern Baptists', *Journal of Ecumenical Studies*, 17 (1980), 49–61, p. 57.

[81] 'The new situation gives all parties concerned a new dimension of ecumenical responsibility for the future, namely, to keep open the channels through which we constantly remind one another of the vices in our own virtues, and even the virtues in the other's vices ... if Catholicism becomes overly enamoured of the "Protestant principle", it may need Protestants to remind it that there is an ongoing "Catholic substance" – and vice-versa. For even with the roles reversed, the underlying problems remain the same, and merely switching the scripts will not remove them.' Ibid.

[82] 'In the Lutheran tradition, polemical reaction against the idea of a so to speak "free-floating" ministry, completely separated from the people of God, has partly contributed towards ignoring the distinction between ordination, and installation into a concrete ministry. Thus the conviction has been expressed that in principle ministry and congregation cannot be separated, but must be related to one another. Yet in the area of the Lutheran Reformation general ordination, not limited to a particular congregation, has usually been practised.' L–RC , *The Ministry in the Church* (1981), 38; *Growth*, p. 260.

[83] 'One phenomenon which the Anglicans encountered and which caused some of them surprise (though perhaps it should not have done so) was that the points of theological disagreement did not mostly occur over Protestant or Reformation doctrine ... The main difference was between the Western Latin and the Eastern Greek theological traditions. The Anglicans ... at times ... felt that it was honestly their duty to defend the doctrine or practice

conducted survey in the United States it was possible to conclude that many Roman Catholics, though rather fewer Protestants, held that 'Protestants and Catholics are becoming more and more alike in their religious beliefs and practices'.

The problem of those who refuse to join in

Some communions have entered actively into the ecumenical enterprise only slowly or uncertainly, or not yet at all. The Roman Catholic Church had pioneers of the movement, such as Yves Congar, within it during the first half of the twentieth century. But its official and wholehearted commitment begins with the Second Vatican Council, as we shall see again and again in what follows. Within the processes of the Second Vatican Council itself there occurred shifts of assumption. One commentator noted the way in which the hopes of the ecumenists were gradually realised.[84] The entry of the Roman Catholic Church into the ecumenical endeavour in this dramatic, and at the time unexpected, way has done more perhaps than that of any other single church to transform the scene, adding wholly new factors and heightening awareness of a number of existing issues.[85]

Others have been associated longer with the movement but have tended to behave as partial outsiders, or to be inclined to present uncomfortable challenges, to be askers of disturbing questions. That can be a good and useful thing. Such questioning stances have often been instructive about the way the movement should be going. 'The distinctive Orthodox abandonment to the Holy Spirit . . . has enabled them to be "welcome troublemakers" in the Ecumenical Movement', comments one observer.[86]

Nevertheless, some caution is needed here.[87] The challenge of the Christian communion which appears to be dragging its feet or asking awkward questions or presenting a radically different viewpoint cannot always be taken to offer salutary lessons, although, in the case

---

of the Roman Catholic Church. Some of us felt, in short, that we were Western Latins, much though we no doubt have to learn from the Eastern Church.'*The Times*, 23 October, 1976.

[84] While the timid, the pessimistic and those disquieted at this development grew fewer. 'D. O. R.', 'Autour du Concile: l'Inter-session', *Irénikon*, 36 (1963), 204–22.

[85] Editorial, *Istina*, 10 (1964), p. 129.

[86] John Pinnington, 'Symposium: Ecumenism and the Modern World' (held at Duchesne University Pittsburgh), *Journal of Ecumenical Studies*, 2 (1965), p. 256.

[87] 'We should not too readily assume that the Orthodox have solutions to our problems in the West just because they appear to have by-passed our mistakes.' Comment of Dietrich Ritsch in John Pinnington, 'Symposium: Ecumenism and the Modern World', *Journal of Ecumenical Studies*, 2 (1965), p. 261.

of Orthodoxy, it almost always has done, for the Orthodox bring perspectives from the ancient Christian world which have kept a freshness among them largely lost elsewhere.

Others have refused to come in at all, and that is a different matter. The position of the Seventh-Day Adventists, for example, is ultimately irreconcilable with Christian ecumenism, and not in a way which can (as far as one can see), be useful to the movement. One apologist speaks of their 'theological distinctiveness', as definitive.[88] It takes the denominationalist case as far as it is possible to take it by holding that the entire justification of Adventism lies in its unique possession of the truth. To seek to unite with other churches would be to lose the *raison d'être* of the church. That is a position other communities have taken or continue to take although not always in such an extreme way.

More common is an intransigent 'immobilism' which arises out of the belief that some historic position of a given community is an absolute, a terminus.[89] On this view it is impossible to talk with any other community with the open mind and willingness to enter into common life which ecumenical rapprochement requires. That willingness requires a knowledge of the history of theology and of the Church itself which such communities have not traditionally found relevant.[90] Without a wider and longer sense of the shape of the Christian story Christians naturally feel more comfortable where they are. The denominational church, with its certainties and sense of identity, provides a reassuring home base.

Some churches have been pragmatic, co-operating ecumenically when it served their ends and withdrawing when it did not. That may be regarded as perhaps a more cynical reason for the failure of ecumenical commitment.[91]

---

[88] 'With such wide divergence from the great body of Christendom, coupled with a deep conviction that our belief on these matters is in harmony with Scripture, how could we possibly come into any kind of genuine and lasting unity with other churches? The attitude of the Seventh-Day Adventist Church toward the ecumenical movement is based, in my best judgement,' he goes on, 'upon the charity of true wisdom ... The very logic of our belief demands that we seek to persuade men to accept the message we preach and to join the Advent movement, and help it accomplish its world-wide task.' R. Dederen, 'An Adventist response' to C. Rubencamp, 'The Seventh-Day Adventists and the Ecumenical Movement', *Journal of Ecumenical Studies*, 7 (1970), pp. 561–2.

[89] 'Without realizing that every "historic position" ... is not the end of the march but merely a bivouac on the route of the pilgrim church.' Arthur B. Crabtree, Editorial, *Journal of Ecumenical Studies*, 7 (1970), p. 100.

[90] We shall come to the implications of that in Chapter 5.

[91] E. Glenn Hinson, 'William Carey and ecumenical pragmatism', *Journal of Ecumenical studies*, 17 (1980), 73–83.

It has long been noticeable that the churches which have grown most strikingly in numbers in the nineteenth and twentieth centuries (that is, when heads could most accurately be counted), have been 'generally the most backward in ecumenical cooperation in the modern period'.[92] There is an ecclesiological reason for this as well as the simple human one that people find the well-defined and familiar most comfortable and will continue for that reason to gravitate towards it rather than risk the ecumenical step into the unknown. Indeed the ecclesiological reason is merely a more sophisticated statement of the same principle. The local church is properly 'the Church in each place'. It is wholly the Church and the Christian can be wholly Christ's within it. In the ancient and mediaeval Church in both East and West this was seen as all-of-a-piece with the unity of the catholic or universal Church. That sense of the articulation of the local and universal was altered in the churches of the West which became divided from the Roman Catholic Church in the sixteenth century.

There came into being in many Protestant communities a belief that 'the local church's primary concern' is with 'strengthening the relationship between man and God through emphasizing individual responsibility'.[93] In other words, there was a shift as far away as possible from an extreme universalist position towards an extreme individualist stance. This has proved fully compatible with the flourishing of a strong local church pattern. It has not proved a large step from here to a suspicion of all enterprises which seem to have in view the bringing together of local churches in a larger whole. The fear of domination which helped to prompt the sixteenth-century break-away and to cause it to repeat itself in the centuries since, easily reasserts itself. 'The Free Church Association', says an apologist for this view, 'will resist ecumenical monoliths and all totalitarian concepts in religion which tend to undermine' this emphasis.[94] But it is inescapable that something which is the beginning of unity happens when even the most reluctant positive response is felt.[95]

[92] Franklin H. Littell, Editorial, *Journal of Ecumenical Studies*, 2 (1965), pp. 278–9.
[93] James DeForest Murch, *The Protestant Revolt* (Arlington, Virginia, 1967), pp. 267–8.
[94] James DeForest Murch, *The Protestant Revolt* (Arlington, Virginia, 1967), pp. 267–8.
[95] 'Their response to the call of ecumenism, no matter how prudent and cautious it may be, automatically draws Christian Confessions into a perspective specifically and intentionally focussed on universality, especially in the matter of beliefs.' Congar, *Dialogue between Christians*, p. 147.

STEPS AND STAGES

The step by step approach

'Our search is for steps in "a process of gradual rapprochement . . . in which various stages are possible"[96] In such an open process of growing together we can and should set our eyes on *intermediate goals* and keep on re-examining the methods of advance.'[97] The Lutheran–Roman Catholic conversation which saw things in this light envisaged a 'moving in this way from an incomplete to a more and more complete communion'. It also saw it as a process such as we have already said that ecumenism must be: a moving forward in trust without necessarily being able to see far ahead along the way.[98] The underlying rule here is to be open to the Holy Spirit's guidance.

The most striking thing about any attempt to trace steps in any systematic way is the difficulty of making it fit the disorderly character of the lived experience.[99] It is tempting, in stocktaking, to think otherwise. Certainly it was a temptation to do so a century ago when many present-day difficulties had not yet become apparent. In the Bonn Reunion Conversations of the 1870s:

Dr. Döllinger said we were now far on the road towards an understanding. He thought that about three-quarters of the matter was already peaceably settled. Respecting the remaining quarter it would perhaps be best to appoint a select committee of two or three of each of the three main bodies,

---

[96] L–RC Malta; 73, *Growth*, pp. 185–6.

[97] L–RC, *Ways to Community*, 1980, 54; *Growth*, p. 225.

[98] L–RC, *Ways to Community*, 1980, 54; *Growth*, p. 225.

[99] This Lutheran–Roman Catholic discussion broke down the 'steps' into categories. The first category, 'implied by the nature of ecclesial fellowship (*communio*) as a gift of God's grace', is spiritual. These are the steps of experiencing a change of heart; of becoming open to the discovery 'of great spiritual treasures in the past and present of other churches'; of the realisation that the Holy Spirit has 'maintained through its work in our churches a fundamental fellowship', despite division. The second category of 'steps' involves 'the mediation of community'. Here the ministry of Word and sacrament and common service in ministry must be brought closer in the understanding of the two communities. Then there is the 'realisation of community' through common study of common faith, trust in going forward in a common hope, and the finding together of a community of love. There is a further series of steps to be taken in achieving unity in 'form of community', through recognition of ministries, 'credible practice', 'collaboration' (here there is an emphasis on the preservation of legitimate diversity). The final category of 'steps' has to do with the 'all-encompassing character of the community', the unity of humankind and Christian responsibility to the world.

Helpful though they are, these are treated rather discursively, and their progressive, stepwise character is by no means always clear. L–RC, *Ways to Community*, 1980, 56 ff; *Growth*, pp. 226–40.

Orientals, Anglicans and Germans, to draw up statements respecting the remaining points of difference, and lay these before the Conference.[100]

It does not look so easy now. Perhaps, as one commentator suggests, we are tending not to examine closely enough the assumptions that there are indeed natural 'steps' to unity, a proper sequence. [101]

But certainly sometimes there has been a consciousness of being at a particular stage. 'Coexistence', for example, was seen at the beginning of the 1960s as not a substitute for unity but a stage through which it is necessary to pass on the way to unity.[102] An observer of the work of the World Council of Churches' Faith and Order Commission suggested a year or so later that Lund, 1952 had marked the end of the period of making comparisons, and the beginning of an attempt to approach problems Christologically and pneumatologically, in the hope that a new and positive light could thus be thrown on them. In 1963 the Montreal meeting was beginning to see further into the complexity of the issues and to suggest that it would be necessary to enlarge the methodology and the choice of subjects and questions to discuss and to take account of their interdependency.[103]

Again, the notion of steps or stages was a model much in evidence in the responses of the 1980s to the *BEM* text:

'a stage along the way';[104]

an 'extremely important milestone ... Theologians representing a
    hundred different traditions have found a common ground on
    which to pursue the dialogue on the issues dividing Christians';[105]

'an important stage in Church reconciliation, dialogue and
    collaboration';[106]

'the distance travelled towards this agreed statement'; [107]

a 'landmark on the road to removal of misunderstandings and
    obstacles in the relationships between the Churches';[108]

---

[100] Alfred Plummer, *Conversations with Dr Döllinger, 1870–90*, ed. R. Boudens (Louvain, 1985), p. 133, August 1875. On these conversations, see further, Chapter 6.

[101] That is, to take the 'incremental approach to Christian unity' for granted, 'without having to explain very much what we understand by it, much less offer a defence or rationale for it'. John F. Hotchkin, 'Bilaterals – phasing into unity', *Journal of Ecumenical Studies*, 23 (1986), 404–11, p. 404.

[102] C. Constantinidis, 'Présupposés de la coexistence', *Istina*, 8 (1961–2), 381–4, p. 382.

[103] J. Vodopivec, 'Foi et Constitution à Aarhus' (1964), *Istina*, 10 (1964), p. 191.

[104] *Churches Respond to BEM*, IV, p. 4, The Roman Catholic Church.

[105] *Churches Respond to BEM*, V, p. 4, Malankara Orthodox Syrian Church (India).

[106] *Churches Respond to BEM*, V, p. 168, Reformed Church in Hungary.

[107] *Churches Respond to BEM*, IV, p. 7, Mar Thoma Syrian Church of Malabar.

[108] *Churches Respond to BEM*, IV, p. 80.

'we now present our response to BEM in the prayerful hope that it will make a small contribution towards the eventual reception of a common expression of the apostolic faith by all churches'.[109]

Its satisfactoriness here seems to lie in its enabling us to see that we have got on, and to feel pleased about it. That has a value in itself, but it is a limited one.

Gradual growing together

Altogether more realistic seems the picture of a gradual growing together, an eventual convergence of the churches through dialogue and practical Christian living together. That can perhaps be achieved on a double understanding of the dynamics: that there cannot be more than a *perfectio currens*, a 'working completeness' in this life; and that the Church will always be reforming herself, *ecclesia semper reformanda*, and can never in this world be what she was created to be, though she must strive for that perpetually. This is closely akin to one of the principles of central importance to the Reformed and Roman Catholics alike, 'the acceptance of "the principle of continuing reformation under the Word of God by the guidance of the Holy Spirit"'.[110]

An essential element here is that both the 'step by step' and the 'gradual growing together' motifs have within them an acceptance that work for the foreseeable future can only be preparatory for union. Cardinal Bea said on 29 January 1962 that Vatican II would not be a council of unity like those of Lyons and Florence, but that nevertheless it would have an ecumenical finality in the sense that it would prepare for union.[111] The Anglican–Orthodox Moscow statement of 1976 prompted the comment that 'while both sides . . . were profoundly encouraged by the *progress* made, they were also conscious that their agreement is only over a limited field, and is often phrased in very general terms.'[112] Report after Report speaks in similar terms of a sense of the smallness of what has yet been achieved in proportion to the great vision of what a truly peaceful fellowship in unity ought to be.

---

[109] *Churches Respond to BEM*, V, p. 180, Melanesian Council of Churches.

[110] Paul A. Crow, 'Ecumenism and the consultation on Church union', *Journal of Ecumenical Studies*, 4 (1967), 581–603, p. 584. The other three principles he outlines are 'commitment to a Church truly democratic in its government'; 'seeking for new ways to recapture and manifest the brotherhood and fellowship of all its members and ministers'; 'the inclusion in its catholicity of a wide diversity of theological formulations of the faith'.

[111] Cited in Editorial, *Irénikon*, 35 (1962), p. 4.   [112] A–O, Moscow, 1976, p. 44.

'The Eucharist is not and never can be the sign of a perfectly achieved unity; it is always the sign of an imperfect unity seeking to become more perfect.' Avery Dulles here proposes a notion very like that of Augustine's *perfectio currens*. He sets it in the context of a discussion of the place of the 'intercommunion' which necessarily falls short of full union. (It should be stressed that 'intercommunion', for the reasons stated below, is a term ecumenists would now prefer to avoid.) 'Intercommunion is to be recommended,' Ramsey suggests:

when it promotes enduring habits, patterns and structures of mutual concern and responsibility among divided Christians and Churches. When this does not happen or is not intended, it may well be more destructive than constructive. It then threatens to become an expression of subjective attitudes of togetherness, rather than as an efficacious sign of God's gift, and can lead to views of the Church as evanescent fellowships of the like-minded.

So among the conditions for intercommunion as he envisages them is a dissatisfaction with it, which is stimulated by 'the will to a more perfect union'.[113]

The dissatisfaction is in a sense a 'divine discontent' with anything but the fullness of a communion before which one need place no qualifying adjective or other modification. 'We see ourselves as having a communion *in via*', said the Disciples–Roman Catholic conversations, echoing the thought.[114] Again, such sentiments are to be found very widely.

Running with a leading idea

The 'steps and stages' and the 'gradual convergence' pictures are not mutually exclusive but complementary. At intervals a stage in ecumenical progress is marked by the fashionableness of a particular theme. From time to time an idea comes to the fore and is run with for a time as a 'leading idea'. At the time of the Malines conversations of the 1920s the notion that churches could be 'united' but not 'absorbed' was proposed. It was thought by Beauduin that the Anglican Church might be 'united to but not absorbed by Rome, in much the same way as some "uniate" Eastern Catholics had preserved a definite liturgical and disciplinary autonomy while yet being united to Rome'. This reflected a realisation that 'group reunion rather than individual

---

[113] Avery Dulles, 'Intercommunion between Lutherans and Roman Catholics', *Journal of Ecumenical Studies*, 13 (1976), 250–7.   [114] Disciples–Roman Catholic; *Growth*, p. 164.

conversions' were 'the real solution to the problem of disunity'.[115] In the 1970s 'united not absorbed' again became a favourite concept, revived at the suggestion of Christopher Butler. He contended that his idea was not exactly the same as Beauduin's; rather, it would involve 'some sort of coexistence in full ecclesial communion'. He admitted that the uniate idea is an imperfect notion from an ecclesiastical point of view.[116] 'Reunion through coexistence will be only a penultimate, or better a preliminary stage.'[117]

Minimum and maximum

At the Bonn Conference of 1875 Reinkens said 'if we are to wait until we can agree about such questions as the number of ecumenical Councils we can no more become one Church than one nation'.[118] It was clear as early as this that there was going to be a problem almost of trade-off between ease and speed of movement towards unity and the number of points on which agreement would have to be reached first. There have continued to be two schools of thought on this among ecumenists.

At the end of the first session of the Second Vatican Council it was clear that there would have to be more sessions. To some that was a disappointment.[119] 'Easy superficial theology' is a danger, said Michael Ramsey, then Archbishop of Canterbury, in an address to the WCC New Delhi meeting in 1961. Such a theology suggests that we need only agree a few simple principles to arrive at unity. There is, he suggests, a risk of inadequate examination of the principles when that happens.[120] The Evangelical-Reformed Church of North-West Germany argued in its response to *BEM* that it was not right to aim at 'the wording of a minimal consensus. Special experiences of faith and theological insights should not be levelled out, but introduced into the ecumenical process of reflection'.[121]

The Bonn agreement of Anglicans and Old Catholics had limited aspirations. Here a minimum agreement gave a minimum union.

[115] S. A. Quitslund, ' "United not absorbed", does it still make sense?', *Journal of Ecumenical Studies*, 8 (1971), 255–85, p. 268.
[116] S. A. Quitslund, ' "United not absorbed", does it still make sense?', *Journal of Ecumenical Studies*, 8 (1971), 255–85, p. 282.
[117] E. P. Echlin, 'Unity without absorption', *Journal of Ecumenical Studies*, 9 (1972), 51–73, p. 67.
[118] Alfred Plummer, *Conversations with Dr Döllinger , 1870–90* , ed. R. Boudens (Louvain, 1985), p. 140, August 1875.   [119] *Istina*, 10 (1964), p. 335. See too Suenens, Stacpoole.
[120] *Istina*, 10 (1964), p. 319 in account of the New Delhi meeting.
[121] *Churches Respond to BEM*, IV, p. 94.

The churches remained ecclesially distinct. Their communion was to be 'intercommunion', understood here as communion between two communions which do not thereby become a single communion. An enlargement is the approach which confines itself principally to a few key problems where there has been disagreement but understands these to lie in a context of what is understood by both sides to be in fact agreement at all other points of faith and order as a whole. This 'seeks to express our basic agreement in the doctrinal areas which have been the source of controversy between us, in the wider context of our common convictions about the ministry'.[122]

But it has become apparent that that cannot be taken for granted in all bilaterals as it could for Anglicans and Roman Catholics, and that nothing short of a 'maximal' approach will really do. That does not mean necessarily seeking identity of view on all points of faith and identity of practice on all points of order. It does mean seeking to arrive at a common understanding of faith and order in which all the richness of diversity is reconciled.

[122] ARCIC *M*, 1; *Growth*, p. 79.

CHAPTER 3

Communication and dialogue

CHURCHES AND PERSONS

It is one of the paradoxes of ecumenical encounter that although what is happening is a meeting of churches, that can happen only in and through the meeting of human individuals.[1] We have already noted that churches are not persons in the same way that individuals are persons, although the Church has a corporate identity as the body of Christ. The problem is that persons do not always keep clear, as they talk, the distinction between their positions as individuals and their positions as representatives of an ecclesial body. 'I cannot put my name to this,'[2] says a member of a commission, speaking in conscience as a person, as much as because he fears to 'betray a constituency' if he does.

We have not got very far in exploring the relationship between personal change of attitude to other churches and affirmation of mutual respect, and that which is now possible in and between communities; for communities are made up of persons and must carry their members with them when they 'move'. J. M. R. Tillard writes (in connection with justification by faith) on the ecumenical problem of 'collective faith'. The bulk of work done over the centuries since Luther has been devoted to the working of justification by faith, in the individual and *a Deo solo*. But in baptism the candidate becomes a member of the Church. The baptismal affirmation of faith includes a collective element. Is there justification by faith *a Deo et ecclesia*?[3] 'There is no Christian group denying that the Church of God is *at least* the community of all those who "receive" the Salvation God offers to

[1] See Extract from a discourse of L. Vischer to the Assembly of Enugu (January, 1965), *Irénikon*, 38 (1965), p. 112.   [2] Roger Beckwith in A–O, Moscow.
[3] J. M. R. Tillard, 'The problem of justification: a new context for study', *One in Christ*, 26 (1990) 328–38, p. 329.

humanity.'[4] In another recent article, Tillard points out the inseparability of tradition, and faith in this collective sense. For the Christian community:

formulating their creed [is] the gaining and naming of their own identity . . . Experience proves that a group does not gain its own identity or become firmly bound together by it unless it has a living 'memory' of its foundational history . . . A group fragments when it allows divergent readings (I don't say different ones, that is another matter) of its founding event[5] . . . The creeds are always the work of communities, not of isolated individuals . . . Church cannot exist without feeling itself *hic et nunc* in communion with the long line of generations which have preceded it and prepared it . . . it is not a spiritual 'happening' which results from a sudden experience on the part of some personality or group. It is the presence, today, of an experience which has the sheen of centuries on it, since it is inseparable from the experience of the apostles, even of Israel.[6]

If saving faith must, by definition, also be shared faith, that shared faith must be the faith of the living community; and not only the shared faith of the whole community of the faithful, but also, in important ways, of the specific community. The Christian who believes belongs. What is at issue ecumenically is the way in which that belonging which he feels strongly in his own community can become a belonging *with* others *in* theirs. For divided churches not to see the force of this imperative is, Tillard suggests, for them to 'postpone everything required by their mutual "recognition" as sister-churches'.[7]

It can be invaluable ecumenically when this profound sense of family with other Christians is felt by individuals who can take a lead. The Roman Catholics at Malines commented on the 'sincerity and freedom of spirit, the openness of mind, the cordiality which have prevailed throughout'.[8] This is an experience most ecumenists can echo. Something characteristically happens in such encounters to create an atmosphere of freedom and charity. 'Further plain talk

---

[4] It has to be asked, he argues, whether the community can mean to recognise in the candidate's confession of faith something different from its own doctrine. J. M. R. Tillard, 'The problem of justification: a new context for study', *One in Christ*, 26 (1990) 328–38, p. 337. Yet can the affirmation of faith in baptism be required as an act of obedience by the magisterium? Ibid., p. 335.   [5] J. M. R. Tillard, 'We believe', *One in Christ*, 27 (1991), p. 4.
[6] J. M. R. Tillard, 'We believe', *One in Christ*, 27 (1991), p. 6.
[7] J. M. R. Tillard, 'Communion and salvation', *One in Christ*, 28 (1992), 1–12.
[8] *The Conversations at Malines: Report Presented to the Archbishop of Canterbury by the Anglican Members* (Oxford, 1927), Supplement, p. 75.

followed'[9] is a recollection which bodes nothing but good. The
Roman Catholics at Malines had a sense that there had been real
honesty. There had been 'an entirely frank conversation' on the
papacy. It had been possible to list points held in common.[10] So the
wider sense of family breaks down barriers and leads to mutual ease.

A pattern of the establishment of a friendliness and trust which
makes it possible to be candid is common. It was noted, for example,
by Methodist and Roman Catholic participants in dialogue in the
conversations which led to *The Denver Report*. 'The friendship and
mutual confidence we were able to establish so quickly . . . ensured a
welcome for the candour of the chief speakers on doctrine.'[11]
Participants in the Pentecostalist–Roman Catholic conversations
found that their 'first gathering was largely an occasion for beginning
to know one another'. But 'at the second meeting in 1971 each side
put "hard" questions to the other, a more purposeful conversation
resulted, and it became clear that it would be possible to undertake
discussions of a more systematic kind'.[12]

But a compounding factor today, which operated less in the first
ecumenical conversations because they had little Third World repre-
sentation, is that cultural expectations can differ radically. That can
make it hard for individuals to be sufficiently aware of the incommensurability of many of their own and their communities' assumptions
with those of Christians from other cultures. 'When missionaries from
a universalist tradition with a canonical literature encounter tribal
peoples with oral cultures, the whole idea of discussions designed to
facilitate the disinterested pursuit of religious truth becomes slightly
absurd,' argues one commentator. 'Yet such is the model of dialogue
that Western Christians, at least, tend to presuppose.'[13] In other words,
the barriers may be on the scale of fundamental differences of world-view
and systems of thought. That makes the task unimaginably harder.
There are as yet few paths mapped out from one philosophical terrain

---

[9] *The Conversations at Malines: Report Presented to the Archbishop of Canterbury by the Anglican Members* (Oxford, 1927), Supplement, p. 14.

[10] That 'St. Peter was accepted as chief or "leader" because he was treated as such by our Lord'; that 'the See of Rome is the only apostolic See known in the West'; that 'the Pope possesses a primacy among all the Bishops of Christendom; so much so that, apart from communion with him, there is no hope or prospect of ever seeing a reunited Christendom'; that 'the primacy of the Pope is not merely a primacy of honour, but it implies a duty of solicitude and of activity within the universal Church for the general good, in such wise that the Pope should in fact be a centre of unity, and a head which exercises authority over the whole'. *The Conversations at Malines: Report Presented to the Archbishop of Canterbury by the Anglican Members* (Oxford, 1927), Supplement, p. 89.   [11] M–RC, *The Denver Report*, 12; *Growth*, p. 310.

[12] *Growth*, p. 422.

[13] John d'Arcy May, 'Integral ecumenism', *Journal of Ecumenical Studies*, 25 (1988), 573–9, p. 578.

to the other. Indeed, it is a rare individual who has a real mastery of more than his own 'scene' in this respect.

So if we are to look for the rules of ecumenical communication and dialogue we probably have to start here, with individuals in the front line, and the relation in which they understand themselves to stand to the communities they represent, and the world-views of those communities.

This presents us with the question 'What is required of a man or woman conducting an ecumenical conversation?'[14] Vocation ought perhaps to come at the head of any list. It is not simply a matter of *deciding* to be ecumenically minded.[15] Many committed ecumenists express a sense of having been put to work which they have then come to embrace for themselves. Hans Küng spoke of 'this life-task of mine' which he came to grasp as 'a great opportunity'.[16] Yves Congar traced his own developing sense of ecumenical vocation in an auto-biographical essay at the beginning of *Dialogue between Christians*.[17] He shows how factors of intellectual discomfort and resistance can intermingle with the vocational conviction that something must be done. Congar saw himself as having been drawn in by a distress which seems as much intellectual as spiritual, at the persistence of 'misconceptions . . . prejudices and . . . specious disputes which prevented Protestants from recognizing the true face of the Church and also perpetuated among Catholics a false idea of the Reformation and of protestantism'.[18]

The 'ecumenical vocation',[19] if we can call it that, tests many qualities: 'sincerity', adds one list; patience; persistence; a willingness to start again when discouraged.[20] Subtlety and flexibility of mind are also developed, by an awareness of the complexity of the problems at issue; and with these, the healing recognition that those who allowed division to occur were often motivated by high vision.[21] To respect the

---

[14] G. Biemer, 'Theology of encounter: Heinrich Fries' theological contribution toward ecumenical understanding', *Journal of Ecumenical Studies*, 1 (1964), 213–43, p.224.

[15] 'Not everyone can be open by wanting to be.' Elwyn A. Smith, Editorial, *Journal of Ecumenical Studies*, 4 (1967), p.303.

[16] Hans Küng, 'Why I remain a Catholic', *Journal of Ecumenical Studies*, 17 (1980), 141–7.

[17] Congar, *Dialogue between Christians*.   [18] Congar, *Dialogue between Christians*, p. 12.

[19] For a recent collection of autobiographical accounts to set beside that of Congar, see *Encounters for Unity*, ed. G. R. Evans, Lorelei Fuchs and Diane C. Kessler (Norwich, 1995).

[20] G. Biemer, 'Theology of encounter: Heinrich Fries' theological contribution toward ecumenical understanding', *Journal of Ecumenical Studies*, 1 (1964), 213–43, p. 224.

[21] 'The Reformers were moved by the legitimate and more than justified desire to strive after and accomplish the reform of the Church'. G. Biemer, 'Theology of encounter: Heinrich Fries' theological contribution toward ecumenical understanding', *Journal of Ecumenical Studies*, 1 (1964), 213–43, p. 224.

other's motives is to be unable altogether to condemn. (Here we should perhaps add a realism about the existence of inner prejudices and mixture of motives, a capacity for admitting that one has been wrong.) There has to be a certain capacity for selflessness, a willingness to work without seeking personal credit towards the production of texts in which one's own contributions are subordinated to the common task; a putting of self at the disposal of others. Some of these may be learnt by dedication and experience. Some of them are qualities of character and intellectual temperament which will make some individuals by nature more useful in this service than others.

But a selection of ecumenists by fitness is not perhaps a road down which we shall want to go, at least without mapping it very carefully first. There seems to have been a pattern of divine interference with the recommended profile, and of surprising disjunctions between the availability of persons for ecumenical service and the churches' use of them ecumenically. Leading ecumenists have not infrequently been condemned by their churches' authorities. When in 1948 Congar revised *Chrétiens désunis* he found that he had to rewrite two chapters and make more than a hundred changes. He was unable to obtain a *nihil obstat* from one of the two censors to whom his Dominican Father General sent it and he was kept waiting for a decision until 1950. It seemed to him, as he puts it, 'that at this juncture I could serve the cause best by keeping silence and by publishing nothing'.[22]

Malines[23] was unofficial and at the time, 'there were many in both Churches who viewed the conversations with scepticism and open mistrust'.[24] Archbishop Lang confessed to Halifax, 'I agree with you that formal conferences are almost useless unless they have been preceded by informal and private conferences to pave the way.'[25] The Lambeth Conference of 1920 said in its Appeal 'The time has come for all the separated groups of Christians to agree.'[26] But without official conversations there can be no commitment of the churches, and no progress. That commitment began with the events which set up ARCIC I and other officially sponsored bilateral conversations

---

[22] Congar, *Dialogue between Christians*, pp. 35–40. Instances of theologians condemned for their views are not hard to find.
[23] On the setting up of the Malines conversations, see Mercier's own account of how Halifax came to see him, printed in Halifax, *Documents*, pp. 83 ff., as Annexe IV. See, too, P. Duprey, 'Développement actuel des relations entre l'Eglise catholique et la Communion anglicaine', *Unité des chrétiens*, 23 (1976), 29–30.
[24] C. Hill, 'The Decree on Ecumenism: an Anglican view', *One in Christ*, 30 (1994), 20–31, p. 20.
[25] J. G. Lockhart, *Viscount Halifax*, II (London, 1936), p. 270.
[26] *Appeal* of the 1920 Lambeth Conference.

after the Second Vatican Council's expression of an ecclesiology of mutual ecclesial respect.[27] This made it possible to progress beyond talks initiated by and held between members of divided churches who were meeting as persons, to a meeting, in some sense, of the churches themselves.

Yet 'group thinking' is a phenomenon of which history ought to make us cautious. Human minds can lose their sense of individual responsibility when in a crowd. Those caught up in a mob are not as a rule at their highest or best. The lesson of which it is important not to lose sight is that 'again and again in Church history the breakthrough in creative thought has come from an individual or small group of Christians'.[28] Anyone who has sat on a committee has observed the modifying effects of the contributions of some of its individual members, how a natural leader or diplomat or person with drive can get things done; how one person will always volunteer to redraft a text; how that is not always the best person for the job but sometimes nevertheless the best choice because his or her version will command the loyalty of certain of the others; how a chairman can enable or impede.

This is to argue that collective thinking is secondary to individual thinking, or to the relatively intimate intellectual encounters of twos and threes. We have said that churches have to talk through individuals, that the actual conversations necessarily take place between representatives of communities, who are themselves individual people, and whose minds perform the actions of give and take directly with the other persons who are their point of encounter. A few persons hold a conversation in a different way from a larger group of individuals. The process of establishing mutual trust and respect, listening to the other, noting the other's reservations, responding with sensitivity to the other's difficulties, advancing the case for one's own view in terms the other can recognise and accept, adjusting one's picture in the light of the other's response – all these can go on with much more subtlety and sensitivity and finer sensibility between individuals and in small groups than in large gatherings, where the factors to be taken into account are multiplied and human capacity to take it all in is much stretched. (Members of ARCIC II, for example, reported a change in the group dynamics with even a modest enlargement of numbers over the quota for ARCIC I.)

[27] Cf. ARCIC I, *The Final Report*, 7, pp. 110–11.
[28] M–RC, *The Denver Report*, 111; *Growth*, p. 334.

Real difficulties of a different order occur, as we shall see in Chapter 7, when the agreements arrived at by small groups are offered to the wider community for reception. Nevertheless in our understanding of the processes we are bound to some degree to extrapolate from individual to church. That is relevant, for example, when Vatican II uses the phrase *par cum pari*.[29] 'In the text of the decree,' comments Tavard, 'this expression applies directly to individual participants in ecumenical conversations. But insofar as these represent their Churches, it is the Churches themselves which, through the participants, are deemed to meet and talk *par cum pari*.'

A quarrel between churches is instrinsically different from a quarrel between persons in that corporate memory and collective hostility and alienation have features peculiarly their own. They are harder to deal with, just as an angry mob is harder to quiet than a furious individual. And just as a person caught up in a crowd's emotions may behave in ways not true to his character, so groups of Christians collectively impassioned on some point may be difficult to reason with. This is the other face of the distinction between persons and churches we have already touched on, and we shall come back to it in due course.

THE PRINCIPLES OF RAPPROCHEMENT

Principles of ecumenical communication were already emerging at the first of the three sessions of 'Unionist' Congresses of Orthodox and Roman Catholics held at Velehrad from 1907 to World War I.[30] These were, first, that there must be equality in the way the two sides treat one another, and secondly, that both must go as far as possible to meet their separated brethren.[31] Thirdly, the richness of tradition and spirituality of the participating churches must be recognised, so that there is never any implication that reunion intends the 'conversion' of one by the other.[32] These were enlightened views for their time.[33] But these ground-rules have proved themselves in the conversations between churches which have taken place since Vatican II. Dialogue

---

[29] *UR*, 9.   [30] Four more took place before World War II.

[31] What was intended in this case was that the Eastern rite must be made to stand equal with the Western; in other words, the Orthodox rite need not be Latinised.

[32] P. Esterka, 'Toward union: the Congresses at Velehrad', *Journal of Ecumenical Studies*, 8 (1971), 11–51, p. 13.

[33] And could perhaps not have been arrived at so readily between Roman Catholic and Protestant Christians then.

may have various purposes,[34] but with these ground-rules, it will always tend to promote better mutual understanding.[35] The ground-rules of ecumenical method we looked at in a preliminary way in Chapter 1 have to do with modes of encounter. We need to look at the mechanics, as well as the dynamics,without trying to separate the two completely, for the mechanics will work only if the dynamics are right. So I propose here to examine the implications of what has been said so far for the actual process of rapprochement.

The Orthodox–Roman Catholic conversations made the methodological decision to begin from common ground.[36] But it can be argued that if the dialogue does not begin from an examination of each side's views, it 'will later meet insuperable obstacles'.[37] The first step for each side in most dialogues has been to try to state its own position absolutely clearly. And in fact the Orthodox and Roman Catholic sides began by meeting separately, the Roman Catholics in Rome in 1976 and 1978 and the Orthodox at Chambésy in 1977 and 1978. At an early stage in the period we are chiefly concerned with in this study, the phase of ecumenical endeavour which extends over the last thirty years, it was possible for each side to do this in the Anselmian confidence that once the other side was properly informed it would see that the side explaining itself had the truth, and be converted to that side's view. Roman Catholic movement through this stage of the process is well documented. 'For many centuries we ... Catholics have thought it would be enough to express our doctrine clearly. The non-Catholics thought the same. Each side expounded its teaching in its own terms' said De Smedt, Bishop of Bruges before the Second Vatican Council had completed its work. The understanding of ecumenical dialogue on which Roman Catholics were then working was that it involved 'a witness to its own faith by each side'. But 'with this method of "clear truth" we made no

---

34 One definition of [bilateral] ecumenical dialogue describes it as 'theological conversations sponsored, directly or indirectly by [two] churches, traditions or confessional families, with purposes ranging from promoting mutual understanding to achieving' full communion in true faith and love, and reconciling hostilities and divisions of the past.' G. Limouris, 'The understanding of the Church emerging in the bilateral dialogues – coherence or divergence', *The Greek Orthodox Theological Review*, 36 (1991), 1–21.

35 'Dialogue ... has the immense advantage of dissipating prejudices and correcting false impressions.' Congar, *Dialogue between Christians*, p. 129.

36 Colin Davey, 'Clearing a path through a minefield. Orthodox–Roman Catholic dialogue, 1983–90, I', *One in Christ*, 26 (1990), 285–307, p. 286.

37 Colin Davey, 'Orthodox–Roman Catholic dialogue', *One in Christ*, 20 (1984), 346–64, p. 361.

progress towards reconciliation', De Smedt acknowledges. 'On the contrary, preconceptions and little quarrels and polemical discussions grew on both sides.'[38]

So it proved not to be the case that what was needed was simply clear explanation of the truth by one side to the other, because 'the truth' proved to be only 'the truth as one side saw it'. At first that prompted more rigorous attempts to refine the unilateral statement to make it yet more exact and clear. But a new understanding was creeping in, that the real ecumenical purpose of trying to do so was to come to a mutual understanding of one another's vision and experience of the one faith of Christ. 'Our Conciliar exposition would have an ecumenical spirit if we employ means truly capable of making it understandable to non-Catholics how the Catholic Church sees and lives the mystery of Christ,' continues De Smedt. Here there was room for the further insight that that would mean seeking to enter in understanding into the position of other Christians so as to be able to present one's own account of what one saw to be the same truth to them, in a way they could accept as their own.

De Smedt suggested a series of working rules to achieve this. Roman Catholic apologists must avoid implying that they are uncertain in any way where they themselves stand. They will need to know the faith of Orthodox and Protestants. They must not be afraid of finding that there is a conflict between expressing themselves ecumenically and stating the truth fully. Working in this spirit of confidence and understanding, they will need to know what they hold to be good in Roman Catholic faith; to recognise what non-Catholics think is omitted or insufficiently clarified in Roman Catholic doctrine; to examine what it is hard for non-Catholics to grasp in the Roman Catholic manner of speaking; to choose terms which will not upset non-Catholics, to consider the context in which non-Catholics will receive what is said. They will want to avoid polemic; and so they will argue against errors, but in a way which will not offend.[39] This is still a strictly unilateralist approach, and it assumes still that the desired outcome is to win others over to the Roman Catholic view as it stands, but it has taken the necessary first steps of seeking freedom from fear, of taking others' views seriously, as held by Christians who will best be won by respect for their faith.

Out of this process, carried on at different times and in different

---

[38] *Irénikon*, 36 (1963), p. 130.　　[39] *Irénikon*, 36 (1963), p. 130.

ecumenical contexts, there emerged a clear understanding that minds have to be won and cannot (and must not) be overridden or overwhelmed or coerced.[40] The next stage involves a systematic attempt to meet the sensitivities of the other side,[41] not because that is a more effective way of winning assent to one's own position, but out of a genuine respect for the others' positions. The proviso is important. It makes it possible to learn from others and even to be open-minded about the possibility of adjusting one's own stance in response. It introduces the willingness to allow oneself to be changed.

As long as it remains natural to think and speak of those with whom the conversation is going on as 'the other side', a conscious *effort* has to be made not only to recognise where their sensitivities lie, but also to enter into them so as to be able to respect them in an informed and respectful way. An area of 'sensitivity', ecumenically speaking, is one where one or more groups of Christians fear to be deceived or misunderstood. It is likely to echo ancient damage to relations between one communion and another. 'Sensitivities' and a sense of the 'otherness' of Christians in separation go together.

We can see something of how important this is by looking at an extreme pre-ecumenical example of failure to see the other side. A number of Protestant 'heresy trials' took place in the nineteenth and early twentieth centuries in the United States of America. Conflict between theological parties would focus on a particular individual who happened to become conspicuous. One such commented, 'I was only an incident in this warfare.'[42] These heresy trials trod on sensitivities, blew up what bridges there were between parties, and created a 'theological polarisation'. The trials provided an opportunity for personal jealousies and hatreds to be magnified in an ugly way. 'The opportunity for the unleashing of vicious personal attacks is one of the more unpleasant aspects of this whole way of trying to maintain doctrinal authority.' 'Complex procedural wrangles, the bitter disputes over jurisdiction, the divisive appeals and counter-appeals to higher bodies that accompanied these events' ... 'piles of briefs, records,

---

[40] 'Christian theology can be most creative and ecumenical when persons of widely divergent backgrounds and stances can understand each other; the effort to crush or silence the opponent closes the channels of fruitful discussion.' R. T. Handy, 'Freedom and authority in doctrinal matters – some Protestant struggles', *Journal of Ecumenical Studies*, 12 (1975), 335–47, p. 345.

[41] That is not of course incompatible with being frank and not afraid of conflict.

[42] R. T. Handy, 'Freedom and authority in doctrinal matters – some Protestant struggles', *Journal of Ecumenical Studies*, 12 (1975), 335–47, p. 344.

papers, editorials, articles, pamphlets, and books' are generated. These are not necessarily all bad 'but for the most part represent a regrettable waste of human and material resources'.[43]

So each partner church must avoid any assumption that its own is the 'senior' or 'better' church or more truly the Church. It represents an astonishing advance on the situation before Vatican II to be able to take that as read in conversations involving Roman Catholic participants. We have suggested that it is not quite clear yet whether the Orthodox can take this stand. Not all Protestant churches can do so.

'Equal' can mean a number of things from 'equivalent' to 'complementary'. Equality in this context seems to involve at the least making the effort to put oneself in the other's place which I have been describing. A Roman Catholic–World Council of Churches Joint Working Group two decades ago described ecumenical dialogue like this, as 'a way of relating to the other person which enables me to put myself in his place, and to try to listen to him and understand him from within, as it were'.[44] This is redolent of the principle of absolute equality of mutual valuing implied in loving one's neighbour as one's self. The aim of such exchange is to value the other's views as one does one's own and to seek to find the two compatible as far as that proves at the time to be possible. 'Each side agrees to consider the formulations of faith of the other side as valid alternatives to its own.'[45] For this group there was, however, a proviso. It saw itself as doing this : 'so that I can assimilate what he says to me in as far as it is compatible with my faithfulness to the essentials of my own faith'.[46] The test against which acceptance is being measured by each side is still not the test of a common faith but the test of the faith of one side or the other.

A further step is needed. Congar argues that there exists 'an absolute value, which the other is capable of recognizing and in which we should be able to arrive at communication'.[47] 'As I understand it,' Tavard suggests, 'this implies that each side considers the other, at least tentatively, as of equal value.'[48] The danger of not making the effort to see things as the other side does is to ignore the sheer human

[43] R. T. Handy, 'Freedom and authority in doctrinal matters – some Protestant struggles', *Journal of Ecumenical Studies*, 12 (1975), 335–47, p. 345.
[44] 'Ecumenism Today: a survey by the Roman Catholic–World Council of Churches Joint Working Group', *One in Christ*, 11 (1975), 30–87, p. 42.
[45] G. Tavard, 'For a theology of dialogue', *One in Christ*, 15 (1979), 11–20.
[46] 'Ecumenism Today: a survey by the Roman Catholic–World Council of Churches Joint Working Group', *One in Christ*, 11 (1975), 30–87, p. 42.
[47] The only *force* at work is that of truth. Congar, *Dialogue between Christians*, p. 55.
[48] G. Tavard, 'For a theology of dialogue', *One in Christ*, 15 (1979), p. 15.

implications of deeming the other's views of no, or lesser, value. 'Being satisfied definitively and exclusively with my own insight, I have reduced the scope of humanity to myself . . . every man is, as man, i.e., as creativity, for me unnecessary. Such a position . . . obviously diminishes in my eyes every other person . . . to indifference toward him as a human being. I do not need . . . his experiences or his thoughts.'[49] This denial of the other belongs with other negatives, with 'attitudes of mistrust, fear of the unknown future', and is ultimately incompatible with a true equality of mutual valuing.[50]

A significant reason for the holding back from mutual commitment is the powerful fear of change which is still evident almost everywhere. Denominational inclinations tend to lead to self-sufficiency and 'exclusivity'.[51] While two ecclesial bodies have not yet become one, there is for both an area of 'risk' in dialogue, 'for it necessarily includes the possibility of being persuaded that one's partner in dialogue might have the right on any particular issue, which would then involve changing one's mind – a painful process'.[52] This must be so, for 'dialogue . . . is a model that is distinctively different from a defensive, or even explanatory, model – the second is really just a less abrasive, kindlier form of the first. They both assume that the first party has the truth. The dialogue model assumes a commitment to truth on the part of all participants, but also a realisation that no one partner has an exclusive or complete hold on that truth.'[53]

We need to distinguish clearly here between 'exclusive' and complete. The possibility of coming together in a common faith must logically rest on the assumption that the truth is not the property of only one side. But although division is always a mark of incompleteness in the Church,[54] it does not follow that either or both may have something lacking in the faith. Both sides may (in principle) have the faith complete, but need to recognise its presence in one another's communities.

[49] N. Basjik, 'The significance and problems of dialogue today', *Journal of Ecumenical Studies*, 9 (1972).
[50] J. Coventry, 'Cardinal Willebrands interviewed', *One in Christ*, 8 (1972), 4–10, and J. Willebrands, 'Prospects for Anglican–Roman Catholic relations, *One in Christ*, 8 (1972), 11–23, p. 16.
[51] G. Stephanopoulos, 'Denominational loyalties and ecumenical commitment: a personal view', *Journal of Ecumenical Studies*, 17 (1980), 626–46, p. 640.
[52] Especially 'for those trained never to be mistaken'. L. Swidler, 'Demo-Kratia, the Rule of the People of God, or Consensus Fidelium', *Journal of Ecumenical Studies*, 19 (1982), 226–43, p. 238.
[53] L. Swidler, 'Dialogue: the way toward consensus', *Journal of Ecumenical Studies*, 17 (1980), iii-viii, p. iv.   [54] Cf. Congar's insight that in a divided Church no Church is complete.

Pannenberg agrees that an ecumenical theology of shared reflection 'should not methodologically presuppose that any given tradition has the definitive truth'. So 'the primordial condition for dialogue is to be willing to have one's theology and doctrine questioned'. It 'means attempting to think and live with other categories of thought, other models of theological imagination, other styles'...The outcome should be something fresh.[55] 'In terms of theology as language,...dialogue obliges each side to adopt a very flexible view of the theology which serves as its [own] point of departure.'[56]

This is less alarming (in terms of an implication that one might be risking a change of mind which might set the identity of one's community at risk), if there can be confidence that 'at a point logically prior to their separation into different confessional bodies, Christians are one in their fundamental faith'.[57] Orthodoxy has always been confident that this common root exists in a manner Christologically and temporally, as well as merely logically, prior.[58] Other communions might prefer to speak in terms of the Gospel, the Deposit of Faith, the Apostolic Faith, with the same sense that the faith was at first one faith. All would agree that faithfulness to that beginning is their overriding concern.

The risk is also less frightening if the parties can arrive at 'shared rules for adjudicating disagreements, should they arise, and agreements, where they obtain'[59] and trust one another to keep them.[60] With this

---

[55] It 'should not be going back to one's own theology after an interesting experiment. If one did one would be doing no more in the dialogue than trying out another kind of apologetics.' G. Tavard, 'For a theology of dialogue', *One in Christ*, 15 (1979), 11–20, p. 17.

[56] G. Tavard, 'For a theology of dialogue', *One in Christ*, 15 (1979), 11–20, p. 15.

[57] Avery Dulles, 'Ecumenism and Theological Method', *Journal of Ecumenical Studies*, 17 (1980), 40–8, p. 41.

[58] 'Churches and confessions, in their multilateral and bilateral conversations, today need this kind of listening theologically to each other's doctrines in order to find the *common roots* [my italics] of the Christian tradition stated by Jesus Christ himself.' G. Limouris, 'The understanding of the Church emerging in the bilateral dialogues', *The Greek Orthodox Theological Review*, 36 (1991), 1–21, p. 17.

[59] P. Devenish, 'Can a Roman Catholic be a historian?', *Journal of Ecumenical Studies*, 20 (1983), 67–85, p. 70.

[60] 'Both sides noted that each had a differing understanding of these facts. However, through dialogue, each delegation had the opportunity to understand the motivations of the other party, and so come to better mutual understanding...The Catholic delegation underlined that all the pastoral structures which had been established...were designed to answer the spiritual needs of the Catholic faithful. The Orthodox delegation expressed the concern that such Catholic structures went beyond the genuine needs of the Catholic faithful, and betrayed a desire for expansion. In order to avoid any misunderstanding, and to develop confidence between the two Churches, the apostolic administrators and Orthodox bishops responsible for the same territory ought to consult each other before putting into effect pastoral plans, such as the creation of parishes or other works of the Catholic Church.' G. Weakland, 'Orthodox–Catholic Relations', *Catholic International*, 3 (April, 1992), 393.

we have not yet progressed very far, because it immediately throws up complex problems of authority thus to adjudicate. But rules are badly needed.

Sticking-points

There is still the possibility of the dissentient memorandum on the majority view. This occurred in a Lutheran–Roman Catholic instance in 1970. 'Four of the seven Catholic participants in this dialogue, in putting their signatures to the report, appended explanations in which they dissociated themselves from the paragraph.'[61] The Malta Report of the Lutheran–Roman Catholic Dialogue on 'The Gospel and the Church', 1972, also has 'Special Statements' by a number of individuals.[62] Two Roman Catholic participants were concerned that the practical suggestions the Report was making went too far too quickly, in proposing 'occasional acts of intercommunion'.[63] They were not able to see themselves as 'with' the others at this point.

Another element of risk is the fact that there must be some acknowledgement of disagreement for there to be dialogue at all.[64] So agreement[65] is always an end to be reached, and there is likely to be some degree of difficulty or effort or risk. Here rules of assessment must be shared if discussion is not to result in a methodological stalemate. 'A stalemate occurs when two parties "agree to disagree".'[66] Goodwill has been only painfully preserved where the only agreement

---

[61] Avery Dulles, 'Intercommunion between Lutherans and Roman Catholics', *Journal of Ecumenical Studies*, 13 (1976), 253. The text in question is 'Eucharist and Ministry', *Lutherans and Catholics in Dialogue*, IV (Washington, 1970).

[62] Professor H. Schürmann had not been present at the third or fifth sessions of the commission or at the final voting. 'I therefore wish to explain my understanding of the "request" in no. 63 And the "recommendation" in no. 73 so as to give specific meaning to my signature,' he says. The tenor of his comments is that these should be interpreted cautiously. No. 73 also troubled Professor J. L. Witte. He had expressed his reservations at the final session. 'I am convinced,' he says, 'that in the present situation the commission should not have done more than recommend to the church authorities, on the basis of what is already shared in faith and sacrament and, as sign and anticipation of the promised and hoped for unity, make possible occasional acts of limited admission to the respective eucharistic celebrations, as for example at ecumenical occasions and in the case of mixed marriages', *Growth*, pp. 188–9.

[63] Para 73; *Growth*, p. 186.

[64] 'Conversation can take place only when there is some disagreement ... if there is complete identity of thinking there can be no real conversation but only a confirmation of agreement ... The essence of conversation is actually people exposing their differences in thinking and information ... Thus by undertaking a conversation the subject-matter of the conversation is in some way questioned.' N. Basjik, 'The significance and problems of dialogue today', *Journal of Ecumenical Studies*, 9 (1972), 29–39, p. 33.

[65] On agreement, see further Chapter 7 on reception.

[66] 'An impasse is reached where mere preference prevails.' P. Devenish, 'Can a Roman Catholic be a historian?', *Journal of Ecumenical Studies*, 20 (1983), 67–85, p. 70.

is to disagree (even if amicably). To agree to disagree is a failure. Dialogue ceases at this point.

Agreeing to disagree

Some have been pessimistic that that is the best that can be hoped for. 'Attempts to remove misunderstanding through dialogue would only get us as far as an agreement to disagree, for there [is] more dividing us than mere misunderstanding.'[67] But the ecumenical experience generally is that that is not right. In practice, it seems that there is likely at present to be mixture of agreement with 'agreement to disagree', in each bilateral conversation, with the points of failure to agree differing from one to another. Anglicans and Orthodox, for example, in their Moscow Agreed Statement of 1976, conceded that 'The Agreed Statement is in part an agreement to disagree, on such points as the existence of a hierarchy of truths, the recognition of the seventh Council, on which the Anglican attitude is still ambiguous, and the Anglican concept of indefectibility, which differs from the Orthodox view of the Church as the pillar and ground of the truth.' These were not, however, seen as ultimately unresolvable. 'Some aspects of our subject need more investigation, and the agreements reached need to be assimilated by our Churches.'[68] Reformed–Roman Catholic conversation recently sees a way beyond agreement to disagree through the recognition of the complementarity of different angles of view. 'There are differences of perspective such that we find in the position of the partner a complementary point of view or a different accent on a single commonly-held truth. In opening ourselves to the partner's critique we can learn to express our own views in a more balanced way and perhaps find a common frame of reference for understanding each other'(91). But the same commission saw that that does not work for all points of difference. 'Some of our positions seem simply to diverge. They appear mutually incompatible or incommensurable.' In an atmosphere of goodwill and the desire for rapprochement, 'That leaves us, for the present at least, with no choice but to agree to disagree, while seeking clarity about the nature of our disagreements.' This commission adds a further warning note. 'We find, among other things, that we disagree

[67] Thomas Thompson, in John Pinnington, 'Symposium: Ecumenism and the Modern World' (held at Duchesne University, Pittsburgh), *Journal of Ecumenical Studies*, 2 (1965), p. 257.
[68] Archbishop Basil in A–O, Moscow, account of Kallistos Ware, p. 57.

about what issues are serious enough to be church-dividing.'(92)[69]
What has happened, then, in a situation of 'agreement to disagree' which makes it a failure? In part it is evidently work uncompleted. That will always relate to the most intransigent issues between the parties, so the uncompleted work will be the most difficult to finish. But most importantly, there must have been a failure either fully to enter into the other side's thinking or to maintain the necessary balance between being oneself and 'being together with the other side' in discussion. If it had truly become possible to think as the other side does and to do it with them, the residual disagreement could not persist.

Agreement not compromise
An accusation frequently levelled at those who have taken part in ecumenical conversations is that they have been able to agree only by compromising. Plentiful comment could be cited on this point, but one example will do here, from a relatively early post-Vatican II stage of the conversation.[70]

Suspiciously, it was remarked in 1967 that the Blake–Pike proposal for union of Protestant denominations in the USA 'bears plainly upon it the familiar stamp of a negotiation'. 'Rare are the theological notes that surmount the spirit of "negotiated settlement",' it was suggested.[71] That is not how it ought to be. 'Ecumenical conversation is not an exercise in diplomacy . . . One is not bargaining or saying, "You can have this *if* we can have that." Once we think of ecumenism as diplomacy, we think that if anything actually moves in the deadlock, that is because some poor fool has made a concession, has compromised with principles, has watered down the truth. This is a disastrous illusion. True ecumenism is listening and kneeling in the presence of God with brothers and sisters in Christ from whom the accidents of history have divided us, and asking how we may together learn the gospel way of authentic reconciliation.'[72] In matters of agreement in

---

[69] *Toward a Common Understanding of the Church: Report of Reformed–Roman Catholic Dialogue 1984–90*, (Vatican, 1990). *Catholic International* 2. 16, p. 786.
[70] 'I remember the amazement of one Roman prelate who had come to take part on a joint commission for the first time and who told me how struck he was by the directness and openness - even, as he thought, the discourtesy - of the discussion, and at the same time the strong feeling of brotherhood and friendship which prevailed among the members. He had thought ecumenism meant compromise. From then on he lost that notion for good.' P. Duprey, 'Aspects of ecumenism', *One in Christ*, 9 (1973), 319–36.
[71] Editorial on consultation on Church union, *Journal of Ecumenical Studies*, 4 (1967), p. 295.
[72] H. Chadwick, 'Lima, ARCIC and the Church of England', *One in Christ*, 20 (1984), 31–7, p. 37.

the faith it is axiomatic for some that there can be no possibility of compromise for churches which have bound themselves permanently to a given position.[73] But if we are looking to something which is not compromise at all, but agreement in a common faith, that difficulty disappears, and is replaced by another: that of recognising existing faith in the agreed common statement of faith.

In the case of dogmas, that is of beliefs which have been officially promulgated in one church, but which may differ from church to church, the questions which present themselves concern not only the content of such statements of faith, but respect for the authorities in the churches in question, and whether churches have authority to make decisions in matters of faith for themselves. Here a new way of looking at things has to be found. If reunion is thought of not as a reattachment or submission of one church to another but as the common acceptance of the 'orthodoxy' of an authentic ecclesial tradition by two equally ecclesially authoritative bodies, the conflict of apparently absolute requirements may be eased, at least insofar as the conflict results from a clash of authorities.[74] But we still have to reconcile the dogmas themselves.[75] This fundamental shift of ecclesiological perspective is a very different thing from arriving 'at a midway point of view in which the faithful of the two Churches could feel at ease at the price of a few concessions'.[76] It does not itself point the way to solutions of the differences themselves. But it addresses the issue of compromise of authority which has often been the underlying difficulty preventing the resolution of a difference of opinion.

Concepts of betrayal are relevant here because it has seemed to some that there is a risk of 'compromise of loyalty'. It is often feared that agreement will involve not only making concessions but even

[73] 'En matière de dogme tout possibilité de compromis est exclue.' N. Afanassieff, '"Una Sancta": en mémoire de Jean XXIII, le Pape de l'Amour', *Irénikon*, 36 (1963), 436–75, p. 438.

[74] This suggestion is put forward by P. A. Schmemann, 'Unité, séparation, réunion à la lumière de l'ecclésiologie orthodoxe', *Contacts*, 26 (1959), 73–88.

[75] The main particular problems here concern decisions of the Roman Catholic Church in the nineteenth and twentieth centuries on Papal Infallibility, the Assumption and the Immaculate Conception, which other churches have not made. The Roman Catholic Church thus seems to have taken a step from which it cannot, in terms of its own theology of ecclesial authority and decision-making, retreat. But other churches cannot be compelled to go the same way. This is a major problem methodologically.

[76] It would be even more wrong to look here for a new synthesis, such that the findings of contemporary theological research might be made to pass into the two traditions. See J. M. R. Tillard, 'Anglican–Roman Catholic dialogue', *One in Christ*, 8 (1972), 242–63, p. 245.

betrayal of one's own communion.[77] Here, too, the difficulty disappears if the fear and suspicion are banished. If all parties can be confident that they are now acting and thinking as one Church there can be no 'betrayal', and no 'compromise of loyalty'.

So ecumenism is not 'some kind of diplomatic or political set of negotiations whereby one side gives up the doctrine and asks for a *quid pro quo*'. That would be to set unity and truth in opposition and to hold that 'the truth is thought automatically to be subordinate to unity... This is not the ecumenical position,' insists L. Swidler. 'Ecumenism means to "keep talking with one another in the hope that with good will and hard work a reconciliation will ultimately be worked out".'[78]

No verbal trickery
Another blockage in the way to mutual acceptance and agreement can be presented by the suspicion that some verbal sleight of hand has been going on. Vatican II's confidence was that 'Doctrinal dialogue... needs sincere truth, thus excluding manipulated doctrinal discussion, discussion which is undertaken for political ends' ['political' here interpreted very broadly]. 'In discussion the truth will prevail by no other means than by the truth itself.'[79] That is the ideal. The hope that it may be so, is naturally coupled with the desire that truth will triumph through its very simplicity. 'The results... are not clever ideas to make reconciliation possible,'[80] presses L. Vischer.

This recalls the early stage of ecumenical conversation where each side believes that if it can only explain its position clearly enough, the

---

[77] 'American denominations... have transmitted and preserved... aspects of the traditions from which they sprang; in that very act of conservation undertaken by uprooted persons utilizing their traditions for new purposes, in a new land, and under new conditions of religious pluralism, freedom, and voluntarism, the traditions were betrayed.' Russell E. Richey, '"Catholic" Protestantism and American Denominationalism', *Journal of Ecumenical Studies*, 16 (1979), 213–231. 'Cooperation is desirable between the various Christian denominations, when the end to be attained is itself justified, and when such cooperation involves no violation of conscience or compromise of loyalty to Christ and his Word as revealed in the New Testament.' Southern Baptist Convention, Baptist Faith and Message, 1925, *The Baptist Source-Book: With Particular Reference to Southern Baptists*, ed. Robert A. Baker (Nashville, 1966), pp. 203–4.

[78] L. Swidler, Editorial, *Journal of Ecumenical Studies*, 4 (1967), p. 297.

[79] Cf. Vatican II, *Humanae Personae Dignitatem*, p. 1007, cited L. Swidler, 'Demo-Kratia, the Rule of the People of God, or Consensus Fidelium', *Journal of Ecumenical studies*, 19 (1982), 226–43, p. 241.

[80] L. Vischer, 'The reception of consensus in the ecumenical movement', *One in Christ*, 17 (1981), 294–305.

other side will be won over. The fact is that there will have to be 'clever ideas' for reconciliation to be possible. We need every aid intelligence can devise. But intelligence and resourcefulness are not incompatible with sincerity and truth. This simultaneity of skilfulness and honesty is a feature of all successful ecumenical conversation. Those who perceive the skilfulness but doubt the honesty have spoken of 'devices' used as if to give an appearance of agreement. We need to look frankly at the devices and acknowledge them to be such, so as to see that the agreement they make possible is not an appearance but a reality. To take some examples:

(i) An obstacle to agreement may need to be deemed to have been moved out of the way. That will involve showing that it is not an obstacle after all, or not the obstacle it was thought to be. There can be redefinition, or recourse to precedent, for example. Orthodoxy – in the tradition of the ancient Church – has held that the Eucharist should not be shared with heretics or schismatics. But if it can be argued that 'the Western brothers and sisters never were officially qualified as schismatics or heretics by a general council' and that 'it is the general practice of the Church in the East not to condemn the West', that obstacle may be deemed not to stand in the way.[81] The Eucharist could in principle be shared. What has happened here is a reclassification. Those who seemed heretics are not heretics.

(ii) A second device is to stress equivalences, in the hope that they will come to be treated as a common basis. In the following example, from Anglican–Lutheran conversation, an attempt is made to say in effect, 'we both have confessional documents; we both have something of equivalent value to place side by side in the arena of discussion'. The contrasts are, however, as telling as the parallelisms. 'Prominent place' compares with 'significant phase', 'still' with 'a formative period', and so on:

(29) On the Lutheran side the confessions of the Reformation still occupy officially a prominent place in theological thinking, in catechetical teaching, in the constitutions of the individual Lutheran churches and at the ordination

---

[81] M. Aghiorgoussis, 'Orthodox–Catholic dialogue', *Journal of Ecumenical Studies*, 13 (1976), 204–31. He cites Demetrios Chomatenos, Archbishop of Bulgaria to Konstaninos Kabasilas, Archbishop of Dyrrhachion, 'the fact that their communion is true (valid), does not mean that we can receive their communion. We cannot abandon our respective customs and reestablish communion with Latins.' 'But as they consider our gifts as holy gifts, we also consider their gifts to be holy,' See too G. Rallis and M. Potlis, *Syntagma ton theion kai ieron kanonon*, V (Athens, 1855), pp. 430–4; I. Kotsonis, *Problemata test Ekklesiastikes Oikonomia* (Athens, 1957), pp. 189–92.

of pastors. They serve as a link between the churches of the Lutheran family.
(30) On the Anglican side the Thirty Nine Articles are universally recognized as expressing a significant phase in a formative period of Anglican thought and life.[82]

(iii) A third device is that of expanding a concept so that it will hold within it the various views held by the partners in dialogue. One commentary speaks hopefully in this connection of 'the expanded notion of sacrament, which focuses sharply on the interrelationship of Christ, the Church and the Eucharist, i.e. of Christology, ecclesiology, and eucharistic or for that matter sacramental, theology'.[83]

(iv) A fourth device is to set aside what is awkward, if that can be done without offending against truth. In this situation to omit mention of a problem is to avoid having to resolve an area of disagreement about it. The question which matters here is not the omitting in itself, but whether that area of disagreement is crucial to the resolution of the problem, because if it is, avoidance cannot be helpful. This was a solution arrived at in the following instance.

Mr. Beckwith said it was important to make clear that we are discussing icons and not three-dimensional Western images: first, because Article 22 speaks of images and the Romish doctrine thereof, and Orthodox are not sure if this refers to icons; secondly, because in the Anglican Church a considerable body of opinion dreads the veneration of three-dimensional images as incurring temptation to the sin of idolatry . . .

Archbishop Stylianos agreed. He said three-dimensional Western images are an expression of the self-sufficiency of this world while icons reflect the other world . . . Archbisop Basil: the Orthodox venerate icons for the same reason as they venerate relics, because both are places of the special action of the grace of God . . .

Mr. Beckwith said he must be able to defend in a credible manner any statement for which he was held responsible. Either this distinction [between two- and three-dimensional representations] must be made, or the Anglicans should make no statement at all.

The Bishop of Truro wished . . . no reference made to Article 22. He thought the philosophy behind Mr. Beckwith's view to be pure nominalism, and to ignore the part played by the body in our knowledge of God.[84]

These are certainly devices; but they need to be looked at as examples of problem-solving, not instances of trickery.

---

[82] Anglican–Lutheran, Pullach; *Growth*, p. 17.
[83] Kenan B. Osborne, 'Contemporary understandings of the Eucharist', *Journal of Ecumenical Studies*, 13 (1976), 192–201, p. 196.
[84] A–O, Moscow, account of Kallistos Ware, p. 60, quoting the Minutes.

The power of dialogue to change things

There seems to be an encouraging common consent that dialogue has power[85] to change viewpoints and alter the landscape.[86] 'Dialogue has the power of forming togetherness, a "we" consciousness,'[87] suggests one commentator. This is perhaps the most important primary consequence of dialogue ecumenically. A new stage is reached when each side tries not only to put its own case and to understand where the other's sensitivities lie, but to accept as much as it is possible for it to do of the other side's faith as its own. Heinrich Fries, for example, saw before the Second Vatican Council that 'what unites Protestant and Catholic Christians is greater and more than what separates them'.[88] So he made an attempt to accept as much as is possible for him as a Catholic theologian; he could then more clearly show 'what he cannot assent to and why'.[89]

This may make it necessary to have the courage to recognise that some elements of faith or life on one's *own* side may look unacceptable[90] in the light of new insights or changes of attitude or priority. The next stage is admitting that there may be, or have been in the past, fault on one's own side. It is not so difficult perhaps to concede in a report or agreed statement that something has been omitted or inadequately covered. (In the Methodist–Roman Catholic Conversations, for example, we find the frank admission that 'it is perhaps an omission that in our conversations, though the attempt was made, tardily and

---

[85] 'Dialectical power', N. Basjik, 'The significance and problems of dialogue today', *Journal of Ecumenical Studies*, 9 (1972), 29–39, p. 33.

[86] The Anglican–Reformed dialogue is helpful here. At the conclusion of *God's Reign and our Unity*, seven 'things which we have tried to keep in view' are listed. These are: 1) 'participation in Christ'; 2) 'the primacy of grace'; 3) the fact that 'the Church cannot be a sign of God's reconciling grace for all humankind while itself remaining unreconciled, stubbornly clinging to the past'; 4) the Church's missionary calling; 5) the other discussions – bilateral and multilateral – in which the two communions have taken part; 6) the experience of united churches in India which 'instead of being the vanguard of a movement for unity, have become isolated' and which need the opportunity to join in discussions so as to share their experience; 7) the experience of member churches of the World Council of Churches. These are self-evidently different kinds of things, but they have in common a consciousness that the processes of talking together and (even imperfectly) being together leave things altered (5–7), and that they do so in the context of a divine plan in which Christians in Christ are at the disposal of grace in witness to the world (1–4).

[87] N. Basjik, 'The significance and problems of dialogue today', *Journal of Ecumenical Studies*, 9 (1972), 29–39, p. 35.

[88] H. Fries, *Das Gespräch mit den evangelischen Christen* (Stuttgart, 1961), p. 61.

[89] Biemer, *Journal of Ecumenical Studies*, 1 (1964), p. 225.

[90] 'Ecumenical dialogue sometimes urges the partners to deal with issues that are embarrassing to them', G. Baum, Editorial, *Journal of Ecumenical Studies*, 4 (1967), p. 124.

with insufficient time for success, . . . we never listed side by side our hierarchies of authorities and studied the place of the varying elements in them in our list of priorities'.) To admit fault in one's own communion is harder, because it may carry huge implications for the justification for becoming separated from others in the first place.

If there is to be progress, the parties have to move next to true reciprocity in their attitudes. That means, as we have argued, treating the other as an equal in a common allegiance to Christ. 'Genuine ecumenical exchange resides in finding reciprocal attitudes that allow us to maintain, together and without any mitigation, the requirements of our common allegiance to . . . the Lord Jesus, and the inevitability of conscientious differences in our concept of his person and message.'[91] 'Reciprocity implies more than respect for one another; it implies learning from one another, and, to go one step further, learning Christ together.'[92] The stage of partnership in a common endeavour is reached when both sides can begin to achieve the fine balancing act of simultaneously entering into the discussion as themselves (that is, on behalf of one side); and as collaborators with the others, where the 'sides' disappear. 'No participant is asked to begin by surrendering anything which he holds to be of the essence of the faith once delivered to the saints. All participants in mutual respect agree to find their starting-point in the things which we hold in common.'[93]

The process of mutually seeking to enter into one another's thinking is only an interim one, for it requires the parties to see themselves as standing on different sides while they do so. 'Courage and sincerity, . . . the greatest of freedom and . . . reverence'; a two-way 'listening and . . . speaking'[94] and the patience to go on trying indefinitely – all the concomitants of treating the other communion as equal and trying to see things its way - go on being needed; but they are emptied at the next stage into 'common effort' . . . to improve mutual understanding, to clarify matters on which the parties 'agree, and if possible to enlarge the areas of agreement'.[95] This is the

---

[91] G. Tavard, Editorial, *Journal of Ecumenical Studies*, 1 (1964), p. 99.
[92] G. Tavard, Editorial, *Journal of Ecumenical Studies*, 1 (1964), p. 100.
[93] A–O, *The Moscow Agreed Statement*, ed. K. Ware and C. Davey (London, 1976), Preface.
[94] L. Swidler, 'Demo-Kratia, the Rule of the People of God, or Consensus Fidelium', *Journal of Ecumenical Studies*, 19 (1982), 226–43, p. 238.
[95] Cf. Vatican II *Humanae Personae Dignitatem*, p. 1007, and see L. Swidler, 'Demo-Kratia, the Rule of the People of God, or Consensus Fidelium', *Journal of Ecumenical Studies*, 19 (1982), 226–43, p. 241.

acceptance of a companionship of the separated churches in the shared search for Christian unity.[96]

But in a not yet united Church, common effort cannot yet be fully a single shared effort, even if that can be seen as the desired way forward, and even if it can be glimpsed by individual commissions as they become single working communities in their meetings. In practice we are still at the stage of two or more parties joining in dialogue. The final stage, and the one at which the real work of ecumenical theology can begin, is one of truly working together. Vatican II speaks of *cooperatio*.[97] This, too, has its stages. The beginning may resemble the following example. At a 'Church Leaders' Conference' including 'the whole spectrum from Roman Catholics to the Salvation Army, Quaker and Seventh Day Adventist' in England in 1972, it was intended that there should be no passing of resolutions, 'despite the at times strong temptation to do so'. 'The aim was rather to bring together four hundred bishops, priests and laymen in positions of leadership and responsibility, together with a hundred representatives of ginger groups and renewal movements . . . to explore together the basic problems all Christians face today . . . The basic assumption was that this fundamental process of theology . . . was something that transcended the denominational boundaries . . . the naturalness of exploring in an ecumenical context questions and problems that are often confined within denominational boundaries.'[98] The intention, limited but crucial to future success, was to familiarise the participants with the notion that they could do theology together, and indeed should and must. At the other end of the road stands the prospect of a confessional affirmation which is also a common affirmation. 'It is as though I, as a Roman Catholic, said, "this is my faith", to which my Anglican brother replied, "It is also mine".'[99]

[96] M.-J. le Guillou, 'Interrogations sur l'avenir de l'oecuménisme', *Istina*, 10 (1964), 7–24, p. 11.
[97] Decree on Ecumenism, 12.
[98] R. Nowell, 'Church Leaders' Conference (Birmingham, 1972)', *Journal of Ecumenical Studies*, 10 (1973), 217–21, p. 217.
[99] 'Ecumenism Today: a survey by the Roman Catholic–World Council of Churches Joint Working Group', *One in Christ*, 11 (1975), 30–87, p. 84.

CHAPTER 4

Ecumenical language

FINDING A COMMON LANGUAGE

If Christians are followers of one Christ, the object of the ecumenical common enquiry must be to know him in one faith, but that faith need not necessarily be expressed everywhere in identical terms. There are all sorts of difficulties about the relationship of diversity and variety of expression to unanimity.[1] We shall be looking at these in this chapter. But I want to put forward at the outset the proposition that we are in search of a single Christian truth.[2]

Then we can argue that it has to be grasped in common. That does not mean that everyone has to describe it in the same words. Yet even if distinct languages (in the broadest meaning of the term) remain as theological vehicles, and it is clearly both inevitable and right that they should, it has to be possible to discuss the one truth in a series of sets of words which give everyone a means of expression and access to understanding. The task is to find a way for everyone to be sure that it is the same truth which is being referred to.[3] It is of course notoriously

---

[1] There was an eager desire at Malines 'that misapprehension on either side as to the actual position of the other should as far as possible be removed, in order that there might be secured a foundation of common faith upon which to build new hopes of a reunion'. 'Attention was focussed at Malines on the principle of diversity within the unity of the Catholic Church, and it was pointed out, with various examples, that this was recognized also within the Roman Catholic Church in certain matters of discipline.' *The Conversations at Malines: Report Presented to the Archbishop of Canterbury by the Anglican Members* (Oxford, 1927), Supplement, p. 11.

[2] 'The object of a Definition of Faith, however it may be reached,' suggested the Roman Catholics at Malines, 'is not to formulate a newly-invented dogma, unknown to Holy Scripture, of the tradition of the Church, but to declare explicitly and with authority, in regard to some given point, what is the faith entrusted by Jesus Christ to the keeping of the Church'. *The Conversations at Malines: Report Presented to the Archbishop of Canterbury by the Anglican Members* (Oxford, 1927), Supplement, p. 75.

[3] 'Behind these criticisms there lies a profound but often unarticulated anxiety that the Commission has been using new theological language which evades unresolved differences ... Does the language of the Commission conceal an ambiguity (either intentional or unintentional) in language which enables members of the two churches to see their own faith in the Agreed Statement without having in fact reached a genuine consensus?' ARCIC E, Elucidation, 4; *Growth*, p. 73.

89

difficult to establish that faith is inwardly identical. 'Il est impossible d'être absolument certain qu'il existe chez tous une conviction intérieure totalement identique.'[4]

This is a problem which has grown with the spread of the Gospel. In the early Church the language in which formal or official statements were made was at first predominantly Greek, with Latin the second language for these purposes. (Although the Acts of the Fifth Ecumenical Council survive exclusively in Latin.) Latin-speakers recognised the superiority of Greek as a language in which ideas could be expressed with exactitude.[5] It took some centuries to develop a technical terminology in Latin to make it a better theological vehicle.[6] But with the (to all intents and purposes) linguistic separation of the two halves of the Roman Empire in the fifth and sixth centuries Latin became the common language of theological discourse in the West. The move to the vernaculars from the late Middle Ages[7] introduced a new level of complication, which has grown infinitely greater with the modern advent of a larger sense of 'language' as consisting not only in words but in colorations of feeling and culture and stance. With that has come the fear of sacrificing identity by conceding changes in what has become a familiar language. (An example is the distress caused to some English Anglicans by the replacement of the familiar and beautiful language of the sixteenth century Book of Common Prayer with the modern English of the Alternative Service Book. Another is the wish of some Roman Catholics to keep the liturgy in Latin.)

That fear of loss of identity with change in a form of words is prompted by feeling as much as reason. It can have an intellectual foundation only if there is in fact more than one Christian truth, and one truth can in some way outweigh another. Put like that, the proposition is manifestly absurd. But it can be emotionally compelling.[8]

There are both epistemological issues and issues of meaning and reference here. These are far from being new problems in theology. But there is something new in the ecumenical requirement that ways should be found not only of expressing what all hold to be one truth of

---

[4] E. Bauduin, 'Réflexions sur l'unité et l'oecuménisme', *Irénikon*, 35 (1962), 499–519, p. 505.
[5] Tertullian, Augustine, Boethius in particular followed in Cicero's footsteps here.
[6] See C. Moohrman, *Études sur le latin des chrétiens* (Rome, 1958–), Vols. I– .
[7] Examples in *English Wycliffite Sermons*, ed. A. Hudson (Oxford, 1983–), Vols. I– .
[8] Bishop Butler is quoted as saying 'let us not be afraid of scholarly and historical truth. Let us not be afraid that one truth may tell against another truth.' J. R. H. Moorman, in Stacpoole, p. 166.

faith, but also of doing so in a manner which will (a) reconcile previous separate statements about them rather than seek to override one with another; and (b) respect the existing ecclesial contexts of the previously separate statements in doing so. The second is especially difficult to achieve. We do not 'relate best to each other in difficult discussions . . . when each suppresses the idioms and metaphors familiar to his or her deepest speech'.[9]

We ought to start with some general points about the lie of the land on language.

Thought is not necessarily wholly tied to its verbal expression,[10] nor always linked with it in definable ways. Those elements in the ecumenical field of discourse which have to do with feeling – both positively and negatively: prejudice, loyalty, fear – reach beyond words and complicate the attempt to put things clearly. There is a broad contemporary and especially ecumenical recognition that language is more than words. 'By language is meant not just the vocabulary, but above all the mentality, the genius of a culture, philosophical tools, traditions and style of life,'[11] says Willebrands. There is a perception of the presence of layers beneath the surface. We have to try to 'overhear . . . what is really being said'.[12]

There is a concomitant understanding that these deeper intentions may be expressed in a language shifted or adapted from its usual patterns for the purpose.[13] The emotional component enters in, too, in the choice of words to evoke a particular response. 'Divisions do not destroy but damage the basic unity we have in Christ,' says the Anglican–Orthodox Dublin Statement.[14] 'Destroy' and 'damage' are powerfully negative words, but 'damage' is made to seem potentially capable of pointing to the positive by its contrast with the finality of 'destroy'.[15]

[9] F. H. Littell, 'Foundations and traditions of religious liberty', *Journal of Ecumenical Studies*, 14 (1977), 572–92, p. 572.

[10] P.-Y. Emery, 'Réflexions sur la théologie du mérite en perspective oecuménique', *Istina*, 9 (1963), 239–44, p. 240.

[11] J. Willebrands, 'Prospects for Anglican–Roman Catholic relations', *One in Christ*, 8 (1972), 11–23, p. 14, quoting Secretariat for Christian Unity, *Reflections and Suggestions Concerning Ecumenical Dialogue*, IV. 4, c.

[12] F. H. Littell, 'Foundations and traditions of religious liberty', *Journal of Ecumenical Studies*, 14 (1977), 572–92, p. 572.

[13] On *translatio*, as understood in earlier centuries, see my *The Logic and Language of the Bible*, I (Cambridge, 1985).

[14] A–O, Dublin, p. 11, para.9.

[15] Cf. G. Limouris, 'The understanding of the Church emerging in the bilateral dialogues – coherence or divergence?', *Greek Orthodox Theological Review*, 36 (1991), 1–21, p. 7.

Within this broad understanding of 'language' as embracing feeling and culture lie several narrower usages which we need to look at. The first is 'language' in the sense of the variety of natural living languages which Christians actually speak in their daily lives. Although the ecumenical language for formal conversations and publication tends to be English, ecumenical conversation is actually conducted in all the world's languages, and the results of ecumenical agreement ultimately have to be received by most Christians in their mother-tongues. Several churches responding to the *BEM* texts comment on having had to make a translation or to use a translation sent to them in another language than their own.[16]

This runs us into difficulties of incommensurability between languages. Word will not always translate tidily into equivalent word. For Augustine of Hippo, *substantia, essentia, natura* were close if not interchangeable. At the Bonn Reunion Conversations in 1874 the problem was already apparent in an ecumenical context. 'There was for a time a debate and some misunderstanding as to whether the word to be used was "enthaltene" (contained) or "ausgedrückte" (expressed). The latter was finally adopted.'[17] In modern ecumenical conversation French, 'concile' and 'conseil' are distinct concepts which may be elided in the English 'conciliar'.[18] 'Prominent among features which distinguish words for concepts such as grace, sacrament, faith, are degrees of concreteness. Generally, Romance languages rely on the descendants of Latin abstract nouns, while German employs concrete nouns of native origin.'[19] In French 'grâce' has a number of associate meanings. The German 'Gnade' is used in 'few and rather specific ways'.[20] The problem crops up in the responses to the Lima Report (*BEM*) from churches whose people do not have English as their first language. 'Certain words in the report are difficult to translate accurately because they do not have a Dutch equivalent . . . Those people who are busy studying and assessing the reports should therefore carefully investigate the correct interpretation of the words

---

[16] 'We did not have the text in Spanish; we had to make our own translation'. *Churches Respond to BEM*, IV, p. 118, Waldensian Evangelical Church of the River Plate (Uruguay).

[17] Alfred Plummer, *Conversations with Dr Döllinger, 1870–90*, ed. R. Boudens (Louvain, 1985), pp. 105–6, note 1, 1874.

[18] P. Duprey, 'The unity we seek', *Journal of Ecumenical Studies*, 16 (1979), 303–10, p. 303.

[19] J. Keller, 'The linguistics of ecumenical theology: a preliminary assessment', *Journal of Ecumenical Studies*, 18 (1981), 292–300, p. 293.

[20] J. Keller, 'The linguistics of ecumenical theology: a preliminary assessment', *Journal of Ecumenical Studies*, 18 (1981), 292–300, p. 295.

that are used. Otherwise there is the danger that the report will be misunderstood and as a result the contents misjudged.'[21]

There is also the historical factor that 'the distinctive genius of a particular language may have a special affinity with a particular confession'.[22] Lutheranism, for example, has always been strong among peoples of German-speaking stock. Anglicanism took something of its character for many centuries from the sixteenth-century English of *The Book of Common Prayer*. There are other reasons than the linguistic for this, but the language is important as a sustainer of such differences of ecclesial style and emphasis.

Even where English is used as a common language it proves difficult to use it well, that is elegantly and cogently. There is a noticeable tendency for a special language to develop which has the marks of being the product of committees rather than of individual minds. This has been briskly condemned as 'a horrible product . . . almost unreadable, known as ecumenical English'.[23] Colin Davey speaks of one Orthodox–Roman Catholic Report as 'a typical "ecumenical document", neutral and impersonal, lacking the character of either the Orthodox or the Roman Catholic tradition'.[24] What is at stake is not merely a matter of aesthetics. It is important to the purposes of language that it should be attractive and a vehicle for the utmost refinements of expression, that it should be capable of working upon feeling as well as exact. A natural language impoverished by artificiality in such ways will not in the long term serve the ecumenical cause.

Over and above such problems, and further compounding them, lies the issue of the difference between ordinary and technical language. Exactitude may require that dogmatic theology retains the right, and has a duty, to use a vocabulary and a formulation proper to it. But there is a perceived (and sometimes real) danger, that that will make it incomprehensible to any but specialists.[25] The positive side is that technical language enables people to communicate real experience

---

[21] *Churches Respond to BEM*, IV, p. 100, Netherlands Reformed Church and Reformed Churches in the Netherlands.

[22] J. Keller, 'The linguistics of ecumenical theology: a preliminary assessment', *Journal of Ecumenical Studies*, 18 (1981), 292–300, p. 292, suggests this is Karl Rahner's position.

[23] Stephen Neill, *God's Apprentice*, ed. E. M. Jackson (London, 1991), p.209.

[24] Colin Davey, 'Orthodox–Roman Catholic dialogue', *One in Christ*, 20 (1984), 346–64, p. 360.

[25] P.-Y. Emery, 'Réflexions sur la théologie du mérite en perspective oecuménique', *Istina*, 9 (1963), 239–44, p. 240.

with precision; the negative is that it can drive 'a wedge between doctrine and life', between official teaching and experience. It can also give an appearance that problems have been finally resolved, definitions made definitive, where experience consistently shows that there will always be a need for re-expression.

An example is the tendency to change vocabulary under the pressure of 'shifting theologies'. 'In the 1930s, for example, when protestant liberalism was at its height' in English Methodism, 'the words conveying sacrificial and eschatological meanings were excised' from the Methodist Eucharistic liturgy, which had hitherto depended substantially upon that of the Anglican Book of Common Prayer. Thirty years later these changes were reversed.[26] A similar reading of a theology into the combination of words and actions or things drove Oswald Baker, a priest in Downham Market in the English diocese of Northampton, to keep to Latin and the Tridentine formula because he objected to 'a man-centred and convivial gathering – the meal aspect of the Eucharist' and wanted to retain an emphasis on the 'sacrifice aspect – an act of worship directed to the honour of God'.[27] It would be easy to multiply examples. For the moment we need simply to bear this complication in mind in connection with what follows.

AMBIGUITY AND EQUIVOCATION

Two giant problems recur again and again in discourse about ecumenical language. The first is the problem of equivocation. This has to do with signification, the relationship between the word and the thing it points to. Words do not signify things tidily. They frequently mean more than one thing and in more than one way, both literally and figuratively.[28] Their reference shifts and multiplies or

---

[26] 'Most Methodists would probably consider such questions of liturgy to be far less important than the preservation of the nineteenth century rubric which specifies "unfermented" grape juice to be used.' Robert Nelson, 'Methodist eucharistic usage: from constant communion to benign neglect to sacramental recovery', *Journal of Ecumenical Studies*, 13 (1976), 278–93.

[27] J. S. Sloyan, 'Roman Catholic eucharistic reforms: a basis for dialogue', *Journal of Ecumenical Studies*, 13 (1976), 286–91.

[28] Further meetings were, the Roman Catholics at Malines concluded, 'much to be desired in order to elucidate further . . . and to secure that there should be no ambiguity or misunderstanding with regard to their deepest significance'. *The Conversations at Malines: Report Presented to the Archbishop of Canterbury by the Anglican Members* (Oxford,1927), Supplement, p. 83.

shrinks over time and it varies from one community of people or discourse to another.[29] In the search for a shared ecumenical language several distinguishable aspects of this problem are awkward. The reverse of equivocation is learning to say things in the same way. 'A growing conviction of mine', says one commentator, 'has been that, if Roman Catholics did not have their particular conceptual tools for expounding Christian faith, they would speak very much like John Calvin when they attempt to convey to others their belief in the real presence of Christ in the Eucharist.'[30]

The inadequacy of theological language

A first aspect of the problem of equivocation has been familiar to theologians in every century. Human language is inadequate for talking about God. So theological and spiritual and liturgical language is always over-stretched and never quite reaches, let alone embraces, the fullness of the mystery it seeks to describe. Language as a means of communication between God and man is only imperfectly heard and understood on the human side.[31] Patristic and mediaeval exegesis took this to be the best explanation of the apparent oddities and obscurities and the seeming-contradictions of Scripture.[32] God was regarded as having made Scripture's language meet human limitations in this way as an act of divine mercy.[33] The result was the development of a sophisticated understanding of the special difficulties of talking about God (or indeed anything theological), because such themes overextend the language available. Modern ecumenical theological language will unavoidably suffer from the same inherent inability to say everything perfectly clearly. If we must look in the same way to divine help in making the best of things, we can do something to help ourselves by recognising the difficulty.

---

[29] 'Phrases have come into currency and have worked their way into the life and thought of Lutheran and Anglican Churches. In some cases the words correspond to those used on the other side and mean much the same thing. Sometimes the words are very strange and foreign in the ears of another tradition on the life of the Church.' Anglican–Lutheran, Pullach, 12; *Growth*, p. 15.

[30] Christopher Kielsing, 'Catholic response', *Journal of Ecumenical Studies*, 13 (1976), p. 266.

[31] This 'personal relationship' aspect was stressed by the Anglican Bishop of Oxford in the Church of England General Synod's debate on ARCIC II's *Salvation and the Church* in January, 1989. [32] See *The Logic and Language of the Bible*, I.

[33] See *The Logic and Language of the Bible*, I.

The figurative character of theological language

A second aspect of the problem of equivocation involves two kinds of difficulty. When a given word has more than one signification, the references may be literal or figurative. In the sense just referred to, all theological language is symbolic, 'a tissue of metaphors'. Because it cannot refer with exactitude to mysteries beyond human comprehension, 'it uses image, simile, metaphor, parable and analogy'.[34] It was plain to exegetes from an early stage that contradictions could be resolved and statements apparently at variance with orthodoxy shown to be acceptable if they were understood figuratively.[35] This was not, for the majority of patristic scholars, an indication that they were signifying in an inferior way; rather the reverse. Later scholars, particularly in the Protestant West, have not found it so easy to accept the figurative as a valid alternative to the literal, with a meaning to which equal, or even greater, weight can be attached. There came to be a tendency to speak pejoratively of the figurative.[36] Today the suspicion is voiced that metaphorical language is being used to cover up deceit or to veil real continuing differences. It is therefore often seen as ecumenically suspect.[37]

Precision and 'ways of putting it'

Within the limitations imposed by the natural tendency of human language to multiplicity of meaning, and its unavoidable creaturely limitations in talking about God, it is a matter of priority that 'we should achieve as far as we can a clarity of thought and expression'.[38] It is a repeating theme of criticism of documents produced in ecumenical conversation that what they have to say is not absolutely clear; or that it is capable of more than one interpretation. We enter here on another classic problem of theological language, which is the second of these difficulties about figurativeness. Augustine's writings are full of talk of 'ways of signifying' and differences of usage. Such issues of *modi significandi* became a focus of extended discussion in the mediaeval centuries from at least the time of Anselm of Canterbury

---

[34] Bishop of Oxford, in the Church of England General Synod's debate on ARCIC II's *Salvation and the Church* in January 1989.   [35] See *The Logic and Language of the Bible*, I.
[36] See my *Problems of Authority in the Reformation Debates* (Cambridge, 1992).
[37] See the Roman Catholic Congregation for the Doctrine of the Faith (CDF), Observations of 1991.
[38] Ross McKenzie, 'Reformed and Roman Catholic understandings of the Eucharist', *Journal of Ecumenical Studies*, 13 (1976), 260–6, p. 260

and increasingly to the period of the Reformation.[39] These *modi significandi* were seen as a richness, a gift of God for the enlargement of the understanding of the Church – in something of the way diversity of ecclesial styles and patterns is often seen now.

In the centuries before the dawn of modern ecumenism there was no clear sense of the need for discussion of the problems of finding common language between persons or parties initially disposed to mistrust one another and therefore to misconstrue the meaning of one another's words. The tendency was for each side to try to see that its own language and formulations came out victorious in a battle between the two. That is not the thrust of things now. But there is still a danger of mutual suspiciousness.

The problem about figurative usages and that of multiple meaning both presented themselves in the framing of Rome's Reponse to ARCIC I's *Final Report*. 'The Congregation [for the Doctrine of the Faith] perceives... a certain equivocation on the nature of the "Ecclesiae Mater", connected with the stress on the idea, not erroneous in itself, of the Church "in constant need of repentance" (n.29) and of "renewal and purification" (n.30).'[40] In several critiques of documents issued by ecumenical commissions, the Roman Congregation for the Doctrine of the Faith points out that the language of these documents is often not 'univocal' and thus allows of differing interpretations. It argues that the document is written in a language which we might describe as symbolic and it is therefore difficult to interpret it univocally. Such an interpretation is necessary given that the purpose is to reach a definitive declaration of agreement.[41] And it appears to be obvious that 'neither is a statement truly agreed, nor is theology really common, if they are interpreted differently by the parties involved.'[42]

But that can be questioned. 'If ecumenical language is not univocal, is it bound to be equivocal, and therefore unsatisfactory to the human reason and ineffective as a means of unity?'[43] enquires Tavard. Limouris asks, 'if equivocation is a fact of theological language, is it one which necessarily gets in the way of the precision

---

[39] Augustine and Anselm make notable use of this notion, see *The Logic and Language of the Bible*, I.

[40] 'Commentary on the Observations of the CDF on ARCIC II, *Salvation and the Church*', *One in Christ*, 24 (1988), p. 385.

[41] CDF Observations on *Salvation and the Church*, November, 1989. In the Church of England's 1989 General Synod Debate there was discussion of these problems as dioceses saw them.

[42] G. Tavard, 'Ecumenical theology and the Catholic Church', *One in Christ*, 25 (1989), 101–13, p. 109.

[43] G. Tavard, 'Ecumenical theology and the Catholic Church', *One in Christ*, 25 (1989), 101–13, p. 109.

we ought to look for in a common ecumenical language?'[44] I think we have to be realistic and say that theological language *cannot* be univocal, and that we must therefore think in terms of some degree of equivocation, including figurative usages, as having to be built-in to ecumenical language. The task is then to work out controls and a framework within which they can operate.

Tavard presses 'the question ... whether theological language should be univocal'.[45] The 'should' may imply that, apart from the practical impossibility of speaking univocally about God, the attempt might be inappropriate in any case, since it would impoverish understanding to rest satisfied with the fact that we must constrain what we can say of God within the limitations of one form of human language.[46] There is plentiful patristic and mediaeval precedent for that picture of things. But Tavard suggests that there is a third alternative, after those of univocation and equivocation. 'The language of faith is always analogical, since no term applied to God has univocal meaning, borrowed as it is from human experience that adds many connotations to its basic denotation.' This too is well-trodden patristic and mediaeval ground. Tavard means by 'analogical' something closer to the setting side by side of the whole culture of individual churches. In this context he seems to see it as a way of expressing the relationship between *res* and *verbum*, thing and word, in which the faiths of separated communities are seen as having likeness or equivalency. 'For the analogical language of ecumenical theology to fulfil a unifying function between Christian traditions and Churches, one has to accept the notion that one faith is compatible with several modes of faith. Or, if one prefers, that the one faith is held, in a given ecclesial context, according to a certain mode.' He further explains that, for him, 'a mode of faith is the sum-total of the ways in which the one Christian faith is held, experienced, formulated, transmitted, in a concrete Christian community'.[47] This is a view which would have

---

[44] 'The basic thesis of a pneumatological Christocentrism is the starting-point of overcoming the recent theological neo-scholasticism while looking for exact exclusive statements in the form of definitions.' G. Limouris, 'The understanding of the Church emerging in the bilateral dialogues – coherence or divergence', *Greek Orthodox Theological Review*, 36 (1991), 1–21, p. 9.

[45] G. Tavard, 'Ecumenical theology and the Catholic Church', *One in Christ*, 25 (1989), 101–13, p. 109.

[46] 'ARCIC has tried to avoid vague and ambiguous language, while recognising that there can be more than one legitimate way of saying things.' H. Chadwick, 'The Lambeth Conference 1978: Roman Catholic relationships', *One in Christ*, 14 (1978), 376–80, p. 377.

[47] G. Tavard, 'Ecumenical theology and the Catholic Church', *One in Christ*, 25 (1989), 101–13, p. 109. Cf. 'We must judge beliefs by their consequences, not alone by their inner truth.' Jacob B. Agus, 'Six Jewish thoughts', *Journal of Ecumenical Studies*, 17 (1980), 10–11, p. 11.

support among ecumenists. Arthur de Vogel stresses that 'all meaning is contextual'.[48] He also insists upon the importance of the concreteness of particular contexts, even if that has to be at the expense of a clarity of expression which seems to claim universality of application. 'Canonical clarity can still be found in Churches, but such clarity is abstract, lacking the concreteness of man himself.'[49] We have to learn to make a 'contextual transfer' between one language and another. Human languages are always contextual, and the contexts give a varied content to what are superficially the same words, so that they can vary a good deal in their implications according to places and times. We may variously hear in them in different times and places different parts or aspects of their range of sense and emphasis.

This seems, roughly, to be a way of saying that language, especially theological language, is so multifariously connotative that we must simply seek to see expression in the one as analogous to expression in the other, with each carrying its cultural and confessional baggage as an acceptable accompaniment. There are problems, however, in knowing when expressions are analogous and when they are not. An example may help. This instance comes from Anglican–Orthodox conversations:

Archbishop Basil: We should differentiate between (i) the fact itself, as expressed in what the Old and New Testaments tell us concerning the glory of God; and (ii) the terminology, which was used in the Patristic period but not fully developed until the time of St. Gregory Palamas. It is difficult to require the Anglicans to accept the terminology of the later period. But do they accept what is said on this matter by the Cappadocians, and especially St Gregory of Nyssa? . . .

Dr Constantine Scouteris: We Orthodox do not seek to force the Anglicans to accept what they find uncongenial; we ask them to express their own tradition in a positive way.[50]

This seems to involve a clear attempt on the part of both sides to find a way of setting each tradition in its context in a way which will make them, if not commensurable, at least able to be seen as equivalent and as equals.

---

[48] A. Vogel, 'Church and Eucharist', one of the papers in the ARCIC process, see E. G. Knapp-Fisher, 'Anglican–Roman Catholic Commission: historical introduction, 1970–1', *One in Christ*, 9 (1973), p. 112.

[49] A. Vogel, 'Church and Eucharist', one of the papers in the ARCIC process, see E. G. Knapp-Fisher, 'Anglican–Roman Catholic Commission: historical introduction, 1970–1', *One in Christ*, 9 (1973), p. 127.

[50] A–O, *The Moscow Agreed Statement*, ed. K. Ware and C. Davey (London, 1976), account of Kallistos Ware, p. 44, quoting the Minutes.

There is, however, another and significantly different sense of 'analogy' which has to be mentioned here.

> In common Christian usage the term priesthood is employed in three distinct ways: the priesthood of Christ, the priesthood of the people of God, the priesthood of the ordained ministry ... The word priesthood is used by analogy when it is applied to the people of God and to the ordained ministry. These are two distinct realities which relate, each in its own way, to the high priesthood of Christ, the unique priesthood of the new covenant, which is their source and model.[51]

Here analogy means 'by extension'. A sort of stretching or transfer is involved. In this case, analogy and analogue are not equivalents; one derives from the other. A notion of analogy in which there is an assumption of dependency of this sort is not going to be ecumenically useful if it is used in comparing ecclesial bodies, because it goes against the first principle of equality.

To sum up: it is never going to be possible to put theological language in a frame which will contain it tidily. Even if that could be achieved for now, it would be impossible to prevent the natural developments and changes of usage over time from introducing fresh differences of emphasis. The way ahead must involve an act of trust that the faith is common and that the expression of it by each community and time intends to be faithful and recognises a responsibility to preserve the faith in what it says. Without such trust it will always be possible to find fault with other ways of putting things than one's own, and to point to ambiguity as though it were the result of deliberate deception. This is really the key to the matter. If ambiguity is seen as unavoidable it is construable as innocent. If it is thought to be done on purpose it is potentially divisive.

Baggage and historical conditioning

A further aspect of equivocal language is what we might call the problem of baggage, the historical conditioning[52] which makes it hard for us to use or even read certain expressions without their carrying for us a loading of polemic or old resentments. Even where

---

[51] ARCIC *M*, Elucidation; *Growth*, p. 84.
[52] 'We agree that revealed Truth is given in Holy Scripture and formulated in dogmatic definitions through thought-forms and language which are historically conditioned. We are encouraged by the growing agreement of theologians in our two communions on methods of interpreting this historical transmission of revelation.' 'Text of the Report of the ARC Joint Preparatory Commission', *One in Christ*, 5 (1969), 27–33, para.5.

the goodwill to do so is apparent, there is an anguished sense of the problems posed by the existence of a vocabulary of 'division' of this sort.[53] There is now a high degree of self-consciousness about this among ecumenists. To take a few examples : 'The customary vocabulary of division does not exactly describe our situation, even though there are still some important things we cannot do together or on which we cannot yet be one.'[54] 'The ecumenical movement has cleared away the atmosphere of suspicion which used to exist in most regions of France and replaced it with one of friendship and better mutual understanding. For example, in the matter of vocabulary, the mutual aversion for certain terms has disappeared: the Eucharist is no longer played off against the Lord's Supper, penitence against repentance.'[55] It has become impossible to employ certain terms without hatred, and so it has seemed sensible 'to remove certain word-usages which have . . . become the centre of controversy'.[56] These principles were expressed in a pioneering memorandum of Jean Tillard to ARCIC I at one of its Windsor meetings.

This commission will have to work according to the Spirit of Vatican II and especially of *Dei Verbum*. This means first that we shall have to discover, under our diverse and polemical expressions, the common 'tradition' from which we came. Our divergences are grounded in something that we shared in common, and probably continue to share even under our own polemical words. Some of these words are used to save it! – it will, thus, be necessary to discover what we were saying together before the division. Perhaps, we shall be surprised to see that we are united precisely in the matters that we consider as 'doctrinal divergences'! To demonstrate that to our two Churches, it will be necessary to use the common vocabulary we were using before the shift (if we discover that our faith was the same), and to express our agreements in using these words, no longer the words from polemical disputes.

This is a practical matter which has to be addressed and resolved, for words of some sort have to be chosen. 'Within the historical mindset of the period and culture in which they live, theologians work at a very concrete task.'[57] But it is also one which raises supremely

---

[53] 'We have learned from bitter historical experience that certain words denote several layers of meaning.' Jacob B. Agus, 'Six Jewish thoughts', *Journal of Ecumenical Studies*, 17 (1980), 10–11, p. 11.
[54] Disciples of Christ–Roman Catholic conversations; *Growth*, p. 155.
[55] 'Ecumenism today', *One in Christ*, 11 (1975), 30–87, p. 59.
[56] 'The Report of the Third Forum on Bilateral Conversations, October 6-10, 1980', *One in Christ*, 18 (1982), 44–54, p. 46 (also published as WCC Faith and Order Paper, 107 (1981).
[57] G. Tavard, 'The bilateral dialogues: searching for language', *One in Christ*, 16 (1980), 19–29, p. 22.

intricate methodological difficulties. These can at present be most directly sidestepped by *avoiding* the use of the offending terms. That was ARCIC I's approach. 'In producing these Statements, we have been concerned, not to evade the difficulties, but rather to avoid the controversial language in which they have often been discussed . . . we have sought solutions by examining our common inheritance, particularly the Scriptures.'[58] But it remains an urgent question whether to proceed in this way is avoiding an issue which will sooner or later have to be faced, and the disturbing terms freed of their divisive connotations. The problem of historical baggage is intricately involved with the difficulties about unavoidable equivocation, and ambiguity. That became sharply apparent in the responses to ARCIC I to which ARCIC's own Elucidations tried to reply. The responses were suspicious that a view rejected by reformers in the sixteenth century was being smuggled back in through the use of the term *anamnesis*. 'Some have been anxious that the term anamnesis may conceal the reintroduction of the theory of the repeated immolation. Others have suspected that the word refers not only to the historical events of salvation but also to an eternal sacrifice in heaven.'[59] ARCIC replied by pointing out the honourable ancestry of the term:

> The Commission has been criticized for its use of the term *anamnesis*. It chose the word used in New Testament accounts of the eucharist at the Last Supper. [1 Corinthians 11.24–5; Luke 22.19] The word is also to be found in Justin Martyr in the second century . . . From this time onwards the term is found at the very heart of the eucharistic prayers of both East and West, not only in the institution narrative but also in the prayer which follows and elsewhere [examples] . . . The word is also found in patristic and later theology.

ARCIC then went on to stress what it itself had understood the term *anamnesis* to express for today:

> The Commission believes that the traditional understanding of sacramental reality, in which the once-for-all event of salvation becomes effective in the present through the action of the Holy Spirit, is well expressed by the word *anamnesis* . . . Furthermore it enables us to affirm a strong conviction of sacramental realism and to reject mere symbolism. However the selection of this word by the Commission does not mean that our common eucharistic faith may not be expressed in other terms.[60]

---

[58] ARCIC I, *The Final Report*, Introduction; *Growth*, p. 64.
[59] H. Chadwick, 'Lambeth Conference 1978: Roman Catholic relationships', *One in Christ*, 14 (1978), 376–80, p. 377.   [60] ARCIC E, Elucidation, 5; *Growth*, pp. 24f.

A different set of suspicions was expressed about the use of deceptively 'ordinary' words: 'Some critics have been unhappy about the realistic language . . . and have questioned such words as "become" and "change".'[61]

The particular anxieties were these:

Criticism has been evoked by the statement that the bread and wine become the body and blood of Christ in the eucharist (E,10). The word *become* has been suspected of expressing a materialistic conception of Christ's presence, and this has seemed to some to be confirmed in the footnote on the word *transubstantiation* which also speaks of *change*. It is feared [NB] that this suggests that Christ's presence in the eucharist is confined to the elements, and that the Real Presence involves a physical change in them

ARCIC's Elucidation strove for fuller definition and greater precision:

Becoming does not here imply material change . . . It does not imply that Christ becomes present in the eucharist in the same manner that he was present in his earthly life. It does not imply that this *becoming* follows the physical laws of this world. What is here affirmed is a sacramental presence in which God uses realities of this world to convey the realities of the new creation: bread for this life becomes the bread of eternal life. Before the eucharistic prayer, to the question: 'What is that?', the believer answers, 'It is bread.' After the eucharistic prayer, to the same question he answers: 'It is truly the body of Christ, the Bread of Life.'[62]

So here ARCIC argues that: 'On the subject of Christ's presence in the sacrament, we can use language of the strongest realism, without the least implication of materialism.'[63]

This process of 'elucidation'[64] thus involved (a) clarification of meaning, (b) the provision of grounds for accepting ARCIC's usage which it could be hoped the suspicious could themselves accept, (c) an attempt to show that anxieties were unfounded. Only the first two are strictly to do with the language. The third has much to do with trust.

A special issue here is always the need to defend the use of language and terminology not found in Scripture but brought into use in the course of the Church's history; for all such language could be accused of carrying an undesirable historical baggage. It is strongly argued by ARCIC that such language has simply had to be employed, because Scripture itself did not provide the necessary vocabulary. 'The early Church found it necessary for its understanding and exposition of the

---

[61] ARCIC *E*, Elucidation, 3; *Growth*, p. 73.   [62] ARCIC *E*, Elucidation, 6; *Growth*, pp.74–5.
[63] H. Chadwick, 'Lambeth Conference 1978: Roman Catholic relationships', *One in Christ*, 14 (1978), 376–80, p. 377.   [64] On elucidation see further Chapter 7.

faith to employ terminology in ways in which it was not used in the New Testament.'[65]

But there remain difficulties about timing and about 'loading'. When these non-biblical terms are employed, a word which in one age is not problematic can become negatively charged in another. 'Wesley spoke of "presenting" Christ's saving work to the Father, and thus virtually employed the concept of "re-presentation" long before it became popular [in some quarters controversial] in the present ecumenical discussion,'[66] notes one author, writing on the ecumenical usage of terminology in connection with the Eucharist. Comparable is the need to reassure the Orthodox participants in dialogue that no significant departure is being made from the language of tradition, especially patristic tradition, which has for them much of the special character of the language of Scripture:

Archbishop Stylianos: . . . What Orthodox value is not just the terminology but the message and mind (phronema) of the Fathers.
Professor Galitis: Instead of 'the Patristic period', we should say, 'the Fathers'. We do not wish to restrict the Fathers chronologically.
Bishop Hanson welcomed the phrase 'mind of the Fathers'. We Anglicans, he said, do not always admire the hermeneutical methods of the Fathers but we do recognise the conclusions to which the Fathers came.
The Revd Mark Santer: Let us say 'the Fathers' method of theology, whereby theology is linked with prayer'.
Professor Romanides: That is precisely what I mean by the Fathers' theological method.[67]

So historical contextualisation, a sensitivity to the mind of the age and its anxieties, are ecumenically essential as tools for resolving problems of double and figurative meaning. It is a particularly demanding exercise of insight which is required here, because it involves the attempt to understand the viewpoints of all sides involved. We shall come back to these problems in the next chapter.

EPISTEMOLOGY AND METALANGUAGE: *VERBUM* AND *INTELLIGENTIA*

The second of the grand issues with which we are concerned in this chapter is the question of the relationship not between word and

---

[65] ARCIC *M*, Elucidation, 2; *Growth*, p. 84.
[66] J. Robert Nelson, 'Methodist eucharistic usage: from constant communion to benign neglect to sacramental recovery', *Journal of Ecumenical Studies*, 13 (1976), 278–83.
[67] A–O, Moscow, account of Kallistos Ware, p. 56, quoting the Minutes.

thing-referred-to-by-that-word, but between language and *understanding* of the thing. In the study of ecumenical language, this is double-barrelled. It is epistemological. But it is also a matter of mutual understanding of persons and positions so that there can be an agreed context for the epistemology. 'A phase of mutual comprehension is elementary and indispensable,' comments George Tavard. 'A Catholic has to understand the sense of Luther's formulations of justification by faith, before arriving at an agreement with Lutheranism.'[68] When that is achieved, 'the phase of mutual understanding [can perhaps lead] to a phase of common discovery and elaboration'.[69] It will be apparent that there is need for trust here, too, as a basis for mutual understanding.

There is a further refinement, because the 'common' language which expresses mutual understanding has to be arrived at by way of the partly separate languages and while leaving them in use. It does not, and cannot for the present, supersede them. 'Often . . . division' has been 'brought about by a progressive estrangement which little by little gave rise to a different language to the point where' groups of Christians 'became strangers to one another . . . Perhaps what often passed as schism was only estrangement. But an epithet once hurled goes on its way and makes relationships "schismatic".'[70] There is, in other words, a tendency in a state of division in the Church towards progressive separation of languages. That becomes the case to the point where what seems a common language may in fact be no such thing. The converse of this phenomenon is the tendency for Christians asked to say whether an agreed statement in a 'common language' is, for example, 'consonant in substance' with the faith of their own church, to request that it be made identical with their own familiar language. 'With each one using the language of his own Communion, the same words may signify quite different realities in one Church and in another, while different words may expect the same reality . . . it is a question of establishing real and complete communication.'[71]

So what is actually required is that ecumenists become multilingual, able to understand the language of the communions they come from and also the languages of other communions, while building up a

[68] G. Tavard, 'The bilateral dialogues: speaking together', *One in Christ*, 16 (1980), 30–43, p. 37.
[69] G. Tavard, 'The bilateral dialogues: speaking together', *One in Christ*, 16 (1980), 30–43, p. 37–8.
[70] 'One Church of God: the Church broken in pieces', *One in Christ*, 17 (1981), 2–12, p. 8.
[71] J. Willebrands, 'Prospects for Anglican–Roman Catholic relations', *One in Christ*, 8 (1972), 11–23, p. 14, quoting Secretariat for Christian Unity, *Reflections and Suggestions Concerning Ecumenical Dialogue*, IV.1, c.

common language together. That is going to require an uncommon degree of clear-sightedness about what is happening in the use of language.[72]

It can be argued that the best way to look at ecumenical language is to do so with the aid of a language in which we are able to speak about it. Two things are easily confused here: the search for a common language in which to do theology together; and the need for a language which will be a means of discussing the whole process. Tavard distinguishes the two by seeing the 'metalanguage' as a means to an end and the 'common language' as the end it makes it possible to achieve. That clearly sets as the objective the framing of a common language, or at least fully mutually comprehensible and acceptable *languages* of ecumenical discourse. 'The ecumenical task is to arrive at a metalanguage which, by pointing out the oneness of faith in a new way, should allow the formation of theological languages that will be mutually comprehensible even if they have to remain different . . . the parity of the dialogue lies in the fact that one recognizes the language of the other as a possible system of expression of the metalanguage of Revelation . . . In the light of the metalanguage . . . there emerges the possibility of a common language which, compared to all the languages previously in use, will be new.'[73] It is not absolutely clear whether the 'metalanguage' Tavard envisages is the medium through which the common task becomes possible or itself a higher theological language, intrinsically superior (or of a higher order), in that it expresses the truth more exactly. It would seem inappropriate to see it as the latter, since if it were indeed the best 'language of Revelation' we have, it would itself be the language we were looking for.

The technique of looking down on the process from above has been consciously in the minds of those engaged in conversations, as a means of refining the linguistic instruments for doing ecumenical theology. But the distinction between metalanguage and common language has not always been clearly made, and, as we have just seen, it is not easily made. Yet one thing is straightforwardly apparent. The old divisive language is obviously no longer of use. 'A common declaration of faith on points which have separated us or have been controversial

---

[72] The task of theology, as George Tavard puts it, is not only 'to speak about God', but 'to investigate the conditions of this speaking'. G. Tavard, 'The bilateral dialogues: searching for language', *One in Christ*, 16 (1980), 19–29, p. 21.

[73] G. Tavard, 'The bilateral dialogues: speaking together', *One in Christ*, 16 (1980), pp. 27–8.

during four centuries supposes a creative[74] work concerning language and expression. There is no sense in repeating the old controversial and polemical formulas,'[75] argued Willebrands in 1972. Similarly, in a forum of 1980, the two seem to be partly elided: 'We try to use a new language in order to express a doctrinal deepening that enables the parties to overcome misunderstandings, disagreements and the partiality of those confessional positions which existed in an earlier polemical context.'[76]

'We have a legacy of polemical language by each side designed to exclude the other side. The [ARCIC] Commission has set aside the old polemics and asks if we can get behind what is really meant by affirming the Eucharist to be sacrificial.' ARCIC set out to see if language can 'be found to express . . . faith . . . common to both our traditions . . . which does not tread on sensitive toes, and at the same time is free of inhibitions in boldly affirming our faith'.[77] ARCIC talk of 'getting behind', used here not historically[78] but with reference to language, has the same sort of thrust, with the same implicit (though not explicit) recognition that a common language is to be arrived at best by way of a metalanguage. A similar sense that one language lies behind another is found elsewhere. 'When divided Churches meet together, they have to turn their attention to the time at which the division happened . . . by entering into the language of that time and by trying to unearth the deepest motives behind their disagreement.'[79]

By far the heaviest emphasis in ecumenical discussion has been on seeking the common language which is to be the end product of the conversation, and the shared possession of those communities which

[74] 'Creative' is a broad notion, embracing both the higher and the common languages.
[75] J. Willebrands, 'Prospects for Anglican–Roman Catholic relations', *One in Christ*, 8 (1972), 11–23, p. 14.
[76] 'The Report of the Third Forum on Bilateral Conversations, October 6-10, 1980', *One in Christ*, 18 (1982), 44–54, p. 46 (also published as WCC Faith and Order Paper, 107 (1981)). The text continues: 'understanding them well will demand an effort of profound comprehension that goes beyond the first formulation to a new perception that tries to embrace all the aspects of the question'.
[77] H. Chadwick, 'Lambeth Conference 1978: Roman Catholic relationships,' *One in Christ*, 14 (1978), 376–80, p. 376. On the historical mode of 'going behind', see Chapter 5.
[78] See 'getting behind' pp. 102ff.
[79] The author continues 'consensus is more than the expression of differences overcome' . . . 'they can decide that the differences are not mutually exclusive and can be understood as complementary statements if they are interpreted in an appropriate way . . . they can come to the conclusion that the differences have become mixed up with secondary factors in the course of history'. L. Vischer, 'The reception of consensus in the ecumenical movement', *One in Christ*, 17 (1981), 294–305, pp.296–7.

have taken part in it.[80] Ecumenical encounter certainly requires the discovery of a common language, and ecumenical statements almost universally recognise the fact.[81] 'We have to learn to speak the same language in order . . . to speak together.'[82] 'If unity is recognisable by the adoption of a common language, this is because there is no unity without communication.'[83] 'Convergence can only result from the development and adoption of a new theological language.'[84]

No natural language now provides a base which is not already heavily coloured culturally. The Latin of Vatican II's discussions had the advantage of being a usable common language but not live enough to be too full of nuances which were liable to shift in present use. There is no possibility of such a universal language being a solution now because Latin is ceasing to be the common currency even of those nurtured in the Roman Catholic tradition. Other communions already wrestle with the polyglot problem. 'Languages cannot simply be invented. They have to grow.'[85] The candidate which is emerging spontaneously as the ecumenical base language is English, but English itself is not one tongue. British and American English are becoming two divergent languages, and elsewhere in the world English is effectively a still further tongue in its own right locally.

Present awareness of the problem of 'contemporary pluralism of the languages of faith and of theological languages' [86] draws attention to the desired end rather than to the linguistic instruments by which it might be attained. But some standing-away from the old adversarial language and from the plurality of alternative languages certainly seems a practical necessity, and perhaps that can indeed only be done by moving for the purpose into a higher language.

We are not talking about a technically different language here, but a mode of discussion. An example of the use of what I have in mind as 'metalinguistic' techniques may be helpful. The word 'is' is

---

[80] It has been suggested that some communions have not shared this common language or experienced real encounter until they entered the ecumenical movement. M.-J. de Guillou, 'Intérrogations sur l'avenir de l'oecuménisme', *Istina*, 10 (1964), 7–24, p. 11.

[81] Even if that common language is an instrument of controversy. M.-J. de Guillou, 'Intérrogations sur l'avenir de l'oecuménisme', *Istina*, 10 (1964), 7–24, p. 11.

[82] G. Tavard, 'The bilateral dialogues: speaking together', *One in Christ*, 16 (1980), p. 31.

[83] G. Tavard, 'The bilateral dialogues: searching for language', *One in Christ*, 16 (1980), 19–29, p. 21.   [84] G. Tavard, 'For a theology of dialogue', *One in Christ*, 15 (1975), 11–20, p. 12

[85] G. Tavard, 'For a theology of dialogue', *One in Christ*, 15 (1975), 11–20, p. 13. There is a lesson here about patience.

[86] G. Tavard, 'The bilateral dialogues: searching for language', *One in Christ*, 16 (1980), 19–29, p. 26. 'The problem is not how to streamline theologies into one; it is to discover the oneness of faith within the pluralism of theologies and doctrines.'

notoriously equivocal. It may imply 'identity with', 'inclusion in', 'equivalence to', among other things. In the Second Vatican Council a move of incalculable importance ecumenically was made in the substitution of *subsistit in* for *est*, 'subsists in' for 'is' in describing the relationship of 'Church' to 'Church of Rome'.[87] Willebrands commented a decade later on the process of analysis which led to this move. 'It would not do to think of Christians outside the Roman Catholic Church as members of it only "by desire". In one sense, they clearly did not desire to belong to it, or they would do so. Yet their baptism is recognised by the Roman Catholic Church and they confess the faith of the Creeds.' The members and consultors of the Secretariat felt they could not do justice to the situation of their brothers belonging to other Churches simply by describing them as members '*in voto* of the Catholic Church since a *votum* even implicit could not without serious difficulties be harmonized and reconciled with the explicit refusal to be a member, while on the other hand the real fact of being baptised in Christ and confessing faith in the Trinitarian and Christological doctrines meant more than a mere *votum*'.[88] What had been done was to stand away far enough from the phrase *in voto* to see why it would not do, and to follow through the implications for the wording which was to be used to describe the relationship between Church and churches. So when it came to describing the relationship of 'Church' and 'Church of Rome', 'is' could not be used without qualification. '*Est* . . . would be too exclusive and not take account of the elements of the Church which exist in other Churches.'[89] In the end another expression was substituted, as far less equivocal, and as resting explicitly on an understanding of the relationship which could be shared by both sides. This was applied at the 'common language' level by manipulation from the 'metalanguage' level.

In another case involving 'is', in the Anglican–Orthodox Agreed Statement of 1976, again we find a standing-away so as to see more clearly what is going on. Once more, there is an attempt to articulate the difficulty so as to perceive how to resolve it. Again, it becomes clear that something more than 'is' was needed to express the

---

[87] Vatican II, *Lumen Gentium*, 8.
[88] J. Willebrands, 'The ecumenical movement: its problems and driving force', *One in Christ*, 11 (1975), 210–23.
[89] J. Willebrands, 'The ecumenical movement: its problems and driving force', *One in Christ*, 11 (1975), 210–23.

relationship between term and concept, with some spelling out of the common understanding which is being implied:

In an earlier draft of paragraph 4, it was said in direct terms, 'The Bible . . . is the Word of God', but this was subsequently modifed to read, 'The Scriptures . . . bear . . . witness to God's revelation of himself' and 'express the Word of God in human language'. The more direct formulation, 'The Bible is the Word of God', was preferred by a number of delegates, in particular by the Revd Roger Beckwith . . . On the other side it was argued by the Bishop of Truro, 'You cannot say univocally that the uncreated Word is to be identified with the created Scriptures.' 'In what sense can a book embody the revelation of God?' asked Professor Romanides; and he observed, 'The Bible speaks to us of revelation, but is not itself to be identified with revelation.' 'It should be affirmed', said Canon Carmichael, 'that God's act of revelation is prior to Scripture. In the Bible we have the witness of the community to whom God made that revelation.' The Revd Mark Santer urged that a distinction be made 'between (i) God revealing himself; (ii) the expression of this revelation in Scripture.' It was for these reasons that the modified text was preferred to the original draft.[90]

In a sense, this is perhaps to dignify with the description 'metalanguage' what can be seen as largely an exercise in gloss or commentary or interpretation. For no statement can be complete; there is always room for interpretation.[91] What has actually happened has been a setting out of boundary-posts. An arena has been delineated within which the agreed area of understanding extends. Persons or ecclesial communities accepting such a formulation may regard themselves as standing here or there within such an area. Mark Santer, Anglican Bishop of Birmingham, commented in a Church of England General Synod Debate on ARCIC II's text, *Salvation and the Church*, in January, 1989, that 'any statement, not of a particular theological position but of the faith of the community, must at once respect the limits of what can be said and also leave room for proper width of interpretation. One could say the same of any of the Church's doctrinal statements which have been designed to deal

[90] A–O, Moscow, account of Kallistos Ware, p. 51.
[91] 'If language is in need of interpretation, then in a strict hermeneutical circle between the external and the internal clarity of a text will be inadequate for the hermeneutical task.' Meg H. Madson, 'Hermeneutic and theological method', *Journal of Ecumenical Studies*, 23 (1986), 529–44, p. 533. 'The boundary-line between dogmas of faith and theological explanations' is touched on by Edward J. Kilmartin, 'The Orthodox–Roman Catholic dialogue on the Eucharist', *Journal of Ecumenical Studies*, 13 (1976), 213–21, p. 215. Both reference to an explicit epiclesis and the term transubstantiation are seen as explanatory and 'outside the scope of that affirmation of eucharistic faith which is a condition for eucharistic sharing'.

with division without making unnecessary exclusions. Take, for instance, the creed of Nicaea or the Chalcedonian Definition. Neither is univocal in the sense of dispensing with further discussion or even dispute as to their meaning.'[92] Interpretation, seen in this light, becomes a standing away to give room, gloss or commentary, a permitting of variety of understanding within what are nevertheless fixed limits.

It has not always been seen in this space-giving way, and the alternative of using interpretation to limit options needs to be borne in mind. At a Conference of Anglicans and Russian Orthodox held in 1956, the Orthodox saw interpretation as a means of bringing into line. Patriarch Pimen of Moscow and All Russia said in his opening speech that Anglicans would need 'to pass their dogmatic resolutions officially, in a council of all their bishops, making them obligatory for the whole Church and for all Anglican communities, so that' the Orthodox 'should be able to see clearly what constitutes and what does not constitute the teaching of their Church'. 'The Anglicans must be prepared to make a solemn announcement on behalf of the whole Anglican Church interpreting the "Thirty-Nine Articles" in the spirit of the Undivided Church.' Articles 5,17,19,22,23,25,28,29,31 were seen as 'not clearly formulated'.[93] This, too, has its ecumenical place if by it we mean to improve precision; it is, however, the reverse of helpful if used as a means of excluding another communion from acceptance.

Clarity, accessibility, comprehensibility

There remains a large complex of problems about the way in which a common Christian language, sensitive to ambiguity and equivocation, using figurativeness consciously and to illuminate not to deceive, is also to be directly intelligible and even attractive to the ordinary reader who has not taken possession of this language by being himself involved in framing it. A comment from the responses to *BEM* is illustrative. 'The text of *BEM* is too theological for the ordinary people to understand and sounds unlike Protestantism but rather like the language used in the early centuries of the church.'[94]

So another 'apologetic' task of commentary is that form of

[92] See C. Hill on the official dicasteries in *Catholic International*, 3.3 (1–14 February 1992), p. 134 ff.
[93] *Anglo-Russian Theological Conference, Moscow, July 1956*, ed. H. Waddams (London, 1957), pp. 42–3.   [94] *Churches Respond to BEM*, V, p. 174, Church of Christ in Thailand.

interpretation which is needed to make what has been agreed understandable to those who have not been involved in the conversations and may have no expert knowledge of the topics at issue. A dialogue can create its own language. It is easy for those who develop it together as they talk not to realise that those who have not been taking part in the conversation will not necessarily understand that language. Readers who have not been involved in the conversation may also feel a sense of loss of familiar language when they see something put another way. 'Such documents also require a pastoral explanation, comments one report. 'Since most of the faithful will be surprised and disconcerted at the loss of the venerable expressions with which they were accustomed to articulate their faith . . . we must show the continuity between these beloved traditional expressions and the surprising new language.'[95] Such exposition will require the use of some sort of 'standing away' language, as well as a 'drawing closer' language.

Conclusion

'The object of a Definition of Faith, however it may be reached,' suggested the Roman Catholics at Malines, 'is not to formulate a newly-invented dogma, unknown to Holy Scripture, of the tradition of the Church, but to declare explicitly and with authority, in regard to some given point, what is the faith entrusted by Jesus Christ to the keeping of the Church.'[96] In Chapter 2 of the Decree on Ecumenism of Vatican II the formulation of doctrine is distinguished from the deposit of faith itself. Christopher Hill comments on the statement of Pope John XXIII when he spoke to the opening session of the Council. 'I find that there is still not a sufficient appreciation of the truth that there is indeed a distinction between a doctrinal formulation and the deposit of faith it is designed to express. Only when this truth is appreciated can *particular formulations* be understood as contingent rather than necessary.'[97] These and other attempts to express a central principle need to be stressed again as we wrestle with the problem of framing a common language. The finding of the language

---

[95] 'The Report of the Third Forum on Bilateral Conversations, October 6–10, 1980', *One in Christ*, 18 (1982), 44–54, p. 46 (also published as WCC Faith and Order Paper, 107 (1981)).
[96] *The Conversations at Malines: Report Presented to the Archbishop of Canterbury by the Anglican Members* (Oxford, 1927), Supplement, p. 75.
[97] C. Hill, 'The Decree on Ecumenism: an Anglican view', *One in Christ* 30 (1994), 20–31, p. 25.

does not set at risk the truth it is intended to convey. That is secure.

We are still at a stage where we can barely see the outlines of the difficulties in the way of developing a truly ecumenical language. But those outlines are becoming clear. They consist in the recognition that language is elusive, associative, always hung about with baggage; that we have to learn to identify that baggage as ecumenically a help or a hindrance; and that we have to try to do it together and as widely as possible with other communions, so as to get rid of suspiciousness about trickery and deception. Mutual misunderstanding is Babel; shared and mutual comprehension of the varieties of Christian language a Pentecost. The task is to make ecumenical language honest, clear and exact, and open and accessible. That is a refining of the instrument with which the work is to be done, but it also colours and shapes. It makes, as well as expressing, community.

CHAPTER 5

Historical method

We have been asking the ecumenically central questions whether there can be differences of expression of what is, or comes to be understood to be, the same faith, and, if so, how we can know it to be the same faith. The ecumenical hope rests on the answer 'Yes' to the first of these questions, as it does to the central historical question of ecumenism, whether a common faith was shared before our divisions and can be rediscovered and shared again. There are difficulties in establishing the existence of an undivided primitive Church historically. Yet if the evident differences of expression of divided Christians do not somehow express the same faith in the same Christ, there is ultimately no basis for Christian unity. And that applies as much to unity of faith with Christians of other ages as it does to unity of faith among Christians now.[1] So the relation between the history and the theology is crucial.

When those holding seemingly different theologies and using different forms of expression to speak of their faith need to know whether they speak of the same faith, there will almost always be a historical problem to be solved, because the differences will be likely to have their roots in a past division or at least a loss of common

---

[1] E. Lanne asks the still more testing question whether there may be not only differences of terminology and expression for the same faith, but also different theologies expressing the same faith. He stresses that although differences of rite have been admitted, differences in theological vocabulary do not have the same history of liberal acceptance between ecclesial communities, because they are suspected of pointing to differences of faith. He is able to point to exceptions, even from an early date, which encourage the view that differences of theological vocabulary at least, may not be a bar to our acknowledging that we hold the same faith. In the Trinitarian debate of the fourth century, Hilary of Poitiers tried to show that the difference between the strictly orthodox and the homoiousians was not unbridgeable; Basil (c.330–79) too attempted this sort of rapprochement. That is not quite the same as saying that there can be differences of theology and the same faith, but it is an indicator that it may be possible. E. Lanne, 'Les différences compatibles avec l'unité', *Istina*, 8 (1961–2), p. 241.

context in the past. So the first methodological requirement here is to try to establish a relation between history and theology.[2]

It is no good being other than rigorous in tackling this because to go 'behind' controversial formulations chronologically is not necessarily to go 'behind' them conceptually. Moreover, there are historical and epistemological questions about the ways in which either can be done without altering meaning.

'History by itself has no method making possible the establishment of norms for the belief and life of the Church.'[3] Different intellectual operations are involved in giving an account of the theological past and in framing theological statements which are intended to be of enduring validity. The first requires the weighing of evidence, so as to establish what was said and what influenced the way it was said at the time. The second strives to balance concerns of the period when the statement is being made against the imperatives of a truth for all time. But the two cannot be kept separate. We have to find a 'way of evaluating historical evidence at points where history impinges upon dogmatic affirmations'.[4]

An example from the Bonn Reunion Conferences of 1874–5 may be helpful here in illustrating how difficult it is to keep a clear head about the relation of history to theology in ecumenical conversation. The Anglican Alfred Plummer kept a record of those sessions he himself attended, with particular reference to the contribution of Dr Döllinger, whose friendship had brought him there. He reports one sequence of reflection of Döllinger's on the relation of history to theology:

'Another very difficult question which will have to be discussed', said Dr. Döllinger, 'is the doctrine of the eucharist. I don't yet see my way out of that difficulty. I must think still more as to what will possibly lead to agreement. One thing I am quite clear about, – that the mediaeval doctrine of transubstantiation, as taught by modern Roman theologians, cannot be maintained. It is at variance with the teaching of the primitive Church, it is at variance with science, it is at variance with itself. I have looked at it in all kinds of ways, and sooner or later it lands you in contradiction. We owe the

---

[2] See D. Thompson, in *Festschrift* for Jean Tillard, ed. G. R. Evans and M. Gourgues (Louvain, 1995). [3] H. Chadwick, 'Unfinished business', *The Tablet* (8 February 1992).
[4] ARCIC does 'not think it either necessary or correct to assert that the Petrine texts of the New Testament are in themselves a sufficient historical foundation for asserting that Jesus intended to found the papacy. That the role of St. Peter in the apostolic age affords strong encouragement to the idea that the Church needs a Petrine office to be an effective bond of unity and universality is a far less controversial proposition, and while grounded in good historical evidence is more than a merely historical statement.' H. Chadwick, 'Unfinished business', *The Tablet* (8 February 1992).

doctrine to the influence of Aristotelianism on mediaeval religious speculation . . . In the Fathers you will find a wide difference of expression on this
question. S. Gregory of Nyssa, for instance, uses very strong language, and
goes almost as far as the mediaeval doctrine of transubstantiation.'

He thus argues from the *history* of the doctrine that we ought not to
have to keep to a position which was arrived at (on perhaps dubious
grounds) at one point in the past when it happened to be appropriate
and its dubious foundations were not apparent. That can be said with
confidence, he thinks, because at another point in the past it was not
seen in that way at all, or not by everyone. There is an attempt here to
get from history to theology, but the logical flaws are plain.

Yet one can, Döllinger suggests, come at the relationship of history
to theology from another angle, by asking how an author, now
himself in the past, utilised what he knew of the more remote past in
framing his own theological position:

'S. Augustine, on the other hand, in this matter is at one with Calvin.
Calvin's statements about the eucharist are identical with those of Augustine;
no doubt derived from S. Augustine, like Calvin's views about grace,
predestination, and election. Not that Calvin was a mere borrower. He was,
I believe, a sincere seeker after truth, and took from the Fathers what
commended itself to him as true.'[5]

The issue, which Döllinger fails to confront here, although he glances
at it, seems to be whether stages in the history of theology, contingent
as they demonstrably are upon historical circumstances, can constitute
evidence for the truth of assertions about the faith.[6]

Döllinger's approach elsewhere in the Bonn Reunion Conversations
was to try to derive the theology from the history in another way.

He briefly stated the history of the controversy. All parties, he believed,
would now agree that the Filioque was introduced into the Creed in an
unlawful manner. The creed drawn up at Nicaea, completed and confirmed
at other Councils, ought never to have been changed. No such addition as
the Filioque could be rightly made except by a General Council.

Döllinger could not refrain from making one or two points here which
have a polemical (at any rate, certainly not a dispassionate)

---

[5] Alfred Plummer, *Conversations with Dr Döllinger, 1870–90*, ed. R. Boudens (Louvain, 1985), pp.
122–3.

[6] It is perhaps helpful to distinguish here between the history of theology and the history of
other kinds of events. There is certainly a history of theology itself, that is, the history of the
ideas of Christian theologians and their formulation. It is impossible to trace that history
without in some sense 'doing theology'. It is here, in the orientation of theological ideas in
relation to the ways they were thought of in different periods, that the disciplines of history
and theology most clearly mesh.

character. He noted that Pope Leo III had specifically 'refused to consent to the addition', saying that the Bishop of Rome had no power to change anything in the Creed or add anything to it. This, 'we may remark by the way', said Döllinger, is 'in strong contrast to the claims of the Pope at the present time'.[7] The time of the introduction of the new words into the Western Creed, he argued, was inseparable in all minds from the schism between East and West, because it coincided. This is not of course strictly right. But Döllinger's belief that it was right made it possible for him to say that it 'inflicted a wound which has festered ever since; which has never been healed and never will be healed so long as this stumbling-block remains'.[8] Döllinger here takes a 'good' historical precedent to be authoritative theologically, and takes it that a 'bad' later example is not only not authoritative theologically but has been lingeringly damaging.

Theological analysis of past ideas and the history of events cannot always be tidily separated. Nor should they be. But the importance of keeping them conceptually distinct is evident in more than one debate about the difference between a 'fact' (something whose existence cannot be denied because it did actually take place), and a 'doctrine' (a belief or theological position formally stated at some point in the past). We might take another example from the Bonn Reunion conversations here. One of the groups framed the following account of a doctrinal position as a fact of history:

We acknowledge that the number of sacraments was fixed at seven first in the twelfth century, and then was received into the general teaching of the Church, not as a tradition coming down from the Apostles or from the earliest times, but as the result of theological speculation. (8a).

This was accompanied by the rider (8b) that baptism and the Eucharist are the principal sacraments, with the assertion that 'Catholic theologians (e.g. Bellarmine) acknowledge, and we acknowledge [it] with them'.[9] A device was tried here which was put

---

[7] Alfred Plummer, *Conversations with Dr Döllinger, 1870–90*, ed. R. Boudens (Louvain, 1985), p. 102.

[8] Alfred Plummer, *Conversations with Dr Döllinger, 1870–90*, ed. R. Boudens (Louvain, 1985), p. 102.

[9] 'As a historian, Döllinger regarded Christianity as a force more than a doctrine, and displayed it as it expanded and became the soul of later history . . . Experience slowly taught him that he who takes all history for his province is not the man to write a compendium' . . . 'While Catholics objected that he was a candid friend, Lutherans observed that he resolutely held his ground wherever he could, and as resolutely abandoned every position that he found untenable.' Alfred Plummer, *Conversations with Dr Döllinger, 1870–90*, ed. R. Boudens (Louvain, 1985), p. 250. Alfred Plummer, *Conversations with Dr Döllinger, 1870–90*, ed. R. Boudens (Louvain, 1985), p. 104, 1874.

to use again in connection with the 'historical episcopate' clause of the Lambeth Quadrilateral when it proved controversial.[10] The idea was to treat the contentious point as a historical fact not a doctrine. This made it acceptable because there is no quarrelling with a fact, and to say that something is a fact is precisely not to require assent to it as a belief. The claim being made for it as a fact would seem to be less than the claim which might be made for it as a belief, since it could be accepted as a fact uncontroversially, but not as a belief. Its status as a belief would give it entailments and implications for now and the future which it did not need to carry if it was simply seen as a past event in the history of ideas. But as the Bonn example just quoted shows, it is extremely difficult to set out such an account without embedding in it implications about the authoritativeness of what is being said. 'Tradition' is set over against 'speculation', and the agreement of otherwise opposed camps. 'We' and 'the Catholic theologians' are taken to weigh in favour of authoritativeness.

There is a further problem here. Not only is a 'fact' likely to prove to be a way of smuggling in a 'doctrine', but historical explanations as to matters of fact are liable to be proved inadequate by further research. That is not the case in the same way for matters of faith, which are, of their nature, not susceptible of such 'disproving' because they do not ultimately rest on proofs of that sort. We believe points of faith on a number of grounds: among them that Scripture is God's direct revelation about them; that the consensus of the faithful through the ages supports them; that they are intellectually satisfying ('reasonable'); that experience shows them to be right. The consensus of the faithful through the ages has been expressed in formal and informal ways, through councils and synods and diffusely through the whole of the Church's varying life. The classic and perennial character of many of the Church's problems, as it emerges in events and debates, is itself evidential. So we find ourselves imperceptibly making an assumption. One historical factor may prove nothing. Many may. Faith is therefore historical in the sense of having continuity through time. That is not the same thing as saying that it is founded on ordinary historical proofs, but it may amount to something very close to saying that it is theologically supported by that very continuity.

In the Bonn Reunion Conference discussion just referred to, 'the

---

[10] On this, see *Quadrilateral at One Hundred*, ed. J. Robert Wright (London, 1988).

history of an idea' is treated (in intention) purely historically, but we can see some smuggling of theology into history going on, even where no weight of continuity can be adduced:

Dr. Döllinger remarked that in earlier centuries the Latin term *sacramentum* was very vague and undefined in meaning, much as the Greek term *mysterion* was and remains still. 'Sacrament' since the rise of scholasticism with Peter Lombard has acquired a special and definite significance unknown to the first ten or eleven centuries, while 'mystery' remains as indefinite as ever. In early Latin writers the Trinity, the Incarnation, and the Procession of the Holy Spirit are *sacramenta* no less than baptism, eucharist, or orders. The proposition . . . is merely a statement of historical fact not of doctrine; but *the fact is of importance in order to remove doctrinal or apparently doctrinal differences* [my italics].[11]

Döllinger was right in essence here. But his understanding of 'scholasticism' would not now stand up. An assertion based on what is known of the history of an idea can thus be dangerous in just the same way as an assertion based on inadequate knowledge of an event, because it is partial and unreliable.[12]

So a theology drawn from historical consistency and continuity must be deemed to have a respectability which a theology drawn from historical interpretation of particular events cannot. Perhaps we can say that history shows tendencies and consistencies within its changes and that these may be deemed a form of revelation and a basis of proof. At issue here is a very old theological debate. Can theological truth be established by reasoning alone, or does it require evidences from things which have happened or been witnessed to? If evidences, can these be taken to constitute a continuing of revelation after the closing of the canon? Experience is always gained in a particular and therefore a historical context. Without allowing anything to compete with Scripture, can we search the historical record for evidences of the working out of God's purposes in the world and legitimately use them as supporting evidence for truths of faith? An example from Anglican–Orthodox dialogue of the weighing of 'oldness' against 'experience' against 'reasonableness' may be apposite here; again for the way it shows up the difficulty of keeping

[11] Alfred Plummer, *Conversations with Dr Döllinger, 1870–90*, ed. R. Boudens (Louvain, 1985), p. 104, 1874.
[12] This exchange raised one more point of importance. Taking points in conjunction can make acceptable what would not perhaps otherwise be acceptable. 'None of the Anglicans objected to 8a when taken in conjunction with 8b', Alfred Plummer, *Conversations with Dr Döllinger, 1870–90*, ed. R. Boudens (Louvain, 1985), p. 104, 1874.

it clearly in view whether a given point ought to be deemed 'historical' or theological:

> Professor Romanides: . . . I wish to ask the Anglicans this question: When the Old and New Testaments speak of the revealed glory of God do the Anglicans consider this glory to be created or uncreated? And if they regard it as uncreated do they consider it to be the essence of God?
> The Bishop of Truro: I am certain that Professor Romanides and I believe the same things. But I wish to ask Professor Romanides: Is it necessary to my salvation to speak about the relation of God to creation in terms of the essence–energies distinction? Cannot this teaching be expressed in other terms? . . .
> Bishop Terwilliger: I am happy about the essence–energies distinction. But how early is it? Is it found in the early Christian sources?
> Professor Romanides: The distinction has roots both in Judaism and in the Greek philosophical tradition. The Church uses the distinction not for philosophical but for experiential reasons.
> Archbishop Basil: We should differentiate between (i) the fact itself, as expressed in what the Old and New Testaments tell us concerning the glory of God; and (ii) the terminology, which was used in the Patristic period but not fully developed until the time of St. Gregory Palamas. It is difficult to require the Anglicans to accept the terminology of the later period. But do they accept what is said on this matter by the Cappadocians, and especially St Gregory of Nyssa? . . .
> Dr Constantine Scouteris: We Orthodox do not seek to force the Anglicans to accept what they find uncongenial; we ask them to express their own tradition in a positive way.[13]

Perhaps 'proving' is not the model we should be looking to, since it will rarely be the case, except for the contents of the ancient Creeds perhaps, that the continuities of acceptance throughout the Church will weigh consistently. History might better be seen as giving meaning and reference to faith and to its enshrining in theological principles. Pannenberg argues that 'All theological questions and answers have meaning only within the framework of history.'[14]

Conversely, it might be more forcefully argued perhaps that history makes sense only in the light of faith, for only trust in God can make bearable the painfulness of historical reality, and only a theology can interpret it to the suffering faithful.[15]

---

[13] A–O, Moscow, account of Kallistos Ware, p. 44, quoting the Minutes.

[14] W. Pannenberg, *Grundfragen Systematischer Theologie*, p. 22.

[15] Paul M. van Buren, 'Historical thinking and dogmatics', *Journal of Ecumenical Studies*, 17 (1980), 94–9 asks whether there can be any such thing as uninterpreted history.

Tillard points out this inseparability of history and faith:[16]

The creeds are always the work of communities, not of isolated individuals . . . Church cannot exist without feeling itself *hic et nunc* in communion with the long line of generations which have preceded it and prepared it . . . it is not a spiritual 'happening' which results from a sudden experience on the part of some personality or group. It is the presence, today, of an experience which has the sheen of centuries on it, since it is inseparable from the experience of the apostles, even of Israel.[17]

I have tried to do no more than point to some of the general difficulties of the study of the past for the theologian. These will all be writ large in ecumenical problem-solving, because these conflicting interpretations of the past have to be reconciled. We shall come to that in a moment. But first we need to look at the uses of history itself.

HISTORY AS A DISCIPLINE

The ecumenical application of historical-critical method

Chronologically, the first disciplinary area to develop in the study of history was the advent of 'historical-critical' method.[18] Understanding why division happened requires the recovery and establishment and analysis of the surviving texts, for which comparatively sophisticated scholarly procedures exist. These are not, however, fully agreed procedures even among secular historians. And for scholars working within a religious context they raise special difficulties.[19] Yves Congar's training at Le Saulchoir consisted chiefly in the assimilation of texts by methods he came to see as essentially mediaeval.[20] But more modern text-critical methods encourage the treatment of sacred texts by the same rules of evidence as would be applied to other ancient texts, and to later Christian texts; and in a similarly rigorous

---

[16] For the Christian community, 'formulating their creed' is 'the gaining and naming of their own identity' . . . 'Experience proves that a group does not gain its own identity or become firmly bound together by it unless it has a living "memory" of its foundational history' . . . 'A group fragments when it allows divergent readings (I don't say different ones, that is another matter) of its founding event.' J. M. R. Tillard, 'We believe', *One in Christ*, 17 (1991), p. 4.

[17] J. M. R. Tillard, 'We believe', *One in Christ*, 17 (1991), p. 6.

[18] Y. Congar discusses Maurice Blondel's query as to whether historical-critical method can be applied to traditional dogmatic affirmations. Y. Congar, 'Tradition et vie ecclésiale', *Istina*, 8 (1961–2), 411–36.

[19] 'The "historical-critical" method . . . is first of all a reaffirmation of loyalty to objective truth even in the most subjective of all domains of spiritual life . . .' Jacob B. Agus, 'Six Jewish thoughts', *Journal of Ecumenical Studies*, 17 (1980), 110–11, p. 111.

[20] Nichols, *Congar*, p. 192.

way. This may depend upon assumptions and techniques and 'evidential rules unacceptable to believing Christians'[21] where 'the dimension of faith' is 'epistemologically blotted out'.[22] The question whether such a methodology could be admitted in Christian theology has remained controversial for a century. Its danger has been seen to be that faith would come to be undervalued. So it is not satisfactory to import a historical-critical method from secular into theological scholarship without at least weighing the concomitant methodological requirements.

The difference was crisply summed up more than a century ago. In 1863 a Congress of Catholic scholars met, with Döllinger as a driving force. He argued that Catholic theology should regard scholasticism as a set of fetters and turn to historical research.[23] The antithesis envisaged here is between an approach to theological problem-solving by reasoning on what are acknowledged to be ultimately non-negotiable matters of faith; and an approach based upon the dispassionate evaluation of evidence as though it had no bearing upon faith at all. In 1964 the Pontifical Biblical Commission published an *Instruction on the Historical Truth of the Gospel* which was at the time variously seen as perhaps (and perhaps not) allowing a possibility of the admission of historical-critical method for Roman Catholic scholars. J. Fitzmyer, for example, took the view that 'the document will go down in history as the first official statement which openly countenances the [form-critical] method itself', but that at the same time it decries 'scarcely admissible philosophical and theological principles [which] have often come to be mixed with this method, which not uncommonly have vitiated the method itself as well as the conclusions in the literary area'.[24]

The Commission listed a number of such 'inadmissibles'. The intention was partly to try to define the area of overlap between matters 'evident to reason'; and matters of faith. The historian should not refuse to admit the existence of a supernatural order, or the intervention of a personal God in the world through strict revelation.

[21] Avery Dulles, 'Ecumenism and theological method', *Journal of Ecumenical Studies*, 17 (1980), 40–8, p. 43. E. Schillebeeckx, *Jesus–an experiment in Christology* (New York, 1979), p. 38, citing Ernst Troelsch.   [22] Nichols, *Congar*, p. 5.
[23] G. Alberigo, 'The authority of the Church in the documents of Vatican I and Vatican II', *Journal of Ecumenical Studies*, 19 (1982), 119–45, special issue on 'A critique of authority in contemporary Catholicism'.
[24] J. Fitzmyer, 'The Biblical Commission's Instruction on the Historical Truth of the Gospels', *Theological Studies*, 25 (1964), pp. 387–8.

He should not refuse to admit the possibility of miracles and prophecies. He should hold that historical truth is compatible with faith. He should not deny that the documents of revelation have historical value and a historical nature. He should not make light of the authority of the apostles as [historical] witnesses to Christ, or of [the historical character of] their task and influence in the primitive community, or 'extol' instead 'the creative power of that community'.[25]

I do not want to take a view here on the acceptableness or otherwise of such structures ecumenically. I give them merely as an illustration of the difficulties about applying a critical method borrowed from another discipline in theology. We clearly have to attempt something different.

The search for ecumenical principles of history

'The understanding of history is to find the rules according to which the phenomena should be grouped, and every advance in the knowledge of history is inseparable from an accurate observance of these rules.'[26] This nineteenth-century view of history is sanguine about the possibility of finding scientific principles of historical interpretation which will apply universally. But there are problems with that. It is certainly true that repeating patterns of human fear and prejudice and optimism occur, and that in that way phenomena can be 'grouped'. But historiography cannot have first principles of the sort which geometry has in its axioms. That was clear to scholars of the patristic period and the Middle Ages, who distinguished between the parts of theology which could be dealt with by reasoning and those about which we could know nothing at all unless we had Scripture's account of events revealed to us. It was equally clear in the eighteenth-century revival of the concern to make a distinction between reason and revelation. But the search for rules does propose a

---

25 'If "Jesus of history" means "rendering Christology more rationally accessible to modern positivist thinking" I would express uneasiness, but if it is suggested for the sake of taking historical reality more seriously, including wordly religious experiences, then I will fully follow the suggestion.' 'The historical Jesus is not accessible directly by theology . . . the "Jesus of history" has been revealed in the Spirit and within the Ecclesia as the Christ of God. That is why a possible clash between the historical Jesus, as he is investigated by critical biblical research, and the Christ of God, as he is experienced by the ecclesial faith and communal consciousness, is unthinkable for a theology of participation over against a rational theology.' Nikos A. Nissiotis, 'An Orthodox contribution to consensus', *Journal of Ecumenical Studies*, 17 (1980), 100–9, p. 103.

26 Harnack, *History of Dogma*, I, tr. N. Buchanan (New York, 1961), p. 12.

way which is at first sight attractive. It seems to suggest that the problems about the Christian past can constructively be tackled in an objective and orderly way which everyone will be able to agree is the right way, if principles for proceeding can be agreed.

A modern attempt in the USA to work out, by way of a historiographical project, what these rules might be is instructive, not only for its positive achievements but for where it shows there to be pitfalls.[27] This scheme began from the premiss that a historical method for ecumenical use would seek not only to interpret the past but to say something about it in common, to do both history and theology.

> The ecumenical movement needs a process by which common accounts can be written of key church-dividing moments in Christian history, so that they might heal the memories of the past and challenge Christians to find a common identity in which their diversity can be celebrated in Christ.[28]

This belief that such a process was wanted led to an experiment. A group set to work to consider what were the possibilities of doing five things: 'appropriating a common history, claiming each other's history, correcting history with challenges from other directions, filling in lacunae, and identifying hermeneutical principles at work'.[29] The group was formed from the then Commission on Faith and Order of the National Council of Churches. It was decided to attempt three projects : an ecumenical historical study of the fourth century[30] and another of the nineteenth century in the United States, taken as examples of periods when division arose in the Church; and a study, to be based on what had been learned from doing this, of the general principles which might be involved in writing 'ecumenical church history'.

It may be useful to underline the huge difficulties which stand in the way of being axiomatic about history by suggesting some criticisms of the universality of the principles which this group tried to formulate. It is of importance here to note that the points stressed included a number which arise from present-day historiographical concerns and from a need to be 'politically correct' in the terms

---

[27] See, too, my article in *Journal of Ecumenical Studies*, forthcoming.
[28] O. C. Edwards, 'The ecumenical church historiography project', *Ecumenical Trends*, 21 (1992), 28–32, quoting Jeffrey Gros, in *Ecumenical Trends*, 16, p. 117.
[29] Edwards, 'The ecumenical church historiography project', p. 29.
[30] In the attempt to tackle the fourth century a wide variety of accounts were first produced, written from various standpoints.

currently approved in the late-twentieth-century West (especially in the USA). There was accordingly a quite proper anxiety to be saying that ecumenical history ought especially to consider women, the poor, the laity, the oppressed and ignored. 'Members of the Ecumenical Church Historiography Group . . . recognized that many issues remain to be covered . . . church historians often overlook the role of women and the poor in the early church . . . it is easier to write a history of the activities of bishops than of those of the laity . . .'[31] Among the 'principles' eventually drawn up by the group, the first states that 'an ecumenical history of Christianity understands church history as the story of all who call themselves Christians, paying special attention to those Christians whose story has been ignored or suppressed'.[32] Clearly the first half of this is unexceptionable; the second, however desirable in terms of redressing an old imbalance, might perhaps create a new one. It also fails to allow for the character of the surviving evidence, and for the realities of what divided the Christians who are now seeking to unite. The laity, the poor, women, the oppressed, although they often joined dissident groups from the Middle Ages, were usually signally uninvolved in the actual mechanisms of division. Their actions do not usually explain the divisions we are seeking to mend, and so the study of their history may tell us relatively little about how to repair them.

The second principle is that 'an ecumenical history of Christianity is global in outlook and seeks to avoid geographic centrism, classism, ethnocentrism, sexism, and the cult of personality'.[33] Here again, there is a mixture of what is incontrovertibly desirable in any age, and the current concerns of modern Western Christianity. An objective account of what moved things forward or caused division may require the writing of a history which focuses sharply on a given class or race or sex or individual, and in that sense cannot be 'politically correct'. Current political correctness can readily be seen as an all-time absolute in a way which fails to take account of the track-record of such 'seeming-axioms' of history.

So the question has to be asked, whether these preoccupations will prove to be durable to the point where they can confidently be taken to be axioms applicable for all time. History tends to answer in the negative. If we take for comparison another attempt to frame axioms in this way, we see similar difficulties arising in the struggle to speak

[31] Edwards, 'The ecumenical church historiography project', p. 30.   [32] Ibid.
[33] Ibid., p. 31.

for all times. Five conditions are suggested by J. A. Nash. The first is designed to oppose 'propositional idolatry'. 'Christian communions are bound not by the specific formulation of the creed but only by the soteriological intentions or meanings underlying the metaphysical and/or metaphorical exterior.' The second says that 'an ecumenical creed should be explicitly self-relativizing'. The third is 'predicated on the stated assumption that orthopraxis[34] is the primary criterion of Christian faith' (i.e. 'that not fixed statements but trusting and loving faith is foremost'). The fourth is a 'waiver for "tender consciences"'. The fifth is 'a succinct summary ... in order to encompass all Christian Churches'.[35] Now these beg several questions. The heart of the matter is the need to free a future united Church from obligation to accept particular formulations, while retaining securely the saving truth these fixed words intend to convey. Mixed in with this are a concern for Christian life as the testbed of faith, and a further concern to allow freedom for diversity. These three really very different issues have been wedded here. The second two belong to the second half of the twentieth century, in their concern to respect and protect diversity. This is certainly right in a number of respects, but Christians are far from agreeing which.

Equally difficult to get right proves to be the expression of the issue at the heart of the third 'universal principle' set out by the USA group, that 'an ecumenical history of Christianity enables Christians to see and hear the full range of catholicity in the churches and to understand apostolicity in a variety of contexts'. So far so good. But to say that 'it also enables non-Christians to appreciate the great diversity of expressions of Christian identity' is to make a statement of another sort, and one altogether less uncontroversial. First, there is confusion here of the need to describe Christian history ecumenically so that all Christians can own it together, with the need to do so so that non-Christians can see it clearly. Secondly, his formulation raises in passing and without establishing its implications, the issue of the existence of a variety of senses of identity among Christians. This is a complex question and still far from being resolved. It cannot satisfactorily be left as an assumption here that diversity of expression or of identity is either neutral or always a good.

Three 'principles of context' follow in the USA study. These state

---

[34] On orthopraxis, see A–R, *God's Reign and our Unity*.
[35] J. A. Nash, 'Political conditions for an ecumenical confession: a Protestant contribution to the emerging dialogue', *Journal of Ecumenical Studies*, 25 (1988), 241–61, p. 242.

that 'an ecumenical history of Christianity recognizes and investigates the interaction between gospel, communities of faith, and culture'; 'an ecumenical history of Christianity takes into account the worship, piety, practice, and teaching of the various traditions, as well as doctrine, history and institutional development'; 'an ecumenical history of Christianity makes significant use of such sources as iconography, liturgy and worship, oral tradition, tracts and other popular literature, and the archaeological record'.[36] Again, this is unexceptionable in itself. But it seems deliberately to tip the balance in the direction of a sociologically conceived 'fairness' and 'spread' which fits late-twentieth-century preoccupations, but whose parameters and limitations remain largely unexamined against a wider background.

The group moves on next to a series of principles designed to address the need for openness; for a willingness to concede that one's own tradition may have been at fault; and for a sense of the provisionality of all churches in history. 'An ecumenical history of Christianity acknowledges that each generation and tradition reads the past in the light of its own lively issues.'[37] We see things our way. We have to learn to accept that others see things differently and may think us wrong. We have yet to settle to everyone's satisfaction where this ought to lead. Mutual respect is clearly a good, and tolerance too. But there have always been limits to tolerance in Christian history, as the group concedes in saying that 'an ecumenical history of Christianity opens each particular tradition to critical analysis by others'.[38] There has to be a balance between acceptance of others in their own traditions (which implies respect for them and a desire to see them continue); and a willingness to see one's church as provisional (which implies that one is open to its changing). 'An ecumenical history of Christianity approaches its task in the spirit of repentance and forgiveness, avoiding defensiveness with regard either to social location or to particular theological, methodological, or ecclesial traditions.'[39] ('Defensiveness' here would seem to mean a hostile erection of walls against others.) 'An ecumenical history of Christianity seeks to understand and clearly to acknowledge its own presuppositions and seeks to overcome its prejudices.'[40] 'An ecumenical history of Christianity acknowledges that no historical account can claim complete objectivity, but seeks fair-minded empathy with the particular stories that comprise the ecumenical history of the

---

[36] Edwards, 'The ecumenical church historiography project', p. 31.   [37] Ibid.
[38] Ibid.   [39] Ibid.   [40] Ibid.

Christian people.'[41] This group of principles also represents a set of late-twentieth-century values. But it differs from the first in reflecting something entirely new – the ecumenical theology principle of 'doing together' which must be the way forward in a future united Church.

So we can perhaps look for historiographical principles for use in ecumenical theology if we look for them here, where the task is addressed as a common task.

HISTORY AND IDENTITY

A detached scholarship seeks only to establish the truth. Historical insight into the ecumenically significant past is coloured at the outset by the observers' being on one side or another. So objectivity is a desideratum to be achieved, and the historical retrieval for ecumenical purposes has to begin without it and work towards it.

Perspectives on history can conspicuously change. A recent Reformed–Roman Catholic text can speak for itself here:

Whence have our communions come? What paths have they followed – together and apart, interacting, reacting and going their separate ways – over 450 years to reach where they are today?(12) . . . Today, in the late twentieth century our churches are not the same dialogue partners they were even a generation ago, let alone in the 16th century. In the past, we tended to read our histories both selectively and polemically. To some extent, we still do. We see the events through which we have lived through confessionally biased eyes. The present reality of our churches is explained and justified by these readings of the past.

The report is optimistic that:

we are beginning to be able to transcend these limitations
a. by our common use of the results of objective scholarly inquiry
b. by the dialogue our churches have had with each other in this consultation and elsewhere.(13)

The key terms here are 'common' and 'objective'. Dialogue begins to make it possible to work and think together. That in its turn tends to diminish confessional bias, for the sake of objectivity. The Reformed–Roman Catholic Report *Toward a Common Understanding of the Church* suggests that technically new breakthroughs have been made possible along these lines:

---

[41] Edwards, 'The ecumenical church historiography project', p. 31.

Historical scholarship has not only produced fresh evidence concerning our respective roles in the Reformation and its aftermath. It also brings us together in broad agreement about sources, methods of inquiry and warrants for drawing conclusions. A new measure of objectivity has become possible. If we still inevitably interpret and select, at least we are aware that we do, and what that fact means as we strive for greater objectivity and more balanced judgement. (41)[42]

This general sense that there has been advance in the discipline of history is endorsed by Congar. 'The ancients had . . . less experience and historical sense' . . . 'for this reason they easily put certain points of local or particular discipline and certain theological categories current in their time on an absolute level.'[43] Notwithstanding, ecumenical history is still at a stage of relatively primitive development which makes its claim to maturity a fragile one.

The root of the problem for ecumenical history is that a sense of having a history peculiar to one's community is often used to define ecclesial identity. 'What is distinctive about us is not our faith, for that we share with the whole catholic Church, but our history. The way that God has led us and what he has said and done among us – that really is our very own.'[44] 'Memories . . . hamper "rapprochement" between the denominations and the Churches' . . . 'many unexpected interruptions in the dialogues remind us that the ecumenical dialogue is still burdened – even unconsciously – with the enmities, prejudices, caricatures and judgements that have been built up in all Churches during centuries of bitter controversies in order to protect and justify one's own position and views.'[45]

Divided Christians have their own views of their history and how it is to be understood and what it means for them. In the nature of things, objectivity cannot be looked for at the beginning of an enquiry to which the participants come *parti pris*, when what were in fact shared events are separately interpreted. 'Divergences since the sixteenth century have arisen not so much from the substance of this . . . common Christian inheritance for many centuries . . . as from our separate ways of receiving it.'[46]

[42] *Toward a Common Understanding of the Church: Report of Reformed–Roman Catholic Dialogue 1984–90*, (Vatican, 1990). *Catholic International*, 2.16, pp. 775ff.
[43] Congar, *Dialogue between Christians*, p. 122.
[44] E. G. Rupp, 'The future of the Methodist tradition', *London Quarterly and Holborn Reviews*, 184 (1959), 264–74.
[45] J. E. Vercruysse, 'Prospects for Christian unity', *One in Christ*, 26 (1990), 185–200.
[46] Text of Report of ARC Joint Preparatory Commission, *One in Christ*, 5 (1969), 27–33, para. 4.

It takes a further effort of sympathetic imagination to see both sides with a view to explaining each to the other in its living heritage now, and that has to be arrived at as a second stage. There is a double task, in which it is essential to keep the old partisan view in sight in order to see more clearly how it is to be transformed by doing history together.

Yet, paradoxically, the more open historical consciousness which makes it plain that the old accounts of things will not do, is relatively recent in ecclesial communities, and there can be apathy about the need to take the past into the life of the present, alongside a fierce clinging to a self-understanding rooted in the past. The history has to be actively taught and kept in view, or it can seem irrelevant. 'Young churches . . . do not see the avenue to their future being opened through the rehashing of historical disputes rooted in European Church history.'[47] The history of the reasons for division can be forgotten from one generation to the next. 'We are growing together . . . youth too are pushing . . . We are very proud of starting ecumenical dialogue, but young people are very shocked that we have not spoken to one another for so long.'[48] That might be a good thing if the history could be relied upon to stay forgotten.

Nevertheless, there is a fundamental difference of approach to the historical method in ecumenism between those who regard it as indispensable and those who see it as irrelevant. The argument that the past is irrelevant may take several directions. It may be based on the view that we should simply try to forget the bad things of the past and give ourselves up to a future which will have different priorities. It is tempting to ask whether it matters now how we became divided. Can we just forget it and get on with unity now? The answer must be no. Old hostilites will always resurface if they are not dealt with.

Or it may rest on the hope that the old disagreements have died a natural death and are simply not important any more. Or it may say that 'controversies arose in a world very different from ours. Consequently it has become to a large extent impossible to make use of a past understanding of the world in the context of our present proclamation. Thus many of our traditional doctrinal disagreements are losing importance'(36).[49] If this were true it would be in many ways extremely helpful ecumenically. 'Ecumenism today is partly a

---

[47] John F. Hotchkin, 'Bilaterals – phasing into unity', *Journal of Ecumenical Studies*, 23 (1986), 404–11, p. 406.
[48] John Coventry, 'Visible unity: an interview with Cardinal Suenens', *One in Christ*, 8 (1972), 336–44, p. 344, Suenens' comment.   [49] L–RC, Malta (1972); *Growth*, p. 176.

movement to reopen the past in order to create a future more pleasing to God.'[50] But as we see again and again, the old disagreements are in fact very reluctant to lie down. Simple attempts to forget are ultimately not helpful bcause memories of conflict will always come back unless the conflicts are resolved. Divisions cannot be mended unless we understand why they happened. Anything else would be like bandaging a dirty and suppurating wound and expecting it to heal. 'Forgiveness has to "work backwards" if it is to have universal value and purpose.'[51] 'Ecumenism is a spirit . . . that . . . recognises and welcomes the ambiguities which lie embedded in our past.' [52]

Here we need to be methodical, and to study the living memory as if it were archival.[53] 'The modern ecumenical movement has run for almost one century. The WCC is close to its fortieth anniversary. It is not such a long history, but it is already too long for us to rely on a "living memory".'[54]

We also need to address a great methodological problem. The rewriting of history easily becomes revisionism. The telling of a story can take place in an atmosphere of sympathy and support; or of disappointment and criticism. The interlocutor accepts the story as such and does not attempt to change it; or there may be a deliberate attempt to revise the story by retelling it. Authorship may be claimed or disowned. Or the story may be offered to the audience to be changed by interpretations, change of emphases, attribution of motivations, causal explanations.[55] Among the documents produced in connection with the Malines conversations was an enquiry by J. B. Kidd 'To what extent was the Papal Authority repudiated at the Reformation in England',[56] in which Kidd analysed the theological implications of events. Lutheran–Roman Catholic conversations speak of 'removing confessionally conditioned prejudices and misjudgements of other churches from the entirety of theological research and consciousness as well as from textbooks of church history and systematic theology, and to develop [sic] an ecumenical view of church history and history of doctrine since the 16th century. The

---

[50] Elwyn A. Smith, Editorial, *Journal of Ecumenical Studies*, 4 (1967), p. 303.
[51] G. Daly, 'Forgiveness and community', in *Reconciling Memories*, ed. A. Falconer (Dublin, 1988), p. 103.   [52] Elwyn A. Smith, Editorial, *Journal of Ecumenical Studies*, 4 (1967), p. 303.
[53] The contrast is conveniently made by G. Tavard, 'Vatican II understood and misunderstood', *One in Christ*, 27 (1991), 209–21. See too examples in Stacpoole.
[54] José Miguez Bonino, 'The concern for a vital and coherent theology', *Report* to the executive committee of the WCC, Kinshasa, Zaire, March 1986.
[55] On historical revisionism see J. Harris, 'Reconciliation as remembrance', in *Reconciling Memories*, ed. A. Falconer (Dublin, 1988), p. 40.   [56] Halifax, *Malines*, pp. 151ff.

joint Roman Catholic–Lutheran study on the Augsburg Confession is a promising example.'[57] Revisionism is a notoriously dangerous game, and we have to think ecumenically strictly in terms of an appropriation of a shared history in which there was conflict, as a common Christian history about which there is now peace.

Asking what the original purpose was: the exercise of historical retrieval

The approach of asking what was the original purpose of a confessional document which has proved divisive may be valuable in those bilateral conversations where such a text seems to stand in the way of rapprochement. What was the Augsburg Confession designed to be? If, for example, it is possible to say that the 'express purpose' of the Augsburg Confession 'is to bear witness to the faith of the one, holy, catholic and apostolic Church', that 'its concern is . . . with the preservation and renewal of the Christian faith in its purity',[58] the text no longer looks like a stumbling-block but like an aid to unity. Here something which is as much historical retrieval as purification of memory is involved. There has to be a retelling of the story. The method adopted is to ask whether Roman Catholic as well as Lutheran theologians, studying together, can say that the contents of the text 'fulfil this intention'.[59] Their work, it is argued, is confirmed by a solid body of scholarly evidence, 'a whole series of recent studies and research efforts in a wide variety of disciplines, including a number of joint studies'.[60] The implication is that such studies will stand as witnesses to progress in achieving objectivity and to the consolidation of knowledge. So it is now possible to 'appeal to the Augsburg Confession' in making a modern joint statement, that is, to take it on board and regard it as pointing the same way.[61] 'Reflecting on the Augsburg Confession, therefore, Catholics and Lutherans have discovered that they have a common mind on basic doctrinal truths which points to Jesus Christ, the living centre of our faith.'[62]

---

[57] *Confessio Augustana*, ed. H. Meyer, E. Schütte et al. (Frankfurt/Paderborn, 1980). L–RC, *Ways to Community*, 1980; *Growth*, p. 227.

[58] *All under One Christ*, Statement on the Augsburg Confession by the Lutheran–Roman Catholic Joint Commission, 1980; *Growth*, pp. 242–3. para. 10.

[59] *Growth*, p. 243, para.11.   [60] *Growth*, p. 243, para.12.   [61] *Growth*, p. 243, paras. 13ff.

[62] *Growth*, p. 244, para.17.

The liberation of not having a common history versus the enrichment of a shared heritage

Paradoxically, the lack of a previous common history may be a help in arriving at a common possession of a history. Methodist–Roman Catholic conversations have spoken of the 'advantage' that 'there is no history of formal separating between the two Churches, none of the historical, emotional problems consequent on a history of schism'.[63] When Methodists and Roman Catholics asked what is most important in their respective histories they looked for common ground. They found it in their nineteenth century traditions of spirituality. 'Investigation of the historical dimension gave special emphasis to the nineteenth century in both Methodist and Roman Catholic spirituality.' This 'leads to the conclusion that what has mattered most in both traditions has been the reality of religion as it brings about the transformation of man's heart and mind in everyday living'.[64] Now this is valuable because it provides a historical base of sympathy. But it is not really historically ground-breaking, because it does not address underlying questions of difference of heritage. (For the Methodists sprang from an Anglicanism which had a history of its own relative to Rome.) And it may throw into prominence one 'interface', to the neglect of the whole picture.

Disciples and Roman Catholics have argued that 'the very diversity of our histories and Christian experiences frees us for a new kind of ecumenical dialogue'.[65] This comment suggests that awareness of a diversity of historical vantage-points may be intellectually liberating. Where that may be true, there is, however, the difficulty that patterns of prejudice and preoccupation can still be present in

---

[63] M–RC, Denver, 6; *Growth*, p. 308.

[64] M–RC, para.54; *Growth*, p. 319. Daniel Brevint's *The Christian Sacrament and Sacrifice* deeply impressed the Wesley brothers and Wesley's eucharistic hymns are arranged according to Brevint's outline, under memorial sign and means of grace, pledge of heaven, sacrifice of ourselves joined to that of Christ, appropriation of benefits. These have been described as 'historic ingredients in Methodist Eucharistic theology'. J. Robert Nelson, 'Methodist eucharistic usage: from constant communion to benign neglect to sacramental recovery', *Journal of Ecumenical Studies*, 13 (1976), 278–83.

[65] Disciples–Roman Catholic, Introduction; *Growth*, p 155. That points up the difference between a common history before division, which all Christians share, yet of which some Protestant denominations have not always been strongly conscious; and a history and historical theology of a time when division happened, which is not shared by all bilateral partners. The particularities of their historical experience are carried as luggage in the traditions of the Churches. Some of this baggage is useful (as it were the toothbrushes and the aspirins). Some of it is enriching. Some of it is just an encumbering load to carry.

the form of the generic sets or 'types' of attitudes which are characteristic of the ecclesial styles of the divided churches.[66] These tend in practice to be far more of a hindrance than a sense of rich pluriformity is a help. But this is a very large issue and we can only touch on it here.

In their Common Declaration of 1966 Pope Paul VI and Michael Ramsey, Archbishop of Canterbury, spoke of a 'serious dialogue which, founded upon the Gospels and on the ancient common traditions, may lead to that unity in truth, for which Christ prayed'. He described the method which has since been used by ARCIC and other commissions to reach that foundation of common faith which, as ecumenism must believe, lies beneath and behind later disagreements and which those intent on mending division have to rediscover.

The confidence that this is possible was endorsed by Pope John Paul II at Castel Gandolfo in 1981 with the reflection that the 'method' of ARCIC I 'has been to go behind the habit of thought and expression born and nourished in enmity and controversy, to scrutinize together the great common treasure, to clothe it in a language at once traditional and expressive of the insights of an age which no longer glories in strife but seeks to come together in listening to the quiet voice of the Spirit'.

Cardinal Willebrands later commented. 'The originality of ARCIC's work consists in this: instead of clinging to the notions and doctrinal expressions which were at the heart of historical conflicts, it has gone straight to the realities in question and to what the "apostolic faith", as lived and handed down until the divisions, says about these realities.'[67] Other commissions have used a similar idea. In the Disciples–Roman Catholic conversations we meet the comment.'We have begun to discover that when we go beneath the current theological description of our traditions, a convergence becomes evident.'[68]

The leading idea in Willebrands' comments is the one I have argued to be ecumenically indispensable: that there exists a common faith behind the divisions, and that it can be reached by going behind the

---

[66] I have explored this problem further in a parallel study, *The One and the Many*.
[67] J. Willebrands, 'Anglican–Roman Catholic dialogue', *One in Christ*, 15 (1979), 290–304, p. 291.
[68] Disciples–Roman Catholic, Introduction; *Growth*, p. 155.

barriers of differences of view of tradition which make it difficult to see clearly. This gives us a nice clear image to work with, but it has its drawbacks. The first is that divisions are never clean. Constructiveness and valuable reform of various sorts are almost invariably mixed in with hostility to those from whom separation occurs. Secondly, the common faith 'behind' the barrier must not be thought of as having been cut off and lost there, but as having continued in the divided churches beneath and behind and within the expressions of faith they have made their own. We meet talk of 'going behind' again in the Anglican–Reformed dialogue. 'From the outset we sought to go behind the historical and traditional problems which have divided us since Reformation times and to put our quest for unity in new perspectives.'[69] This 'going behind' is certainly a historical exercise. But it has to do with more than going behind in time. So, thirdly, there are issues between churches which had never been raised in the undivided Church (such as that of justification by faith alone), and they can form a top-dressing which can make it hard to see what lies beneath or before.

So 'going behind' or 'going beneath' can be and ought to be both historical and epistemological. It involves the use of 'metalanguage'. For to 'go behind' or 'go beneath' our present divided positions, it is necessary not only to change the way one thinks, but also to become aware of the assumptions which have been guiding the way that one thinks, so as to achieve some self-understanding about prejudices which may be partly buried and therefore not wholly conscious.

The implications, and what the experiment was seen to involve in one bilateral dialogue, were spelt out by ARCIC I. 'We have endeavoured to get behind the opposed and entrenched positions of past controversies. We have tried to reassess what are the real issues to be resolved. We have often deliberately avoided the vocabulary of past polemics, not with any intention of evading the real difficulties that provoked them, but because the emotive associations of such language have often obscured the truth.'[70]

This is a risky business. Digging up foundations can disturb what has been built upon them. 'To examine the roots and causes of disunion, to isolate and evaluate the basic issues which separate us . . . This immediately raises the specter for adherents of any individual confessional belief that they may perhaps have to modify credal positions that have been the foundation of their faith for decades and centuries.'[71]

---

[69] *God's Reign and our Unity*, p. v., Preface.   [70] ARCIC *AI*, 25; *Growth*, p. 98.
[71] B. Cooke, Editorial, *Journal of Ecumenical Studies*, 1 (1964), p. 520.

It involves going behind in labelling and in language and also in concept with a thoroughness and openness which may lead to radical shifts of self-understanding.

Purifying memory

Ecumenically speaking the most important thing about history is that it is memory. Most of the divisions which persist in the Church today took place in a past which can still seem a vivid present. 'Travelling round Ireland I find I am confronted by an experience of pain which I have come to interpret as being in touch with the experience of the past,' comments one observer.[72] Each community's understanding of why it is where and what it is depends upon its view or interpretation of the past as it signally affected that community. Here there are 'mentalités' from which it is hard to break away.[73] Memory can be modified to fit an account which resists reconciliation, and reconciliation can seem like betrayal.[74] So just as it is an 'urgent task to reconcile our memories', so also we have to 'purify our memories'.[75] Where two communions remember their common past in terms of conflict and polemic they will not be able to remember it together in a future united Church unless that memory is purified of those elements in it which are hostile to the other side.

That could in principle be done in various ways. One or both sides might say that they now see that they were mistaken about the other's actions; or if not about the actions, about the motives. Or they might continue to feel that the hostility was justified then, but all should now be forgiven. Either of these involves continuing to see things, as it were, from one side or the other, and in that respect will be an interim stage of historical analysis.

Purification of memory is attempted in many bilateral Reports. In, for example, *The Ministry in the Church*, the Lutheran–Roman Catholic Statement of 1981, the method (as for the Reformed–Roman Catholic group just discussed) was to begin by stating squarely that 'in the past, Catholics and Lutherans had different starting-points

---

[72] J. Harris, 'Reconciliation as remembrance', in *Reconciling Memories*, ed. A. Falconer (Dublin, 1988), p. 44.

[73] Cf. G. E. Aylmer, 'Collective mentalités in seventeenth century England: the puritan outlook', *Transactions of the Royal Historical Society*, 36 (1986), 1–25.

[74] 'Reconcilation will mean "transgression", for reconciliation is not about the repression of difference, but about us jointly transgressing the contraints, the boundaries that have solidified into our precious "differences",' suggests the same author, J. Harris, 'Reconciliation as remembrance', in *Reconciling Memories*, ed. A. Falconer (Dublin, 1988), pp. 37ff.

[75] J. E. Vercruysse,'Prospects for Christian unity', *One in Christ*, 26 (1990), 185–200.

when defining the ordained ministry',[76] and then to describe these starting-points from either side. This is done in terms of the reasons why each side wished to emphasise one aspect rather than another. 'The Reformers protested against tendencies in the Middle Ages to emphasise almost exclusively the sacramental functions of the ministry of the priest, particularly the offering of the sacrifice of the mass.' Accordingly, they emphasised as a 'task of the ministry the proclamation of the gospel in which word and sacrament are closely connected with each other'.[77] On the other side, 'the medieval understanding of the ministry remained influential in the Council of Trent which placed the emphasis primarily on the administration of the sacraments'. A gloss is provided here to explain that although this was so, 'the Tridentine decrees are meant positively and not exclusively: according to the Council of Trent the proclamation of the gospel is included in the task of ministry'.[78] Thus eirenic language seeks to 'purify' and purge the ill-feeling so as to make it possible for the two sides to say something together.

The text goes on to draw out points constituting a balanced pronouncement about ministry, to which both sides can now subscribe (which 'our churches are thus able today to declare in common').[79] It includes the key elements stressed by either side in the sixteenth century. It is deemed to describe the 'essential and specific function of the ordained minister', that is, what he (and only he) is in the Church.

One way of purifying memory is by accepting the original purpose of a text or action or position as having been something which makes that text or action or position no longer a justifiable ground for maintaining division. 'In the past, Roman Catholic teaching that the bishop of Rome is universal primate by divine right or law has been regarded by Anglicans as unacceptable. However, we believe that the primacy of the bishop of Rome can be affirmed as part of God's design for the universal *koinonia* in terms which are compatible with both our traditions. Given such a consensus, the language of divine right used by the First Vatican Council need no longer be seen as a matter of disagreement between us.'[80]

Another method of purifying memory involves the frank acceptance that the earlier intention of a document or decree of one side was divisive, but that now the issue can be agreed about. In the light of modern agreement the previous text, while unavoidably standing in

---

[76] *Growth*, p. 256, para.26.   [77] *Growth*, p. 256, para.26.   [78] *Growth*, p. 257, para.26.
[79] *Growth*, p. 258, para.31.   [80] ARCIC *AII*, 15; *Growth*, p. 110.

the tradition of a church which does not disown it, is not a reason to remain divided.

Admitting we were wrong: history and the problem of going astray in development

The 'providential' understanding of history will say that God has everything under control, and will bring, even out of division, a consummation for the Church which will be for the best. That makes room for the possibility that something may have gone wrong in the past, which can now freely be admitted to have gone wrong. It may even be possible to point out the inadequacies of the manner in which some of the dogmas or formulations of the past were framed, or to speak of 'prematurely proclaimed definitions'.[81]

The Anglican–Lutheran conversations suggested that: it is 'an accident of history (i.e. something that depended upon the availability or otherwise of Reformed bishops in good standing with their monarchs in the sixteenth century) that in modern times Sweden and Finland find themselves on one side in the matter of succession and the other Lutheran Churches on the other'.[82] The concept of an 'accident' of history has the drawback for ecumenical purposes that it seems to set in question providential purpose in events. It must therefore be used with careful definition. Here it is taken to imply that there was nothing theologically binding in the circumstances which resulted in Swedish and Finnish Lutherans maintaining the 'historic' episcopal succession while other Lutherans have not.

What have we achieved if we say that a past disagreement is not one now? In most cases we have acknowledged an imbalance or incompleteness in the past ruling or decision or interpretation. Sometimes we may have to go so far as to admit that our communion was wrong. Some commentators have confronted this implication squarely. One suggests that Roman Catholics should admit the inadequate manner in which some of the past dogmas were promulgated; the inevitable incompleteness of the proclamation of faith made apart from the full participation of all Christians. He has in mind the dogmas which have tended to be ecumenical barriers: that of the Immaculate Conception, the Assumption (but also

---

[81] P. Chirico, 'Dogmatic definitions as ecumenical obstacles', *Journal of Ecumenical Studies*, 14 (1977), 51–65.
[82] Anglican–Lutheran, Pullach, note by Anglican Chairman; *Growth*, p. 30.

others). 'Suppose . . . that after much joint study Roman Catholics discover that neither they nor their partners in the dialogue have been able to find any saving meaning or operational significance in the dogma of the Immaculate Conception . . . Roman Catholics would find themselves in the unenviable position of having defined as dogma (which by definition is saving truth) something that has no saving meaning and operational significance.'[83] 'On the other hand', he continues, 'suppose that joint study reveals that genuine saving meaning and operational significance do lie embedded in the acceptance of the dogma,'[84] then the other side must equally be prepared to admit it has been wrong. 'We must not be afraid to reconsider, on both sides, and in consultation with one another, canonical rules established when awareness of our communion . . . was still dimmed,' said Pope John Paul II in an address of 30 November 1979, in the context of Orthodox–Roman Catholic rapprochement. 'These rules perhaps no longer correspond to the results of the dialogue of charity.'[85] This is partly an acknowledgement that 'agreements formed in the face of ancient challenges may no longer correspond to new challenges and this situation demands new agreements'.[86] But it is also an acknowledgement that positions stated by only a proportion of the body of the faithful must ultimately be tested by the whole.

It also tests the notion that the Church (or a church) can be authoritative as the arbiter of history.

This line of argument accepts that not only can there be development in doctrine, there can also be development in the understanding of doctrine and that changes in historical circumstances can alter cases. The old emphasis is not forgotten. It is taken into the process as a stage of incomplete vision of what can now be seen better or more clearly or more comprehensively.

What is going on here has to do with 'the recognition . . . that in order for the gospel, as saving event, to remain the same in every historical situation, it must always be proclaimed anew'.[87] This is the perennial issue of how to preserve the identity and continuity of the

---

[83] P. Chirico, 'Dogmatic definitions as ecumenical obstacles', *Journal of Ecumenical Studies*, 14 (1977), 51–65, pp. 61–2.
[84] P. Chirico, 'Dogmatic definitions as ecumenical obstacles', *Journal of Ecumenical Studies*, 14 (1977), 51–65, pp. 61–2.   [85] Stormon, p. 362.
[86] 'The Report of the Third Forum on Bilateral Conversations, October 6-10 1980', WCC Faith and Order Paper, 107 (1981) and *One in Christ*, 18 (1982), 44–54, p. 45.
[87] L–RC, Malta; *Growth*, p. 169.

Gospel in varying circumstances. But it has the new ecumenical dimension of the requirement that the 'proclaiming anew' is also a 'proclaiming together'. 'The representatives of the Evangelical Church of Latvia, . . . hope that the Church of Latvia in its historical development in the future will adopt such forms of the episcopal office and give it such validity as will promote the working out of the oecumenical unity of the Christian Church.'[88] So this is a theology of development with the admitted possibility of error; and the built-in confidence that error which has divided can be mended so as to unite.

Purifying memory by forgetting?

The Orthodox–Roman Catholic conversations leading to the *Tomos Agapis* contain a number of references to 'oblivion'. On 7 December 1965 a Common Declaration expressed the decision by both sides 'to remove from memory and from the midst of the Church the excommunications of 1054'.[89] 'The memory of the decisions, actions and painful incidents which came to a head in 1054' are seen as 'obstacles along the way'. It is acknowledged that 'nothing can be done to change the fact that these events were what they were in that particularly disturbed period of history'. But they can now be seen to have involved 'excesses' and to have 'brought in their train consequences which, as far as we can judge, went beyond what was intended or foreseen by those responsible'. If these consequences were not intended they can now be deemed not to be binding. The device used is to consider that 'their censures bore on particular persons and not on the Churches, and were not meant to break the ecclesial communion between the sees of Rome and Constantinople'.[90] On that understanding all that seems to be needed is an act of repentance, an expression of 'regret' for 'the offending words, the baseless reproaches, and the blameworthy symbolic acts with which both sides marked or accompanied the sad events of this time'.[91] The bad memory is thus consigned to oblivion. But it is not really 'buried'.[92] Rather it is retained but purified. On 7 December 1966 Pope and Patriarch sent each other telegrams remembering the lifting of the

---

[88] Evangelical Lutheran Churches of Latvia and Estonia in conversation with the Church of England, 1936–8, *Lambeth Occasional Reports, 1931–8* (London, 1948), p. 243.
[89] Stormon, p. 126.   [90] Stormon, p. 127.   [91] Stormon, p. 127.
[92] Despite the use of the expression in *Ambulate in dilectione* of Paul VI, 7 December 1965, Stormon, p. 129.

anathemas, and the Pope's telegram made the point that God is not tied to time. 'May he who is and was and is to come cause the past to be purified by his mercy.'[93] This notion of an oblivion which is really a 'taking in' to the continuing story would seem helpful in showing how the good and the bad in the vicissitudes of history can be accommodated within the unchanging character of the Gospel.

Backwards or forwards?

It is always a key question for the historian whether he can take it that those who lived in earlier ages can be judged to have had responses much like ours. 'I wonder what Küng – or Schillebeeckx, whom he quotes – means when he says that the New Testament authors had "a completely different world of experience" from that which we have. The difference could not be complete, for if it were, we would not be able to understand them at all.' Nevertheless, 'Historically conceived, the difference between the author of Matthew, for example, and ourselves is the nineteen-hundred years that lie between us in which so many important developments have taken place.' There are bound to be differences of attitude or assumption overlaying the common humanity.[94]

This is an important point. All talk of 'common consent' and *consensus fidelium* must rest to some degree upon it. If it is true that there is a common humanity in us all in every age, we can hope to speak with, and even for, one another in its terms. The task is then to re-express what happened in the past in this common language. If not, then the model we are working with is one of responsibility chiefly for today and the common mind of the present. It is true that, even if we are sanguine about the existence of a common humanity, it is doubtful whether we can enter fully into the mind of an earlier age. We cannot know enough about it. We read about it with the preconceptions of our own. This problem of getting back by an effort of historical imagination into the situation which created division in order to understand it, is compounded by the need we have been addressing to see clearly at the same time where fault and misapprehension lay.

There is also the question of shifts of prejudice over time. That is

---

[93] Stormon, p. 141.
[94] Paul M. van Buren, 'Historical thinking and dogmatics', *Journal of Ecumenical Studies*, 17 (1980), 93–9, p. 98.

especially a problem for an ecumenical historiography, which must be sharply alert to the divisive and the potentially unitive alike. We have to try to stand away from, as well as within, a given set of assumptions. 'In the search for the tools of theological elaboration . . . the members of all Churches have to rely on the same resources and documents . . . It is essentially a matter of claiming the past of all the Churches as one's own.'[95]

Here, as elsewhere, we lack a solid foundation of technique which would enable us to explain the past to the understanding of the present and confront the divisions of the past with the present's concern for unity. Dealing with historically generated bias, in which there is huge vested interest in partners in conversation, also requires skills in which ecumenical historical scholarship is as yet not very far developed.

Suggestions have been made as to how these limitations might be methodically overcome by the direction of approach. One might begin with Biblical events and go forward in time, so as to build a chain of cause and effect and thus see how things came to happen. Or one might begin with the situation at a later date where it seems clear what is at issue, and work chronologically backwards, so as to illuminate what had been unclear at the time in earlier events.[96] We have the advantage of hindsight. We know the consequences and that makes it easier to see from the way things went wrong where the roots of the disaster may have lain. 'When Catholics and Lutherans look back to the Augsburg Confession today, we do so from a situation which differs considerably from that in 1530.'[97] Both these approaches seek to find a point of departure which is secure, in order that the conclusions reached may be as firm as possible. The difficulty with that is that there can be no universal confidence about the security of the proposed starting-points. Nor is it necessarily safe to ask how one thing came after another as a means of explaining outcomes.

Another approach tries to look down upon the history from a sufficient height for it to be possible to see the grand patterns and large strategies of events. Möhler, for example, tried in a preface for his *Symbolik*, published in 1940, to trace the movement of relations

[95] George Tavard, 'Ecumenical theology and the Catholic Church', *One in Christ*, 25 (1989), 103–13, p. 105.
[96] G. I. Konidaris, 'De la prétendue divergence des formes dans le régime du Christianisme primitif', *Istina*, 10 (1964), 59–92, pp. 59ff. and 78ff.
[97] *All under One Christ*, Statement on the Augsburg Confession by the Lutheran–Roman Catholic Joint Commission, 1980; *Growth*, p. 241. para.1.

between Christian communions 'from a period of hostile polemics through controversy (up to the middle of the seventeenth century), to the stage of objective presentation and discussion which we would call irenic controversy (mid seventeenth to mid eighteenth century).' He suggested that then 'the incursions of naturalism, which menaced all the opposing confessions equally, led Christians to adopt a new method, that of the *symbols* (creeds), the purpose of which was to show historically how and on what points oppositions had arisen. It was this method which Möhler wished to follow, not as a pure historian, but as a theologian armed with the beginnings of a new dialectic which would allow him to interpret anew the whole process of disagreement and then the endeavour to re-establish unity.'[98] Such pattern-making may be illuminating, but it has the fault of the 'cause and effect' approach, that it unavoidably over-simplifies.

Changed perspective

A more promising line seems to be the recognition of the illuminating power of changed perspective, that as events occur, the perspectives of those who observe them, or are able to look back on them because they come after them, unavoidably shift. The Reformed–Roman Catholic group which produced *Toward a Common Understanding of the Church* proceeded by first taking stock as separate 'confessions': 'The method used in our present dialogue has also deepened our shared historical understanding. We first drafted our respective parts of this chapter separately.' This proved instructive. 'Reading and reviewing these drafts together we learned from each other and modified what we had written. We were reminded that over the centuries our forebears had often misunderstood each other's motives and language . . . We occasionally heard each other speak vehemently and felt some of the passions that dictated the course of historical events and still in some ways drive us today' (15). This hearing of historically based prejudices cleared the air. 'We have begun to dissolve myths about one another, to clear away misunderstandings.' It pointed the way towards common endeavour. 'We must go on from here . . . to a *reconciliation* of memories, in which we will begin to share one sense of the past rather than two' (16).[99]

---

[98] Conveniently summarised by Congar, *Dialogue between Christians*, p. 135.
[99] *Toward a Common Understanding of the Church: Report of Reformed–Roman Catholic Dialogue 1984–90*, (Vatican, 1990). *Catholic International*, 2. 16, pp. 775ff.

The very recognition that this is the case marks important progress in our attempt to rid our memories of significant resentments and misconceptions. We need to set ourselves more diligently, however, to the task of reconciling these memories, by writing together the story of what happened in the sixteenth century, with attention not only to the clash of convictions over doctrine and church order, but with attention also as to how in the aftermath our two churches articulated their respective understandings into institutions, culture and the daily lives of believers.(63)[100]

But above all, this methodology made a cross-reference from present to past:

These reviews of our respective histories... have shown us, 'whence we have come,' so that we can better understand where we are – so that we can better understand what yet needs to be done in reassessing our past. We see more clearly how our respective self-understandings have been so largely formed by confessional historiographies of the 16th and 17th centuries. These differing self-interpretations have, in turn, fostered the establishment of whole sets of differing values, symbols, assumptions and institutions – in a word, different religious and ecclesiastical cultures. The result is that today, as in the past, the same words, even the same biblical expressions, are sometimes received and understood by us in quite different ways.(62)[101]

So this is the temporal dimension of the problem of unity and diversity. Just as we have to reach a consensus on the place of diversity in a future united Church so we need to understand the role of seeming-diversity over time in the Church, what 'Harnack recognized' as 'the issue of theological unity and diversity, as viewed from the historical perspective'.[102] Perhaps the most important thing ecumenically is to strive for a kind and degree of familiarity with events and especially fashions of thought which makes it possible to begin to

---

[100] *Toward a Common Understanding of the Church: Report of Reformed–Roman Catholic Dialogue 1984–90*, (Vatican, 1990), *Catholic International*, 2. 16, p. 785.

[101] *Toward a Common Understanding of the Church: Report of Reformed–Roman Catholic Dialogue 1984–90*, (Vatican, 1990), *Catholic International*, 2. 16, p. 785.

[102] W. H. Capps, 'Harnack and ecumenical discussion', *Journal of Ecumenical Studies*, 3 (1966), 486–502, p. 487. Similarly, a geographical difference can alter a standpoint. 'The American experience of the ecumenical movement... differed... from the experience in most of the rest of the world... Ecumenical Christianity in America exhibited strong continuity with American culture... Church cooperation had a cultural latitudinarian base; missions, a base in ideas and attitudes drawn from the frontier and the American Dream; and Christian social action a base in the agrarian and Progressive tradition of American reform.' R. S. Bilheimer, 'Let American ecumenism be ecumenical', *Journal of Ecumenical Studies*, 16 (1979), 197–205, pp. 201–2. So a cause-and-effect, or antecedent-and-consequence approach is too linear to be altogether satisfactory.

move about the territory with some degree of sureness. That seems the best way to gather together the consistencies and to give due place to the variables.

Historical relativism

Nevertheless, as ecumenical historians we are certainly dealing with more variables than we can handle.[103] We have already touched on one of the major problems in establishing a common picture of a common story so as to possess the history together; the effect of continuous alteration upon a tradition which seeks to be 'always the same' in its essence; the perpetual tension of change and continuity. Statements to that effect abound in the ecumenical literature. 'The Church's faithful mutation is to be seen as consistent with the Church's historical character. This means that apostolic continuity, perhaps quite diversely defined, is integral to the Church's identity through change.'[104] Congar also argues that 'knowledge of history makes possible a healthy relativism, which is quite different from scepticism. Relativism is, on the contrary, a way of being and seeing oneself more truly, and by perceiving the relativity of that which is really relative, it is a way of attributing absoluteness only to what is really absolute. Thanks to history we take proper stock of things, we avoid the mistake of taking for "tradition" that which is only recent and which has altered more than once in the course of time.'[105] This takes a view of the value of history as lying in giving a sufficiently grand perspective to make it possible to get things in proportion; and to see what lasts and what repeats itself. So historical relativism becomes a relating of patterns.

There is another unresolved issue here, of the relationship of later formulations of doctrine to those which came earlier.

(i) One school of thought stresses the essential *identity* of orthodoxy in every age, with variation in expression being put down to linguistic, cultural and other kinds of change.

(ii) Another takes what might be called a 'Whig' view: that some *progress* is made over time, or at least that the full articulation of truths

---

[103] Nichols speaks of 'competing doctrinal claims rendered anodyne through their massive relativisation as so many symbols or sensibilties expressing in diverse ways relationship with the single Christian God'. Nichols, *Congar*, p. 97.

[104] Reformed–Roman Catholic, para. 65; *Growth*, p. 449.

[105] Congar, 'Church History as a branch of theology', *Concilium*, English edition, 57 (8 June 1970), p. 88.

requires time. [106] 'Generally speaking, the recent efforts to overcome *past* disagreements have proved beneficial to the participants. The exercise has helped the churches to correct the one-sidedness of their own previous positions and to advance toward a more contemporary understanding of the gospel.'[107] Does this imply that 'more contemporary' is better? 'It is not sufficient to say that the substance of the doctrine remains the same in each age, but the formulation of it can be changed and perhaps improved.'[108] But Karl Rahner suggests that 'every formula in which the faith is expressed can in principle be surpassed while still retaining its truth'.[109]

(iii) A third way of dealing with the problem of too much 'relativism' has been to fix on one key point in a given tradition, or the tradition of the whole Church, and take that as normative. For the whole Church this is usually taken to be 'apostolic times'. For divided Churches it can often be a point early in their existence as distinct entities. 'Churches have shown a dominant tendency to select one moment of their theological past and make it classical, erect it as normative for all future theologizing.'[110] The solution to the divisive effect of clinging to such a 'moment' is perhaps to learn to see it as a moment in a longer story. 'Each one of the main streams of the Christian tradition will learn to understand itself as a moment, be it an important one, in the on-going diachrony of Christian doctrine [as] together, they will build a valid alternative to their own past positions.'[111]

The axis of inter-confessional historiography in theology is crossed by another axis, equally important ecumenically. The complete history of the ideas embedded in a doctrinal formulation will normally extend back long before there was division on the matter. Without knowing the whole story, we cannot understand the theology. 'The Church is now acquiring a new awareness of how important it is to know the whole history of a dogmatic formula in order to interpret it accurately,'[112] comments one author. 'The ministry, in its successive

---

[106] W. H. Capps, 'Harnack and ecumenical discussion,' *Journal of Ecumenical Studies*, 3 (1966), 486–502, p. 486, note 1. Newman 'stresses the necessity of time for the articulation of great truths, for instance, while [Rahner] tends to refer the occasion for doctrinal development to the incompleteness of human language in which divine truth is expressed'.

[107] Avery Dulles, 'Catholic response to G. A. Lindbeck's *Lutheran–Catholic Dialogue*', *Journal of Ecumenical Studies*, 13 (1976), p. 248.

[108] L. Swidler, Editorial, *Journal of Ecumenical Studies*, 4 (1967), p. 131.

[109] *Theological Investigations*, I, tr. C. Ernst (Baltimore, 1961), p. 44.

[110] G. Tavard, 'For a theology of dialogue', *One in Christ*, 15 (1979), p. 14.

[111] G. Tavard, 'For a theology of dialogue', *One in Christ*, 15 (1979), p. 15.

[112] L. Swidler, Editorial, *Journal of Ecumenical Studies*, 4 (1967), p. 130.

forms, . . . constitutes a typical example of a doctrine that cannot be understood apart from its history,'[113] notes another. There are implications here that theology cannot be done at all without its history.

That brings us back full circle to our starting-point, the complex questions of the relation between history and theology; and between continuity and change. Ecumenical methodology in the historical arena has been wrestling hard with these, but there is still a long way to go. The most that can really be glimpsed as yet is that just as 'doing theology together' is essential for dialogue, so 'possessing together' must be the historiographical goal, 'whole history' the ecumenical ideal. ⁄

[113] G. Tavard, 'The bi-lateral dialogues: speaking together', *One in Christ*, 16 (1980), 30–43, p. 37.

CHAPTER 6

The process in close-up

In his youth Ignaz von Döllinger had been a leader of renewal of the Roman Catholic Church in Germany. He also had a strong interest in the institutional growth of Protestantism, and developed friendly relations with Protestants in Germany and outside. After 1850 his work seems more and more strongly marked by his realisation of the value of historical criticism. In *Kirche und Kirchen. Papstthum und Kirchenstaat* (1861) he argued that churches which separate themselves from the Pope end in chaos. At the same time, he himself was beginning to resist papal claims to absolute power. In 1871, unable to accept the teaching of Vatican I on Papal infallibility, he was excommunicated. Students were forbidden to attend his lectures. He was thus placed in circumstances which encouraged him, although they were personally very painful, to work actively for unity in the Church in such arenas as were open to him.

The protest against the Vatican I decrees in Germany contributed to the formation of the Old Catholic Churches. Döllinger was uncomfortable with anything which would set up 'altar against altar',[1] and he found a constructive outlet for his concern in the Bonn Reunion Conferences of 1874 and 1875. These were held under Döllinger's presidency and included Old Catholics who had recently separated from Rome over the decrees of the Vatican Council, German Evangelicals, and a number of Anglicans. To the Bonn Conferences went a younger English friend of Döllinger, Alfred Plummer, himself an Anglican scholar. He recorded the events in an intimate, conversational way which reproduces the flavour and tone of the gathering better perhaps than any other device could have done. The example is valuable. It shows both the constants – the

---

[1] See P. Neuner, *Döllinger als Theologe der Ökumene* (Paderborn/Munich/Vienna/Zurich, 1979), pp. 171–219.

patterns of personal and ecclesial interaction which repeat themselves still today in ecumenical conversations – and that we have learned something about how to set about the task which ought to help us to see more clearly than these pioneers were able to do. I shall draw a good deal on Plummer's account in what follows, because it provides the kind of intimate details of the process in close-up we need in this chapter, without the disadvantages of any risk of upsetting work in progress, which might come from using close-up accounts of more recent work.

Framing the enterprise

On the first morning of the Bonn talks, 14 September 1874, Döllinger invited Plummer to come to the house of Bishop Reinkens in the early afternoon 'to prepare some subjects for discussion, with a view to avoiding questions which might cause unnecessary difficulty'.[2] This was a common-sense procedure with honourable precedent.[3] But it is also the kind of thing about which we have to ask the question whether it is fair play ecumenically. What may be acceptable in, say, business or civil service meetings may not be proper ecumenically, if the principles of freedom and trust and respect and 'doing together' which we have been underlining are sound. Döllinger's intention was to avoid the difficulties by the way he framed the subjects for discussion. If the topics he thus eliminated would be construed by everyone as 'unnecessary' that would clearly be right. The operation would simply be removing clutter. But if there was some inadvertent or conscious suppression of matters which others would consider necessary, that would only be deferring discussion; and it would be damaging to trust to try it.

On the other hand, to go to a meeting without planning beforehand what is to be addressed is to run the risk of doing harm, or at best, not achieving any useful end. The Anglican Stephen Neill distinguished three kinds of ecclesiastical assembly. The first two are those which have no effect on the Church or the world; and those which do harm by speaking in an unconsidered way or by reinforcing existing prejudices. The third are those which have an effect through their prophetic style or by moving the conscience of the Christian

---

[2] Alfred Plummer, *Conversations with Dr Döllinger, 1870–90*, ed. R. Boudens (Louvain, 1985), p. 100.
[3] Bernard of Clairvaux did something of the sort in connection with the trial of Gilbert of Poitiers in 1148.

world.[4] This is supremely the work of the Holy Spirit. Insofar as it is at human disposal, to a considerable degree it is the governing vision brought into focus beforehand which determines which sort any given assembly will be. The Lambeth Conferences have consistently tried to work to a leading idea in this way. For example, the Encyclical Letter of the 1920 Conference says, 'One idea runs through all our work in this conference . . . fellowship.' 'Witness' was seen as the Conference's theme in 1930, and in 1988, the idea of the bishop's 'bringing his diocese with him'.[5]

To avoid the second of Neill's possibilities is partly a matter of taking care in the use of language and being conscious that there may be buried assumptions inimical to peace between the churches. To achieve the third and avoid the first is not entirely in the hands of planners. It is not always possible to predict what will catch imagination and set hearts on fire. But largeness and simplicity of vision will often do it. The value of good preparation before a meeting is that it makes it possible to achieve the maximum at the meeting itself.[6] But it also to some degree predetermines at least what is covered.

THE SCALE OF THE OPERATION

Limiting the agenda and not expecting too much

Should ecumenical method set itself large or small goals? Experience suggests that it has to do both. It was found as early as the Bonn Reunion talks that it was helpful to set limits. Not expecting too much is itself a methodological decision, and it is not incompatible with considerable achievements – indeed, at the right stage, it may foster them. 'Prof. Reusch of the University of Bonn opened the proceedings at the Bonn Reunion talks by stating what the wishes of the Germans, who had taken the initiative in the matter, were. 1. The Conference was not a *public* one, although the invitation to it had been very general. It was not intended that detailed reports should be published; and it would be well if reports sent to newspapers were brief and couched in general terms. 2. Noone was present in any *official* capacity. Each member was to be understood as stating only his own personal convictions, not anything which could bind others. We were

[4] D. O. R., 'A la veille du Concile', *Irénikon*, 35 (1962), 213–35, p. 229.
[5] Report of the 1920 Conference, p. 147.
[6] D. O. R., 'A la veille du Concile', *Irénikon*, 35 (1962), 213–35, p. 217.

there to suggest, and discuss, and prepare the way for agreement, not to determine the exact terms.'[7] A similar modest sense of the unofficial and limited character of the proceedings marked the Malines conversations.

The way in which difficulties are compounded when anything more ambitious is attempted was apparent in the preparations for Vatican II. At the beginning of the Second Vatican Council seventy-two schemata were proposed. They were uneven in value, and in any case far too much in their total volume for the Council to cover.[8] Decisions were needed as to what were the major issues, and the time needed for adequate coverage of these had to be balanced against the length of the Council. 'At all costs,' notes Cardinal Suenens, 'we [had to] avoid the bishops having the impression that they did not have time to deal seriously with the matters put before them because the Council had got bogged down in details.'[9]

The future Pope Paul VI, in the December before he became Pope, suggested that in the preparatory material 'a vast amount of excellent material has been brought together, but it is too disparate and uneven. A central controlling idea is needed to coordinate this immense material.'[10] Suenens' plan, as he submitted it to Pope John XXIII, was that the Council should see itself as continuing the work of the First Vatican Council, which had made statements on Papal Primacy and Infallibility but had not completed an account of the Church as a whole, which would 'place' the bishops and the laity within it. To do that would be to give a better doctrinal balance and that would make possible steps towards rapprochement with separated Christian communions.[11] Congar would add to that a stress upon the Council's taking seriously the concept of the 'pilgrim Church', in a world where there is cultural variation, so that ideas have their own geography.[12]

Karl Rahner was successful in opposing the use of the first drafts prepared in Rome for the Council. He saw these as conservative, neo-scholastic and triumphalistic,[13] and unlikely to provide fertile ground for reforming work by the Council. In a letter to Pope John XXIII, 4 July 1962, Suenens argued successfully that the prepared

[7] Alfred Plummer, *Conversations with Dr Döllinger, 1870–90*, ed. R. Boudens (Louvain, 1985), p. 100, September, 1874.   [8] L.-J. Cardinal Suenens, Stacpoole, p. 89.
[9] L.-J. Cardinal Suenens, Stacpoole, p. 93.   [10] Stacpoole, p. 8.
[11] Stacpoole, p. 97.   [12] Congar, Stacpoole, p. 129.
[13] Herbert Vorgrimler, Stacpoole, pp. 40–1.

texts should not be sent out without planning. He wanted to see 'maximum possible use of the schemata which had been drawn up'. 'A massive and important amount of work has been done,' he commented, 'and we must take advantage of it, while removing its fragmentary and mosaic character.'[14]

This experience echoes that of one ecumenical commission after another, as the net is cast wide to begin with, and perhaps a great deal of detailed work done in areas on which it is later decided not to concentrate.

Deferring other work

As to what was to be done with the topics, or aspects of issues which would thus be moved off the Second Vatican Council's agenda, Suenens suggested that post-conciliar Commissions should be set up to deal with unfinished business and with 'monitoring the practical outcome of the decisions taken by the Council'. This would achieve the purpose of 'decongesting' the Council and 'setting them up would give the feeling of serious intent to our endeavours that the whole world expects to see'.[15] It was thought sensible for bishops representing the various continents to be named by the Holy See for this purpose. 'They should not be too numerous.' 'Experts could be called in in a consultative capacity.'[16] Suenens wanted these to become 'permanent bodies, attached to each Congregation of the Roman Curia'. This 'would allow the diocesan bishops to make their pastoral concerns known, so as to rethink the problems tackled by each Congregation in a pastoral way'.[17] This is an instance of a practice which has, again, had to be adopted by all ecumenical commissions. Work which the commission comes to recognise to be outside its scope for the present is deferred. There are attempts to plan how it may be tackled later, so as not to let it be neglected by default.

Thinking big

Yet it is not a contradiction to set this practical talk of limiting the topic beside the imperative to think on the largest possible scale

---

[14] L.-J. Cardinal Suenens, Stacpoole, pp. 95–6.
[15] L.-J. Cardinal Suenens, Stacpoole, p. 94.
[16] L.-J. Cardinal Suenens, Stacpoole, p. 94.
[17] L.-J. Cardinal Suenens, Stacpoole, p. 94. He points out that Congregations tend to be 'by the nature of things more attuned to the canonical and administrative aspects of their work'.

ecumenically. That must above all mean thinking eschatologically. It can be partly a matter of setting the struggle to express the faith together today in a context of ultimate and enduring Christian truth.[18] It can also be a matter of unashamedly looking to an ideal beyond the shortcomings of real life in the churches. ARCIC I was criticised for doing so, when the realities of church life so conspicuously fail to approach the ideal. 'There lies ahead the task for both parties of moving from the actual (and the situations in which actual churches find themselves are governed by formularies, canon law, sentiment, custom and their understanding of truth) onwards to the joint realisation of a common ideal,'[19] argued Hugh Montefiore. 'The Joint Report [ARCIC I] does recognize the cultural relativism of credal formulae . . . It only permits restatement that builds upon the truth intended by the original definition . . . But cultural differences cannot be disposed of so easily,'[20] he continued. Yet to be satisfied with an imperfect reality, as others stressed, may be to sacrifice the chance of achieving the ideal. In this same debate of 1977, Henry Chadwick presented the alternatives in terms of 'painful rock-climbing with rope and ice-axe' or 'a faster . . . route to the summit, by cable-car' which could be reached by immediately establishing 'intercommunion'.[21] He comments that 'ARCIC has not gone about its task as if the limited goal were a charitable get-together through the hospitality of inter-communion between bodies agreeing to differ benevolently about matters of weight, some of which appear of the very substance of the faith . . . ARCIC has sought rather to examine, and where possibe to remove, obstacles to communion.'[22] He recognises that Montefiore thinks ARCIC 'confuses what ought to be the case with what is the case', and asks, 'is this complaint really as damaging as it may seem to those who have never tried to construct a doctrine of the Church in coherent terms'? 'A satisfactory exposition of the essential being of the Church can hardly be attempted at all if the data available exclude any element of the ideal and heavenly and are

---

[18] 'This statement starts with the grandiloquent and glowing rehearsal of accepted verities which they do so well in Rome.' John Drury, writing on ARCIC I on Authority, Editorial, *Theology* (May, 1977), p. 167.

[19] Hugh Montefiore, *So Near And Yet So Far* (London, 1986), p. 17.

[20] Hugh Montefiore, 'Authority in the Church', *Theology* (May, 1977), p. 17.

[21] Henry Chadwick, 'A brief apology for "Authority in the Church" (Venice, 1976)', *Theology* (September 1977), p. 325.

[22] Henry Chadwick, 'A brief apology for "Authority in the Church" (Venice, 1976)', *Theology* (September 1977), p. 326. Henry Chadwick dislikes 'a relativistic or sceptical doctrine of a multitude of ecclesial groups, all equally right or equally wrong, none of which mirrors or approximates to the true form of Christ's holy catholic Church'. Ibid.

strictly confined to the not too militant community of frail believers whose treasure is in very earthen vessels.'[23] It is not without significance that this exchange was prompted by the publication of a text which has caused more controversy than any other ecumenical agreement of recent years. ARCIC's Venice Statement of 1976 on 'Authority in the Church' challenged the reality by its portrayal of an ideal. That is what an ecumenical methodology has to attempt, and why it must always seek both to 'think big' and never to lose sight of the limiting realities of the Church's daily life in the world.

HUMAN RESOURCES

The experience of being there

Something of all this carries over into the processes at an actual meeting. Hans Küng encapsulates this infinitely subtle and complex interworking of individual and formal in the processes, with the consequent 'imperfect, unfinished, mysterious, partial, fragmentary character . . . of all our doctrinal utterances',[24] in his description of the experience of Vatican II:

One who is there experiences concretely what the thousand 'chance happenings' of a council workday mean to a particular decree and its individual expressions. He sees . . . that . . . it was this introduction and not another one that opened the debate, that it was followed by precisely these interventions and not others . . . he also sees that . . . at one of the countless 'ricevimenti' a particular Protestant observer was able to call a certain problem to the attention of this particular bishop or theologian, that the moderators' third question for provisional voting used this term and not another, that at this session a certain member was present or absent, that a specific bishop or peritus, because of his fluency in Latin or lack of it, was able to be persuasive, or had to be silent, that in this commission or in that secretariat no up-to-date exegete could be found, . . . that a certain private coordinating group of bishops or theologians correctly anticipated the course of a debate or vote, that this particular bishop was able to use that particular theologian for the working out of his intervention, that that theologian found a bishop ready to bring his matter to the floor . . . it often depends on a single man whether one or another important matter comes up for discussion before the Council or not . . . Later on it will often be hardly possible to be sure why a particular point of view, perhaps an important one

---

[23] Henry Chadwick, 'A brief apology for "Authority in the Church" (Venice, 1976)', *Theology* (September, 1977), p. 327.

[24] Hans Küng, Editorial, *Journal of Ecumenical Studies*, 1 (1964), p. 109.

for the ecumenical dialogue, was included in the schema concerning the Church, and another left out.'[25]

We cannot hope to convey the subtleties of these processes here. But we can underline their complexity and draw out a series of factors for consideration.

The common table but not the common table

I give you welcome to my own house, and I was particularly glad to be able to give you the deepest welcome in the celebration of the Holy Communion of our Blessed Lord in the Chapel this morning. That was not only by my own wish, but by the authority of the Church of England in the case of such conferences as these.

I remember that round this table have gathered in recent years representatives of many of the Churches in Christendom. I think of the representatives of our own protestant Churches here in England and of the Church of Scotland.

Round this table also have gathered representatives of the Holy Orthodox Church, of the Old Catholic Church, and, particularly, of the Church of Sweden. And, most recently, the representatives of that Church which is very akin to your own, the Church of Finland.

In all these cases, relations of cordial friendship have been established, and, in some, relations of close communion and even of complete and full communion.[26]

These words of the Archbishop of Canterbury in the 1930s painfully underline the paradox of all ecumenical conversations, that those who gather round a common table to talk cannot gather together round the Lord's Table in a single Eucharist. Some worship together is possible, and meals taken together, coffee-breaks, walks, outings, build up fellowship. But it remains a fellowship frustrated of its proper eucharistic consummation. Here the need to look to the ideal while living with the reality makes its sharpest point.

The dynamics of conversation and the role of leadership

In all ecumenical conversation there is what might be called tidal flow. A chairman or draftsman may try to create a sense of urgency

---

[25] Hans Küng, Editorial, *Journal of Ecumenical Studies*, 1 (1964), p. 109.

[26] Archbishop of Canterbury, addressing the first session of the Evangelical Lutheran Churches of Latvia and Estonia in conversation with the Church of England, 1936–8, *Lambeth Occasional Reports, 1931–8* (London, 1948), p. 215.

and purpose in order to sweep through on the substantive issue without risking complications; and find he cannot do it because the tide turns. So timing is important. An optimism about the speed with which things could be cleared up characterised the inexperienced ecumenists who met at Bonn in the 1870s. The first topic to be attempted was the *Filioque*. Döllinger thought that the best plan was for a preliminary 'understanding' to be reached by the rest during the afternoon before the meeting with the members of the Greek Church took place at 6 o'clock.[27] Avoiding all discussion at this point of the theological difference the addition might be said to make, Döllinger tried to confine the proposal to the relatively simple one of removing the offending words in Western usage. This proved to carry its own difficulties. Two of the Anglican bishops pointed out that they had 'sworn to maintain the Creed in its Western form'. 'Dr. Döllinger said no question of principle was involved. It was the rectification of a wrong, which all parties acknowledged to be a wrong.' Döllinger tried to stop the discussion running away in a direction which would wreck its chances of success. But he unwisely engaged in the (ecumenically unforgiveable) blackmail of threatening to close down the talks. 'He argued', says Plummer, 'that if members of the English Church there present were seriously of opinion that the *Filioque* could not now be surrendered, he conceived that the present negoti-ations . . . were at an end.' Ecumenically unforgiveable it may be, but it can also be a way of bringing participants to see that they are going in a direction which must result in a dead end; and perhaps this was Döllinger's real intention here.

'The next meeting was a more stormy one,' comments Plummer.[28] The Greeks went straight for the jugular vein. They found 'inadmissible' the Bishop of Winchester's amendment: 'Without sacrificing the truth of the doctrine embodied in the form of the creed now in use in the Western Church.' Greek after Greek stood up and said the same. Döllinger called a halt and said that he agreed that it could not be correct to say that 'there was no essential difference of *doctrine* on this point. It was clearly not just a matter of difference of form.

Bishop Reinken saved the situation by an ecclesiological argument. If there remained a difference it could not be the case that the whole Church had agreed. 'The Orientals had no right to lay an anathema

[27] Alfred Plummer, *Conversations with Dr Döllinger, 1870–90*, ed. R. Boudens (Louvain, 1985), p. 102.
[28] Alfred Plummer, *Conversations with Dr Döllinger, 1870–90*, ed. R. Boudens (Louvain, 1985), p. 104, 1874.

on a proposition, about which the whole Church had not yet spoken.' 'The Greeks had at first taken a very high line' ecclesiologically, points out Plummer. They had claimed that 'Their Church was a mighty stream flowing in one unbroken course from the fountain-head of Christ and His Apostles. After Bishop Reinkens' speech they became more moderate' and were indeed able to accept the clause if it said 'may be embodied' instead of 'is'.[29] The episode with Reinkens illustrates very well the influence which can be achieved by the Chairman who steps in at the right moment. It also demonstrates the impact which can be had by the individual whose insight wins minds and makes a difference. Reinkens here was able to see a way through and point it out to others in such a way that they could see it too.

Ecumenical conversations are usually chaired, and commonly co-chaired, by representatives of each of the participant communions. The dynamics here are of course subtly different from those of a meeting with a single chairman. Where a chairman can see his way, much can be done directly through his steering of the conversation. Dr. Döllinger saw his role very much in this light.[30] The fault in Döllinger's chairmanship, when he made mistakes, seems to have been that he sometimes saw his role primarily as that of leader and guide rather than as that of co-worker. We should perhaps now want to see the chairman's role rather differently, as properly one of collaboration rather than primarily of direction, though there will certainly be a place for direction. But just as a sense of there being 'sides' has to go, so must any notion of compulsion such as a directing chairmanship might carry.

An example of the chairman's intervention being used to direct a discussion which threatens to take off uncontrollably occurred at the 1875 Bonn meeting, with, again, some fault lying with Döllinger. Here he used what is colloquially called the 'put-down'. As Plummer relates it, 'The debate ... on the doctrinal question was not edifying, and proved what a mixed multitude the members of the Anglican communion were. We included ultra-Protestants of the Irish Church. Things reached a climax when Dr. Schaff, the Presbyterian secretary of the Evangelical alliance, came forward and almost insisted upon

---

[29] Alfred Plummer, *Conversations with Dr Döllinger, 1870–90*, ed. R. Boudens (Louvain, 1985), pp. 104–5, 1874.

[30] 'Another very difficult question which will have to be discussed,' he said during the Bonn conversations, 'is the doctrine of the eucharist. I don't yet see my way out of that difficulty. I must think still more as to what will possibly lead to agreement.' Alfred Plummer, *Conversations with Dr Döllinger, 1870–90* , ed. R. Boudens (Louvain, 1985), pp. 122–3, 1875.

being heard. "He had come a long way," and had a speech which had evidently been composed with some care . . . Schaff's view was that we should agree in adopting certain statements in S. John's Gospel and S. Paul's Epistles, and leave everything else to take care of itself. As soon as he had finished Dr. Döllinger came forward and said, "The last speaker, not being a member of those Churches which have preserved the episcopate, has no claim to be heard at this Conference. But as a matter of courtesy I thought it well to allow him to speak. If his opinions are shared by the other members of the Conference, it follows that we all of us should have done far more wisely if we had remained at home." I have seldom seen a man so quietly, and at the same time so effectually, snuffed out,' says Plummer. 'I walked with Liddon when it was all over. He was greatly distressed, and thought that little good could come of these mixed gatherings.'[31]

Ecclesiastical machinery is heavy and slow.[32] It is cautious and suspicious of the charismatic where that seems to threaten order. That can make it difficult for the personal vision of the individual to make itself felt. An isolated voice is sometimes first shouted down but later turns out to be right and to change the course of events. We have already seen how, where a blockage threatens, one side, or an individual, may propose a way through. At such a vexed point in the Anglican–Rumanian Orthodox conference of 1935, 'a statement was submitted by the Rumanian Commission to the Anglican delegation, concerning the Holy Eucharist and was accepted unanimously by the latter in the following form'.[33] Behind 'in the following form' we must read some process of revision. But it is important that this was recognised and accepted to have been a success because of the Rumanian initiative.

The role of experts and observers

In most ecumenical conversations individuals who are not full or voting members have a place. These are now normally of two sorts – 'experts' called in to advise, and 'observers' from other communions, often there to provide a balancing viewpoint, or to sound a warning note about consequences of a proposed solution for other dialogues.

[31] Alfred Plummer, *Conversations with Dr Döllinger, 1870–90*, ed. R. Boudens (Louvain, 1985), p. 134, August, 1975.
[32] D. O. R., 'A la veille du Concile', *Irénikon*, 35 (1962), 213–35, pp. 214–5.
[33] *Lambeth Occasional Reports, 1931–8* (London, 1948), p. 197.

Experts and observers make a contribution in ways which can be highly significant for the outcome. This was already apparent in the first major Roman Catholic conciliar experiment to include non-voting theologians but also observers from other churches. Experts (*periti*) appointed to the Second Vatican Council had to find informal ways of making themselves useful, by working through the bishops. The position of the observers was even more difficult to define. At the Council, all observers from other churches were treated equally. They all received all Council texts and were able to attend all General Congregations. They were able to make their views known to the Secretariat for Promoting Christian Unity each week. They had opportunities of contact with the Council fathers and the *periti*. It was informally possible for an observer as it was for the theologian *peritus* to ask a friendly bishop to get up and make a point on his behalf. These provided useful channels. It has been argued that the reason why Anglicans won something of a 'special place' in the Council documents 'may be due to the conversations which the Anglican observers had had with the bishops and with members of the Secretariat for Christian Unity which drew up the schema'.[34] The observers may also have had an effect on the Dogmatic Constitution on Divine Revelation which began by calling the Bible and Tradition a 'double source' of revelation. 'Anglicans and protestants objected very strongly to it as it reduced the authority of the Bible as the sole source of revelation,' and some modifications resulted.[35]

It was a new experience at the Second Vatican Council to have observers from other communions present. It created a new awareness that texts submitted for deliberation in the Council could have ecumenical repercussions according to the way they were drafted.[36] One comment pointed out that observers, by being actually present, could see by the operation of the Church in its very life, things which could not be learned by reading the resulting documents.[37]

But they also had an effect by simply being there, by making other Christian communions present to the Council. There was a resulting powerful mutual presence. This in itself can constitute an influencing factor. The same proved true in the Synod held in Rome in 1985 to review the work of the Council. There, in their Report to the council

---

[34] J. R. H. Moorman, Stacpoole, p. 163.   [35] J. R. H. Moorman, Stacpoole, p. 165.
[36] Editorial, 'Aux premières heures du Concile', *Istina*, 8 (1961–2), 385–9.
[37] Editorial, 'Aux premières heures du Concile', *Istina*, 8 (1961–2), p. 360

the ecumenical observers were able to say, 'Observers are not detached spectators: we are deeply engaged in your discussions.'[38] So, in a sense, experts and observers share a role in the dynamics of conversation which is by no means only a matter of giving background support.

WRITTEN RESOURCES

Background papers, position papers and producing a statement

Ecumenical conversations produce texts – reports and agreed statements. But the notion that this is a natural end result was not obvious at the beginning. It was arrived at by trial and error. The idea of making a statement as a mode of publication of results probably first arose in the last letter written by Cardinal Mercier to Halifax.[39]

At the Malines conversation, Halifax's *Memorandum* was of the first importance in limiting the agenda and shaping and directing the discussion. Halifax himself saw his *Memorandum* for the first conversations at Malines as 'an attempt to state . . . a position which might afford a basis for discussion and agreement between Roman Catholic and Anglican theologians. I have ventured . . . to make some tentative suggestions as may facilitate discussion, promote agreement and perhaps suggest the possibility of bridges where the difficulty of arriving at an agreement seems greatest.'[40] Halifax's *Memorandum* 'was by general consent taken' by the participants at Malines 'as the basis of discussion and carefully considered paragraph by paragraph'.[41]

---

[38] Report of the Ecumenical Observers to the Synod, Rome, 1985, delivered by Henry Chadwick, *One in Christ*, 20 (1984), 98–101, p. 98.

[39] Lord Halifax, *Notes on the Conversations at Malines, 1921–5. Points of Agreement* (London, 1928), pp. 12 ff. , p. 64 of text of Anglican report. Cardinal Mercier wrote a last letter before his death to the Archbishop of Canterbury, on 25 October 1925. 'If the goal remains the same, the means to reach it vary according to circumstances and raise new problems at every step' . . . 'the difficulties in the way of final success loom larger on the horizon and the reasons for hoping seem less convincing' . . . 'inveterate optimists and obstinate pessimists' . . . 'not only have our meetings brought hearts together which is already a very appreciable result, but . . . they have also, on important points, harmonized our thoughts and achieved progress in agreement' . . . 'We must bring to light progressively whatever favours reunion, and set aside or defer whatever stands in the way' . . . 'we met face to face like men of goodwill and sincere believers . . . we set to work without knowing either when or how this union hoped for by Christ could be realized, but convinced that it could be realized since Christ willed it, and that we had, therefore, each one of us, to bring our contribution to its realization.'

[40] Halifax, *Les Conversations de Malines* (London, 1930), p. 72.

[41] *The Conversations at Malines: Report Presented to the Archbishop of Canterbury by the Anglican Members* (Oxford, 1927), Supplement, p. 10. *The Conversations at Malines. Original Documents*, ed. Halifax (London, 1930), p. 10.

It is accessible in two versions. The first was printed by Halifax himself in his collected documents of the conversations. But Walter Frere, Bishop of Truro, pointed out in his own *Recollections*[42] that 'by some oversight' it was an earlier version which had been included. He gives the significant variants. It is instructive to compare the two. (I number the versions 1 and 2.)

1. Perhaps not dissimilar considerations might facilitate agreement in regard to the Papal Supremacy and the Decree of the Vatican Council. In regard to the first Leo XIII has explicitly declared that the Supremacy of the Pope implies no claim to authority in temporal and civil affairs and that every Bishop derives his spiritual power direct from God, whilst in regard to the Vatican Decree it is I believe admitted that no power is claimed for the Pope to declare new dogmas apart from the Church, but only after having taken every means to ascertain what the teaching and mind of the Church is on any given point implicitly contained in the deposit of faith committed to the Church's guardianship, to declare what that faith is in an authentic manner.[43]
2. Perhaps not dissimilar considerations might facilitate agreement in regard to the Papal Supremacy and the Decree of the Vatican Council. In regard to the first, it is well to remember, with a view to reunion, two pronouncements of Leo XIII, when, speaking of the independence of the civil society from the temporal, he said with regard to religious society (1) that the Supremacy of the Pope implies no claim to authority in temporal and civil affairs; and (2) that the powers of bishops exist *iure divino*. In regard to the Vatican Decree a great difficulty is removed if it is admitted that no power is claimed there by the Council for the Pope apart from the Church; and that what it claims for the Pope is simply the power, after having taken every means to ascertain what the teaching of the Church is, on any given point, to declare what that teaching is in an authoritative mannner. In short the power of the Pope is not the power to declare or impose a new dogma, but only the power to declare explicitly and authoritatively what is the faith committed by the Lord Jesus Christ to the Church's guardianship.[44]
1. The Eucharist is the same sacrifice as that of the Cross offered mystically and by way of sacrament and that in consequence when we assist at the sacrifice of the Mass it is as if we were kneeling at the foot of the Cross on Calvary and pleading the one all sufficient sacrifice that has been offered for every member of the human race.[45]
2. That the Eucharistic sacrifice of the Mass is nothing else than the offering made by our Lord Jesus Christ to His Father, under the sacramental species, of His Body and His Blood, separated in a mystical manner the one from the other by the consecration, in memory of the death and bloodshedding; which he suffered once for all upon the Cross for the sins of the whole world,

42 Frere, *Malines*, pp. 14 ff.   43 Halifax, *Malines*, pp. 73–4.
44 Frere, *Malines*, pp. 15–16.   45 Halifax, *Malines*, p. 75.

past, present and future. That the Eucharist is the same sacrifice as that of the cross offered mystically and by way of sacrament.[46]

1. Noone can expect the Roman Church to go back upon what it has authoritatively said, any more than England can be expected to repudiate its history during the last three hundred years. There must be accommodations in regard to all such matters.[47]

2. Noone can expect the Roman Church to go back upon what it has authoritatively said. Nor, equally, can the Orthodox church or the Anglican church be expected to accept formally what forms no part of their traditional faith, and was not an article of faith for Roman Catholics until 1854. There must obviously be accommodations made in regard to all such matters.[48]

Frere says that the *Memorandum* ended with the words,

'From this we may surely feel certain that any proposal that came from Rome for the holding of conferences with a view to discussing reunion, would be welcomed by the authorities of the Anglican Church.'[49]

The changes here tend to expand in order to make explicit and to underline key concepts for both sides, with the intention of winning minds to embrace a single statement.

In 1935 a conference was held at Bucharest between the Rumanian Commission on Relations with the Anglican Communion and a Church of England delegation appointed by the Archbishop of Canterbury in which the procedure was different. The method of this conference was unusual among ecumenical encounters in the use made of background papers. In this case they formed the stuff of the conference itself, with each side contributing a paper on each of a series of topics. These were read in pairs and the topic then discussed. This process is described as 'the method of the conference'.[50] It has not always been the case that background papers have been so thoroughly used. Position papers and background papers are usually produced by members of the commissions and others invited to help in this way, and they are of immense usefulness in clearing minds. But there is a danger of their being partly wasted as instruments for helping others to arrive at the same stages in their thinking. Practice is variable here. The 'Niagara' Report's background papers have been published; the ARCIC ones so far not, except individually in some cases by their authors. The papers covered such matters as 'the apostolic succession and the validity of Anglican ordinations from the historical point of view'; 'the necessity of the priesthood and its sacramental character';

---

[46] Frere, *Malines*, pp. 15–16.   [47] Halifax, *Malines*, p. 78.   [48] Frere, *Malines*, p. 18.
[49] Frere, *Malines*, pp. 18–19.   [50] *Lambeth Occasional Reports, 1931–8* (London, 1948), p. 196.

'holy Scripture, holy tradition, the Prayer Book and the Thirty-Nine Articles of religion'. It can be seen from these examples that care was taken in framing the topics to juxtapose elements of special concern in each tradition, and thus to foster the discussion about points of likeness and difference which was needed. Here the method was not to try to frame a single text which both sides could, with modifications, accept, but to try to express the balance of the two sides' distinctive views.

Ecumenical conversations have almost uniformly settled on the attempt to produce a single agreed text by both sides working together, though not as a rule in Halifax's way. This is the characteristic product of the 'doing theology together' we have been discussing.

That has come about because the dynamics of conversation which have led to 'doing theology together' interact with those of writing. It was evident at an early stage that to put something in wrting is to move the conversation forward; a proposal put on the table has the effect of clarifying at once the points at which each participant community feels uncomfortable with it. At the Anglican–Orthodox conversations of the 1930s one 'Term' (*Of the Christian Faith*) initially read as follows:

We accept the Faith of Christ as it has been taught by the Holy Scriptures, and as it is expounded in the dogmatic decisions of the Oecumenical Councils as accepted by the Undivided Church.

The Metropolitan of Thyateira then rephrased it 'in an Orthodox fashion':

We believe and confess the Christian Faith which is the whole of the truths of Divine Revelation, and which is contained in Holy Scripture and in Holy Tradition, which is partly declared in the Creed and the decrees of the Oecumenical Synods of the Undivided Church, and which is taught by the Church.

It seems that the Anglicans, in framing the first draft, had tried, as it were, unilaterally, to make it an exercise with which the Orthodox could engage. They had drawn on an Orthodox source, in trying to make it a text which spoke Orthodox language. Canon Douglas read out quotations from Professor Zankov. 'Accepting the Bible as basis, dogma consists chiefly in the doctrine of the Oecumenical Councils concerning the Trinity and the Incarnation, and this dogma finds its best and briefest expression in the Nicaean–Constantinopolitan

Creed.' The Metropolitan of Thyateira was not prepared to accept this as anything more than a private and minority opinion among the Orthodox. The exchange had usefully thrown up a key difference which the Anglicans had not perceived before. 'The Archbishop of Dublin inquired whether there were yet undeclared stores of tradition.' Professor Arseniev replied that 'the *lex orandi* is largely the *lex credendi* in the Orthodox Church'. Dr. Goudge then asked how, in that case, it was 'possible to discover what belonged to dogma and what to theological opinion'. The metropolitan of Trikkes said that the official Exposition of the Orthodox Faith was contained in the writings of St John of Damascus. All this made it clear that an attempt to list the commonly accepted sources of faith which the two churches shared was not going to be straightforward, and further discussion of this Term was deferred until after others had been considered.[51]

When the meeting came to Term III, the terms of intercommunion, Professor Arseniev 'put forward a provisional statement' for the Orthodox:

The Spirit of God lives in the Church and manifests Himself in the living stream of the life of the Church. The Holy Scriptures form only a part of this living stream of tradition, coming down from our Lord and the apostles, of this living manifestation of the life of the Spirit of God in his Church. There is nothing which is necessary for our salvation which could not be founded upon or deduced from Scripture, or is in contradiction to it. Therefore the Scriptures ought to be consciously used as a control for the Faith of the Church. But it is only in the light of the Spirit of God who lives in the Church that the true meaning of the Scriptures can be understood.

The dynamic thrust of this, as opposed to the static statement the Anglicans had attempted for Term I is evident. These conversations of the 1930s were confronted in discussing their sixth Term ('that noone may put forth any other Creed') with the problem of clarifying its purpose of safeguarding the use of the Apostles' Creed as the baptismal Creed of the Western Church. 'It was agreed that this Term should be redrafted by the Chairman and the Metropolitan of Thyateira,'[52] again working together.

In more recent conversations involving Orthodox and Roman Catholics, the difficulty has been voiced that when a full committee meets only to agree with minor alterations a text prepared by

---

[51] Anglican–Orthodox Conversations, *Lambeth Occasional Reports, 1931–8* (London, 1948), pp. 64–5.
[52] Anglican–Orthodox Conversations, *Lambeth Occasional Reports, 1931–8* (London, 1948), p. 71.

subcommissions, that means that any dialogue has already taken place before the Full Commission has met.[53]

We can see in these examples patient and exploratory 'feeling the way' through conversation and writing to being able to say something together. [54]

It is not surprising, in view of their still experimental character, that the level of finish of more modern reports and agreed statements varies. Sometimes what is published is really a summary of work in progress. 'The final report' of the Pentecostalist–Roman Catholic conversations 'deliberately refrained from any attempt at a synthesis and offers instead the agreed revision of the five separate reports with which each session was invariably concluded'.[55] There is also considerable variation in the degree to which the text reflects the texture of the living process of interaction in conversation and drafting which we have been describing. A final report 'cannot . . . reproduce all the diversity of styles, plurality of theological method, heat of conviction and novelty of insight which went into the position papers and their discussion', stresses the Pentecostalist–Roman Catholic Commission. 'The commission's method was determined, among other things, by the desire in the case of each separate theme to produce a survey of the degree of agreement, disagreement and unresolved issues'; 'the following pages occasionally may still reveal certain inconsistencies, obstacles, reactions and surprises, we felt it impossible to eliminate these realistic features completely'.[56] There is an acknowledgement here that because the level of finish varies and because much has to go to keep things short, and also because the result is offered for discussion and modification, what a report gives is '. . . necessarily provisional "results" '.[57]

Sometimes, as in the case of the ARCIC texts, what is offered is a polished and substantive statement. But no report or agreed statement is envisaged as the last word. They are offered for reception and so for potential modification.

---

[53] Professor Megas Pharandros, one of the Greek Church's delegates made this point. See Colin Davey, 'Orthodox–Roman Catholic dialogue', *One in Christ*, 20 (1984), 346–64, p. 360.

[54] But the meeting had still not done what it had to do. 'The Bishop of Novi-Sad said that it was clear that they now agreed about what the Roman theologians called *traditio declarativa*. They had now to reach an agreement on *traditio constitutiva*. The Chairman intervened here because he saw that Canon Douglas was about to start a discussion of development ("Does the Orthodox Church . . . admit any change, addition or subtraction to be possible from the Faith of the early Church?") to say that he thought the Anglicans would be able to accept Professor Arseniev's statement.' Anglican–Orthodox Conversations, *Lambeth Occasional Reports*, *1931–8* (London, 1948), pp. 68–9.   [55] P–RC, 45; *Growth*, p. 430.

[56] P–RC, 45; *Growth*, p. 430.   [57] P–RC, 45; *Growth*, p. 430.

THE 'THESIS' METHOD

The participants in the late-nineteenth-century Bonn Reunion talks found the 'thesis' method useful as a means of stating their position at key points succinctly. It is striking that although the main axis of the debate was with the Orthodox, the propositions to which they achieved on the whole very ready agreement in this way were in areas traditionally in dispute with Roman Catholics. This was a false focus, and an indication of two besetting problems of bilateralism. There was no overt concern for implications for Roman Catholic relations because the axis of the present talk was with the Orthodox. At the same time, there was a blindness to many of the real central concerns of the Orthodox and a focus on issues which had been or continued to be live between Protestant and Roman Catholic churches in the West.

Plummer describes what happened:

We had now less than an hour left for the following propositions. 1. We agree, that the apocryphal or deuterocanonical books of the Old Testament are not of the same canonicity with the books contained in the Hebrew Canon. 2. That no translation of Holy Scripture can claim an authority superior to that of the original text. 3. That the reading of Holy Scripture in the vulgar tongue cannot lawfully be forbidden. 4. That, in general, it is more fitting and in accordance with the spirit of the Church, that the liturgy should be in a tongue understood by the people. [All these four were passed at once.] 5. That faith working by love, and not faith alone, is the means and condition of man's justification before God.[58]

This too was passed easily with a small change of wording 'to avoid misconception'. 'And not faith without love' was substituted for 'and not faith alone'. There followed a series of items on good works. 'Merit of condignity' was condemned 'because there is no proportion between the infinite good of the salvation promised by God and the finite merit [changed to 'good'] of man's good works'.(6) The doctrines of works of supererogation, *opera supererogationis,* and of the treasury of merit were condemned(7).

There is a sense in which almost all modern ecumenical reports and agreed statements use the 'thesis' method. They divide the text into brief paragraphs or even sentences, each of which is meant to stand on its own or in connection with the others, as compelling assent by its intrinsic reasonableness or its clear foundation in authority, especially

[58] Alfred Plummer, *Conversations with Dr Döllinger, 1870–90,* ed. R. Boudens (Louvain, 1985), p. 103, 1874.

scriptural authority. 'Recommendations' too have the format of theses or commonplaces. In some cases there is explicit identification of these statements as *theses*. The Anglican–Reformed dialogue produced a list of General Questions in their Report *God's Reign and our Unity*.[59] A list of theses was proposed by the Evangelical Church of Lippe, to add in front of *BEM* on Gospel, Scripture, tradition, Spirit and Word, mission and the ministry of the Word of God.[60] ARCIC I is in part an exception, with its 'onion' of concentric layers of interdependent argument.

Theses can be attempted only when the subject-matter of the conversation has been broken down into aspects. An example is the Eucharist text of *BEM* on institution. This stressed that it is a gift from Christ to Church, and uses the term *anamnesis* in citing the institution texts. It draws out the meal aspect, the kingdom aspect, the sacrament aspect.[61] It stresses that in each Eucharist God does work, renewing, giving assurance and pledge and gift of salvation.[62] It divides up aspects ((i) thanksgiving to the Father, (ii) memorial to Christ, (iii) invocation of the Spirit (done in a Trinitarian way),[63] (iv) communion of the faithful, (v) meal of the Kingdom).

So the 'thesis' method sees it as desirable to aim at brief, clear encapsulations of key points, to which it is hoped all may be brought to assent either because they are self-evidently true or because they can be demonstrated to be true. The self-evidency or demonstrability rests on assumptions deemed to be convincing to all reasonable people once they have grasped them.[64] This was an approach profoundly attractive in the Middle Ages, although, because it really only works for geometry, attempts to apply it in theology, politics and elsewhere were unsuccessful.[65] Its inherent limitation was discovered by Alan of Lille and Nicholas of Amiens at the end of the twelfth and the beginning of the thirteenth centuries. Both tried to use it to show how all Christian theology might be demonstrated to be true. Both found that the sequence could only be sustained so far, and then it fell into untidiness.[66]

---

[59] These vary a good deal in difficulty and answerability, and in what they expect by way of prior theological education in the user.

[60] G. Wainwright, 'Word and sacrament in the Churches' response to the Lima text', *One in Christ*, 24 (1988), 304–27, pp. 326–7.   [61] *BEM*, Eucharist, para. 1; *Growth*, p. 475.

[62] On meaning, para. 2, p. 476.   [63] Para. 14, p. 478.

[64] The *communis animi conceptio quod quisque probat auditam* of Boethius' *De hebdomadibus*.

[65] See my *Alan of Lille* (Cambridge, 1983) and *Problems of Authority in the Reformation Debates* (Cambridge, 1992).

[66] See my *Alan of Lille* (Cambridge, 1983) and *Problems of Authority in the Reformation Debates* (Cambridge, 1992).

In form, theses or articles allow for a good deal of flexibility. They can be 'presented tentatively'[67] rather than as a *fait accompli*, and they can be tested by debate. They may take the form of questions, as in this example: 'What are the points which constitute the fundamental expression of "our unique Orthodoxy"?' asks C. Constantidinis; 'What are the points which represent the differentiated aspects of our unique Orthodoxy in its autocephalous parts without breaking unity?'; 'What are the points which can reinforce the expression and manifestation of the unity existing in "our Orthodoxy"?'[68] Theses may be propositions.[69] Or they may be seen as 'guiding principles'. All these have respectable ancestry in the scholastic and Reformation traditions. In fact they are one of the chief continuations from scholastic to post-scholastic theological methodology which are still found valuable.

The problem with the thesis method is that statements, even though presented in the intention that they shall compel assent by their reasonableness, always carry with them a baggage of unstated assumptions. Hans Küng, for example, devised such 'guiding principles for contemporary theology' in *Existiert Gott?* They demonstrate the adaptability of the thesis method to the concerns of the modern world. The fifth of his principles, for instance, states that 'We need neither hostile confrontation not easy coexistence, but rather a critical dialogue especially between theology and philosophy, theology and natural science.' Here, several value-judgements are made – that critical dialogue is a good, midway between a vague tolerance and outright confrontation, and that the focal interface is between theology, and philosophy and natural science. The sixth says, 'problems of the past should not have priority over the wide-ranging, multifaceted dilemmas of contemporary humanity and society'. Another makes the assumption that there is an unavoidable rivalry between the need to mend old hostilities, and giving energy and concern to the problems which press in modern society; and that a choice has to be made in preference for the latter. The tenth has it that 'we must avoid a confessionalistic ghetto mentality. Instead we should espouse an ecumenical vision that takes into consideration the

---

[67] G. Tavard,'Theses on future forms of the ministry', Editorial , *Journal of Ecumenical Studies*, 5 (1968), 726–9, p. 729.

[68] C. Constantidinis,'Les points d'unité et de différentiation de notre unique Othodoxie', *Istina*, 8 (1961–2), 83–100, p. 84.

[69] Edward J. Kilmartin, 'The Orthodox–Roman Catholic dialogue on the Eucharist', *Journal of Ecumenical Studies*, 13 (1976), 213–21, p. 214.

world religions as well as contemporary ideologies: as much tolerance as possible toward those things outside the Church, toward the religious in general, and the human in general, and the development of that which is specifically Christian belong together.'[70] 'Ecumenism' here is at its most broadly conceived. Küng seeks to include interreligious relations and every aspect of modern thought and political concern without exploring the crucial difference between Christian ecumenical purpose and the wider one.

Fries and Rahner produced 'theses', too, with a more specifically Christian ecumenical slant. These, in comparison with Küng's, rely less on a conviction of the compelling quality of certain assumptions and more on a set of structural dynamics of mutuality. But these, too, contain assumptions. They say, for example:

1. The foundational truths of Christianity, as these are expressed in Scripture and Creeds 'are mandatory on all particular Churches (teilkirchen) within the future single Church'.

2. 'In no particular Church may a doctrinal proposition (Satz) be rejected in a deliberate and confessional way if that doctrinal proposition is a mandatory dogma in another particular Church'... 'no express, positive confessional statement in one particular Church is to be required as mandatory in another particular Church' (except what is comprised in it).

3. 'In the single Church of Jesus Christ, formed from the uniting Churches, there are regional particular Churches which can continue to keep their previous structures... in one and the same territory.'

4a. All are to recognise the Petrine ministry of the Pope as 'a concrete guarantee of the unity of the Church in truth and love'; the Pope is to recognise and respect the independence of the Teilkirchen.[71]

As an example of 'theses' produced not by individual theologians but at an official level we might take the Lambeth Conference Resolutions.[72] Here, as in the case of the Küng, Fries and Rahner examples, there are assumptions behind. The text of Lambeth Conference Resolution I states 'That each Province respect the decision and attitudes of other Provinces... without such respect necessarily indicating acceptance of the principles involved, maintaining the highest possible degree of communion with the Provinces which

---

[70] H. Küng, 'Toward a new consensus in Catholic (and ecumenical) theology', *Journal of Ecumenical Studies*, 17 (1980), 1–17, pp. 13–4.

[71] A. Nichols, ' "Einigung der Kirchen": an ecumenical controversy', *One in Christ*, 21 (1985), 139–66, pp. 141–53, on H. Fries and K. Rahner, *Einigung der Kirchen – reale Möglichkeit* (Friedberg, 1983), tr. R. C. I. Gritsch and E. E. Gritsch as *Unity of the Churches – a Real Possibility* (New York, 1984).

[72] See my article in *Quadrilateral at One Hundred*, ed. J. Robert Wright (London, 1988).

differ.'[73] Tillard points out that the acceptance of the first Resolution by the 1988 Lambeth Conference was unequivocally an approbation of the principle of local autonomy. Even if this was done to avoid worse, he suggests, Lambeth 1988 'chose an ecclesiological option'.[74] It would be easy to multiply instances of the problem of hidden assumption which always bedevils the thesis method.

A set of theses was prepared by the Baptist–Reformed conversations at their meeting at Rüschlikon in 1976.[75] The commission italicise the key points which constitute the theses themselves, and each is provided with an explanatory gloss, which sometimes also serves the purpose of taking the argument forward to the next thesis.

The Holy Spirit, baptism and membership in the Church of Christ.

1. *Both in the Reformed and in the Baptist tradition, there has been emphasis on the work of the Holy Spirit in bringing men and women to salvation and on baptism as a sign of this regenerating activity of God himself . . .*

2. *In our discussions we have made progress in relating these two viewpoints by considering that a sign exists for purposes of communication.* We have therefore asked ourselves to whom the sign of baptism is addressed. Our answer is twofold. . . . it is addressed to man with good news from God, of incorporation into Christ and the benefits of his death and resurrection . . . It is addressed from man to God in a confession of faith . . . this dual character of baptism . . . leads us to affirm its character as action of God by his Holy Spirit . . .

3. *Hence, Christian baptism is to be understood in relation to the work of the Holy Spirit . . .*

4. *Baptism is a powerful sign of God's saving grace and, by virtue of the action of the Holy Spirit in it, an effective instrument of grace, actually imparting what it promises . . .*

5. *Because of the Spirit's action, baptism is effective through personal response . . .*

6. *The Reformed emphasis on the priority of God's grace in baptism and the Baptist accent on man's active participation in the baptismal event are, in a sense, complementary and as such contribute to ecumenical rapprochement . . .*

7. *Our conversations have made us realise again that the ecclesiological and sociological context of baptismal practice must always be carefully considered . . .*

8. *While we affirm the New Testament view of Baptism as a once-for-all incorporation into the church, the body of Christ, we propose to view baptism in the context of the Spirit's total action upon the total life of the individual and the Christian community . . .*

It is at this point that the crucial difference between Baptist and Reformed thinking has to be addressed. This is attempted in a commentary on the thesis just stated.

[73] *The Truth Shall Make You Free* (London, 1988), p. 201.
[74] J. M. R. Tillard, 'La leçon œcuménique de Lambeth 88', *Irénikon*, 61 (1988), 530–6, p. 532.
[75] *Growth*, pp. 135 and 144 ff.

Baptists hold that the work of the Spirit in Christian nurture begins before baptism and that baptism should take place only when the Spirit has engendered the beginnings of an answer of faith . . . The Reformed recognise this as an appropriate order of events in the case of adult converts, but also believe that the Spirit's work of nurture can appropriately take place after his work in baptism for those who are brought to receive baptism within the community of faith . . .

9. *We propose to regard the children of believers – Baptist and Reformed – as being involved in a process of preparation for the full privileges and responsibilities of membership in the church of Christ: they are already within the operational sphere of the Holy Spirit . . .*

10. *In either case, the Spirit willing, the result is actual membership in the church in the Full New Testament sense of the word 'member'.*

The thesis pattern breaks down at this point, in that the last two italicised 'theses' are mere statements of record.

11. *We are thankful to God for this mutual recognition of each other's good standing as Christians . . .*

12. *Our conversations have not produced any arguments or excuses for indiscriminate baptism or for the relaxation of baptismal discipline.*

This text offers two more series of theses, one on ministry and one on the Church. The series on 'The Church – local and universal' preserves the 'thesis and comment' pattern of the first series.

2. *The church is first and foremost an event,* rather than an institution; the church 'exists' in that it continually 'happens', namely where the Lord effectively exercises his rule and where it is recognised and accepted.

3. *The one holy universal Christian church becomes concrete in the local congregation.* The local congregation is not a sub-department of the one church of Christ, but manifests and represents it. This is generally recognised today, as for example by the Roman Catholic Church at its Second Vatican Council.

4. *At the same time the local congregation is necessarily related to other local congregations.* In itself it is not the universal church of Christ. The local congregation which isolates itself from its sister congregations impairs the character of the true church and becomes sectarian.

5. *Thus the wider church relationships . . . have ecclesiological significance.* Church 'happens' not only where Christians gather as a congregation, but also where congregations meet as such or through their appointed representatives. There also the one Lord builds his one church.

This experiment illustrates clearly the naturalness of trying to frame ecumenical statements in brief, clear units, and at the same time the limitation that they will rarely stand without explanation or proviso. It also underlines the need for a good deal more study and development of the uses of this method.

THE MECHANISMS OF WORKING TOGETHER

Each ecumenical commission has had to find machinery to enable it to work effectively. I shall take the example of ARCIC I here because in many respects it was a pioneer. There were three meetings of the Joint Preparatory Commission of ARCIC I, culminating in the Malta meeting. Two joint sub-commissions were proposed, one to examine 'the question of intercommunion'; the other to look at 'the question of authority'.[76] Eight of those who had been on the preparatory commission continued on ARCIC. The Malta Report sets out basic principles. It saw that a 'new stage' had been reached.[77] It commented on the mood of charity and frankness at the three meetings. It spoke of the realisation that penitence was needed for cherishing animosities and prejudices which 'for four hundred years have kept us apart and prevented our attempting to understand or to resolve our difficulties'.[78] So there was an awareness that something qualitatively new was afoot, that sense that something has moved within an apparently intractable situation, with which renewal and reconciliation begin.

It is possible to identify an ARCIC I methodology at several levels. The first and simplest is that of devising machinery for getting the job done.[79] At the first meeting (Windsor, 1970), the themes of Eucharist, ministry and authority were discussed in relation to the common concept of *koinonia*, with position papers prepared beforehand. More preparatory papers were brought to the second meeting later the same year, including some drawn from outside the commission.

The problem of shortage of time began to be felt at this meeting. Three consultants presented papers on moral issues, but it proved impossible to give detailed consideration to these as well as the subjects of Eucharist, ministry and authority on which the commission was now focussing its efforts. The same problem of crowding made the commission decide to take one subject at a time at its future meetings.

The working texts of the 1970 meeting on Eucharist, ministry and

---

[76] M. Richards, 'Twenty-five years of Anglican–Roman Catholic Dialogue – where do we go from here?', *One in Christ*, 18 (1992), 126–35, p. 131.

[77] Text in ARCIC I, *The Final Report*, Malta 1, p. 108.

[78] Text in ARCIC I, *The Final Report*, Malta 1, p. 108.

[79] Practical doing together what can be done together and an acknowledgement that things will take time, which makes it necessary to ask what can be done for the present, also came into the reckoning at Malta. ARCIC I, *The Final Report*, 9–10 and 18.

authority were published in three journals in 1971.[80] This was done with the express purpose of inviting discussion. 'It is vital that the work done and the progress made should be shared by a wider public, especially by other theologians. Hence the commission cannot wait to utter until it has reached finality. The present documents simply indicate what has so far emerged . . . They express work done in hard and serious collaboration and discussion.' . . . 'Members of the commission would each feel free to participate in the further, wider discussion which it is hoped the publication of the drafts will promote.'[81] This policy was not followed up by subsequent meetings, and there has been a good deal of variation of practice in bilateral conversations on this point.[82]

For the main meeting of 1971 the concentration was upon the statement on the Eucharist. A set of short papers on eucharistic sacrifice, and Anglican and Roman Catholic position papers on the real presence prepared for this meeting had made it possible to arrive remarkably quickly at an agreed statement. There was a meeting of a sub-commission, or smaller working group, at Poringland in April, which produced a draft for the commission to revise, and at the September meeting there was again work in three sub-groups, concentrating on problems of presence and sacrifice. This method of taking soundings on an issue through position papers, settling on key points of difficulty, and then sharpening concentration upon them by working in close-up on an experimental text, often in small groups, became the consistent pattern of work. The use of 'sub-commissions' has had the double value of spreading resources (so that the commission could work on more points at a time); and perhaps also of creating a special dynamics of intimacy among a few minds at a time, from which a drafting-group can benefit.

It is instructive to compare the 'working together' which was taking place here with the much more limited process at the end of the Malines conversations. The Anglicans and the Roman Catholics who took part in the Malines conversations prepared separate accounts

---

[80] *The Clergy Review, Theology* and *One in Christ.*

[81] *The Clergy Review*, 56 (1971), 126–145, pp. 126–7.

[82] For example, in the Methodist–Roman Catholic conversations a first series of conversations which produced the Denver Report (1971) was followed by a second which built on it as ground-work on many of the same topics, and resulted in the Dublin Report of 1976. See *Growth*, pp. 307 ff. for the texts. The Anglican–Lutheran *Niagara Report* (London, 1988), published the background papers in a supplementary collection. ARCIC I has left it to contributors of such papers to publish them independently as they choose and has not put its own working papers together in a published form.

afterwards, the Anglicans for the Archbishop of Canterbury. Both sides' versions were then 'read, discussed and amended by both parties acting in collaboration'.[83] There was still a sense at Malines that two 'sides' were trying to collaborate. ARCIC had by now got beyond that to a full working together. The setting out of 'what Roman Catholics think' and 'what Anglicans think' had been attempted by ARCIC at an early stage. It is reflected in the working texts published in 1971. The piece on 'Authority in the Church', for example, gives first a Roman Catholic view of *koinonia* and authority, and then the contrasting Anglican emphasis is set out. 'Measures of complete and imperfect or incomplete communion' encourage Roman Catholics to 'associate other bodies with the Roman Catholic Church to the extent that these other bodies possess, acknowledge, and utilize elements of that Christian wholeness which as a whole and indefectibly survive in the Roman Catholic Church'. 'The Anglican Communion has never claimed to be the unique and complete embodiment of the Body of Christ.' 'Anglicans share with the Roman Catholic Church the fundamental doctrinal pattern, and are divided from it principally by the problem of papal authority (and what seems to Anglicans the occasionally autocratic style of *magisterium*, with the attendant problems of doctrines such as the Assumption which have been declared binding by papal declaration).'[84] But it quickly became plain that the 'sides' did not line up tidily. On any given point, Anglicans and Roman Catholics professed a mixed grouping of opinions. Doing together became natural as the 'sides' melted away.[85]

It proved possible to spend a little time at this meeting on social and cultural factors, too. Throughout the commission's work a consciousness of this larger agenda of issues concerning the Church's life was never far away, but again and again the extra matters had to be held over.

The next year's work (1972) concentrated upon ministry. Again there was a casting-about to get the general picture of the issues through position papers, not all from members of the commission. Asking for outside help has always been a feature of the working method of ARCIC. The result for this year was the drafting of two texts on ministry in the New Testament, and on apostolicity. This again is an important repeating motif. It is never possible in

[83] *The Conversations at Malines: Report Presented to the Archbishop of Canterbury by the Anglican Members* (Oxford, 1927), Supplement, p. 75.
[84] Paras. 9–14, *The Clergy Review* (1971), p. 129.
[85] See the discussion of 'role-reversal' earlier, pp. 55ff.

ecumenical work to foresee the exact shape or subject-matter of the final text, and working drafts may be concentrated about more than one pole before a sequence of topics can be settled on.

Before the meeting of 1973 there was joint work in Oxford on apostolic succession, on priesthood in Montreal and on ordination in South Africa. All this preparatory work was drawn together in a draft in June 1973, before the main meeting in September. There the draft's principal themes were laid down, and it was decided that the text of the final statement should concentrate on ministries in the life of the Church, the ordained ministry (with coverage of the terminology of 'priesthood'), and ordination (with a treatment of apostolic succession). This text, revised at the September meeting, was published the same year.

The Commission now turned back to authority in the following year. The areas of concentration which had emerged from preparatory work were upon the authority of Scripture, on *koinonia* and ecclesiology; on indefectibility and infallibility. Additional position papers were contributed by members of the Commission on schism, on *magisterium* in the early Church, on Vatican I and on the *sensus fidelium*. The primary themes to which the Commission addressed itself at its main meeting in 1974 were the authority of Scripture and the *sensus fidelium*. These were developed during 1975 to embrace the Lordship of Christ and the gifts of the Spirit. It also became plain that the exercise of authority in the Church would have to be explored, especially in relation to the primacy of the Bishop of Rome and jurisdiction. Two sub-commissions tackled, respectively, primacy in relation to unity and infallibility; and truth in relation to councils.

In 1976 all this began to be co-ordinated by a series of meetings of sub-commissions, and material was added on primacy, collegiality and conciliarity, to produce the Agreed Statement on Authority in the Church, finished in 1976 and published in January 1977.

The main meeting of 1977 addressed itself to the responses which had been received to the three published statements. A policy decision was taken to produce elucidations.[86] These Elucidations, on the Eucharist and Ministry texts, were published in June 1979. From 1979 to 1981 work focussed on the authority issues of the Petrine texts, *ius divinum*, jurisdiction, infallibility, which were to form the second Statement on Authority, together with reaction to responses received

---

[86] On ARCIC's 'Elucidations' see further Chapter 7.

to *Authority in the Church I*; and upon the framing of the introduction which was to deal with the ecclesiological basis, and especially with *koinonia*.

The Final Report was published in January, 1982.

During the period of ARCIC I's work, in 1977, a new Common Declaration was made by the Pope and the Archbishop of Canterbury. This invited comparison with the Common Declaration of 1966, which had spoken of 'fraternal relations', 'respect, esteem and fraternal love'. The new text emphasised the existence of 'communion with God in Christ, . . . even while between us communion remains imperfect'.[87] The Preface to *The Final Report* commented on this second Common Declaration that it provided 'a striking endorsement of a central theme of our Statements' in what it thus had to say about a brotherhood which was also communion *in via*. 'In other words, the *koinonia* which is the governing concept of what follows here is not a static concept – it demands movement forward, perfecting.'[88]

Foundation principles

When the First Anglican–Roman Catholic Commission began its work it also had to fashion a methodology at a deeper level than that of a method which made it possible to use its time efficiently and to utilise preparatory work in these ways. At both the practical and the deeper levels of methodology it was possible for the commission to say 'we learned as we progressed'.[89]

A number of topics were proposed for dialogue in the Malta Report, on which in the end no report was published by ARCIC I, but which were discussed at a methodological level in the course of its conversations: the relationship between the notion of fundamentals (Anglican) and that of the hierarchy of truths (Roman Catholic); the relation between revealed truths and the manner of their formulation; how far what had once been seen as conflicting could come to be seen as complementary.[90]

The last of these has proved invaluable as an underlying motif in many bilateral conversations as the sixteenth-century polarities of 'Scripture' against 'tradition', 'faith' against 'works' and so on have become a balancing of one with the other in their profound complementarity.

---

[87] In ARCIC I, *The Final Report*, para 9. cf. *The Clergy Review* (1966), p. 117.
[88] In ARCIC I, *The Final Report*, pp. 2–3.   [89] ARCIC I, *The Final Report*, Preface, p. 2.
[90] ARCIC I, *The Final Report*, 6, p. 110.

The first and second are deep issues philosophically as well as theologically. ARCIC I did not get far with them in the time available to it. Christopher Hill comments on the 'distinction between truth and the varying importance of truths as regards the ecumenical dialogue' and notes that 'ARCIC I attempted to use this theological distinction but in the end found it extremely difficult to do so.'[91] 'The object of a Definition of Faith, however it may be reached,' suggested the Roman Catholics at Malines, 'is not to formulate a newly invented dogma, unknown to Holy Scripture, of the tradition of the Church, but to declare explicitly and with authority, in regard to some given point, what is the faith entrusted by Jesus Christ to the keeping of the Church.'[92] In Chapter 2 of the Decree on Ecumenism, formulation of doctrine is distinguished from the deposit of faith itself. This is the line laid down by Pope John XXIII when he spoke to the opening session of the Council. 'I find that there is still not a sufficient appreciation of the truth that there is indeed a distinction between a doctrinal formulation and the deposit of faith it is designed to expresss. Only when this truth is appreciated can *particular formulations* be understood as contingent rather than necessary.'[93] The principle of making the distinction may be plain but the actual making is proving very difficult in modern ecumenical practice. In these areas ARCIC I's chief achievement was to see and begin to explore the difficulties at this deepest methodological level.

Explorations were more fruitful along another line. To agree is, at its best, to have in common. Anything less is mere toleration of persisting difference. So the first task was to discover what could be listed uncontroversially as 'common'. Here the obvious place to begin was the fifteen hundred years of shared tradition between Anglicans and Roman Catholics. Jean Tillard saw this clearly. It will be remembered that in his 'Windsor intervention'[94] he suggested to the commission that:

This commission will have to work according to the Spirit of Vatican II and especially of *Dei Verbum*. This means first that we shall have to discover, under our diverse and polemical expressions, the common 'tradition' from which we came. Our divergences are grounded in something that we shared in common, and probably continue to share even under our own polemical

---

[91] Quoted by C. Hill, 'The Decree on Ecumenism: an Anglican view', *One in Christ*, 26 (1990), 20–31, p. 28.
[92] *The Conversations at Malines: Report Presented to the Archbishop of Canterbury by the Anglican Members* (Oxford, 1927), Supplement, p. 75.
[93] C. Hill, 'The Decree on Ecumenism: an Anglican view', *One in Christ*, 26 (1992), 20–31, p. 25.
[94] J. M. R. Tillard provides this text.

words. Some of these words are used to save it! – it will, thus, be necessary to discover what we were saying together before the division. Perhaps, we shall be surprised to see that we are united precisely in the matters that we consider as 'doctrinal divergences'! To demonstrate that to our two Churches, it will be necessary to use the common vocabulary we were using before the shift (if we discover that our faith was the same), and to express our agreements in using these words, no longer the words from polemical disputes.[95]

From the attempt at establishing common ground a number of difficulties emerged. There is a class of issues on which the two churches proved to be not agreed, and yet not confessionally disagreed. (I.e., there was no official position at the time of the formal division of the two communions.) An important example is the topic of justification which was addressed by ARCIC II.[96] In such circumstances what is required is not simply a going back to shared faith, and expressing it for today, but a formulation of faith which can now be affirmed by both partners in conversation as faithful to their continuing traditions. That will be further complicated by the problem of issues which have become topical since, and sometimes in a way which challenges Christian tradition over against that of other faiths. ARCIC II found itself, for instance, asked to address the problem of the salvation of unbelievers.[97]

Both in the case of matters on which there was explicit disagreement at the Reformation, and of those on which there was not, divergences in formulation and emphasis since division have to be seen as 'separated reception'. Once that begins, it leads to separated experiences, formulations, elaborations, understandings,[98] and the separation of the common tradition into distinct traditions. Here we need an ecumenical historiography which is methodologically capable of doing two different things. It must be able to retrieve the common past, where that past existed. It must also be able to retrieve a part of the past which was not common, and make it something which can now be shared. That is much more difficult, as we saw earlier.

It has a third task, which is to look forward. The last major area of

---

[95] On this text, see also earlier, p. 45.
[96] ARCIC II, *Church as Communion*, 2, also notes that it 'does not focus specifically on doctrinal questions that have been historically divisive'.
[97] ARCIC II, *Salvation and the Church*, 'A question not discussed by the Commission, though of great contemporary importance, is that of the salvation of those who have no explicit faith in Christ. This has not been a matter of historical dispute between us.'
[98] ARCIC I, *The Final Report*.

methodological enquiry entered into by ARCIC I was that of the forward movement of what was agreed, the task of assenting to and apprehending dogmatic truths and agreeing legitimate means of understanding and interpreting them theologically. The Appeal of the 1920 Lambeth Conference spoke of 'forgetting the things which are behind and reaching out towards the goal of a reunited Catholic Church'. But that is not quite enough. We cannot 'forget' what remains and ought to remain living memory and has been constitutive for the lives of our churches as they are. ARCIC I thought it might be possible 'to discover each other's faith as it is today and to appeal to history only for enlightenment, not as a way of perpetuating past controversy'.[99] Certainly the last is right. But it has not proved possible or right to treat history as a source of information only and to concentrate entirely upon faith for today. The common and the separated past both have to be take into the present, and also into the future.[100]

That is necessary because as part of the processes of separated reception there has been historical conditioning of thought-forms and historical conditioning of language. The historiographical and the linguistic issues are shown in Tillard's 'Windsor' text to be intimately interrelated. ARCIC's assessment speaks of the importance of 'avoidance of the emotive language of past polemics'.[101] But again 'avoidance' will not work. The bad language has to be used in order to purge it of hatred, while at the same time a fresh vocabulary is found in which it will be possible to see the separated communions 'seeking to pursue together that restatement of doctrine which new times and conditions ... regularly' call for.[102] There has been real success here. There is much less linguistic tension. 'People are now talking to us as they do normally among themselves.'[103]

But the experience about language has also generated a salutary warning. A useful analogy can be drawn with learning languages.

---

[99] Preface to *The Final Report*, p. 2.
[100] ARCIC I's 1971 working piece on *Church and ministry*, speaks of a 'new situation' in which 'we have to show that a development of doctrine has occurred with regard to the theological presuppositions of the Bull [of 1896]. This ... would have to be shown to be consistent with the principle which has supported a quite different practice in the past ... if a consistent development of doctrine is to be demonstrated, we must show that no dogma has been denied, but that theological presuppostions have been changed', paras.15–16, *The Clergy Review*, (1971) pp. 142–3.   [101] Preface to *The Final Report*, p. 2.
[102] Preface to *The Final Report*, p. 2.
[103] M. Richards, 'Twenty-five years of Anglican–Roman Catholic dialogue – where do we go from here?', *One in Christ*, 18 (1992), 126–35, p. 127.

'After the first painful steps, we are delighted to find ourselves being understood and understanding other people.' Then we discover it is not so easy after all and that communication has run into difficulties.[104] ARCIC I defended its use of *anamnesis* and of 'become' in the Eucharist text, in its Elucidations, because the former has been thought to 'conceal the reintroduction of the theory of a repeated immolation, and the latter had been 'suspected of expressing a materialistic conception of Christ's presence'.[105] 'Behind these criticisms', ARCIC commented, 'there lies a profound but often unarticulated anxiety that the commission has been using new theological language which evades unresolved differences.' Critics ask, 'Does the language of the commission conceal an ambiguity (either intentional or unintentional) in language which enables members of the two churches to see their own faith in the Agreed Statement without having in fact reached a genuine consensus?'[106] 'Our intention', says ARCIC, 'has been to seek a deeper understanding of the reality of the Eucharist which is consonant with biblical teaching and with the tradition of our common inheritance, and to express in this document the consensus we have reached.'[107]

The Lambeth 1920 Appeal:

pointed to an external unity which was not to be a mere federation, but a re-incorporation of the severed parts into one united body. The second suggested a policy, not of surrender, but of revision and reunion founded on the acceptance of what was held to be de fide by the Universal Church from the beginning. Further, that all controversies of the past should be reconsidered in this spirit, as was exemplified by the fact that the Anglican Bishops assembled at Lambeth had stated for themselves and their clergy that they were ready to accept from the authorities of other Churches whatever form might be considered necessary in order that the Anglican ministry could be fully recognised by them, providing an agreement has already been reached upon all the points which had hitherto divided them . . . setting a conspicuous example of humility and making a great sacrifice for the sake of unity.[108]

It thus foresaw to some degree the cost of the mutuality which requires humility and sacrifice and willingness to change; but which

---

[104] M. Richards, 'Twenty-five years of Anglican–Roman Catholic dialogue – where do we go from here?', *One in Christ*, 18 (1992), 126–35, p. 127.

[105] ARCIC I, *The Final Report*, Eucharist, Elucidations, 5, 6.

[106] ARCIC I, *The Final Report*, Eucharist, Elucidations, 3.

[107] ARCIC I, *The Final Report*, Eucharist, Elucidations, 1.

[108] Lord Halifax, *Notes on the Conversations at Malines, 1921–5. Points of Agreement* (London, 1928), p. 8.

also commands respect for 'things as they are' in each community. That above all is what the ARCIC methodology has been working at. It needs to be said that it is paradoxical to proceed on the assumption that each side is willing to change while not requiring change of the other. It is an ecumenical 'after you, Claude', in which there is a contest in ecclesial courtesy. It is inseparable from the other paradox of ecumenism, that we become one by being one. Both require risk and commitment to a future in trust. Christopher Hill points in a recent article[109] to the tension between the unity signified by the Eucharist and the grace of unity given through the Eucharist. To meet in one celebration of the Eucharist is a sign that unity has been achieved. To celebrate the Eucharist together is to be open together to the work of grace which alone will bring that unity into being.

[109] C. Hill, 'The Decree on Ecumenism: an Anglican view', *One in Christ*, 26 (1992), 20–31, p. 26.

CHAPTER 7

Ecumenical reception

WHAT IS ECUMENICAL RECEPTION?

Pope Paul VI spoke, in front of the non-Catholic observers at the Second Vatican Council, of 'the true treasures of truth and spirituality which you possess'.[1] This was an acknowledgement of a need for all churches to address not only ways of receiving and maintaining the common truths of the faith together, but the task of receiving from one another things which each is especially qualified to contribute.[2]

Conversely, reception cannot be complete while separated traditions cling to consciousness of difference of belief. In the 1930s we find 'The representatives of the Anglican Church would say . . .'; 'The representatives of the Eastern Orthodox Church would say . . .'.[3] Such assertions can still be heard, as we shall see in a moment. Such clinging amounts to a 'looking backward to particular traditions', and that (argues Lukas Vischer), clearly cannot be the last word if we are looking forward to unity.[4]

That is not to imply in any way that the separate traditions have to be abandoned. Within each, reception has been going on. The problem is simply that it has been going on in division. The separated reception-processes with their varied emphases and special insights therefore stand in need of completion by being received by the rest of

[1] A. Ganoczy, 'La structure collégiale de l'Eglise chez Calvin et au IIe Concile du Vatican', *Irénikon*, 38 (1965), 6–32, p. 32.
[2] A useful summary of aspects of reception is given by Harding Meyer and Lukas Vischer, *Growth*, pp. 8–9. See W. Rusch, *Reception: An Ecumenical Opportunity* (Philadelphia, 1988); E. Sullivan, 'Reception – factor and movement in ecumenism', *Ecumenical Trends*, 15 (1986), 107; A. Houtepen's articles in the *Dictionary of the Ecumenical Movement* and in *Ecumenical Perspectives on Baptism, Eucharist and Ministry* (Geneva, 1983). See, too, the article by Roger Greenacre, in *Christian Authority: Essays in Honour of Henry Chadwick*, ed. G. R. Evans (Oxford, 1988).
[3] Anglican–Orthodox Conversations, *Lambeth Occasional Reports, 1931-8* (London, 1948), p. 50.
[4] 'The summons to unity is too deeply rooted for it to be possible to ignore or overlook it.' L. Vischer, 'The reception of consensus in the ecumenical movement', *One in Christ*, 17 (1981), 294–305, p. 295.

Christendom.[5] The recognition that there has been separated reception is an acknowledgement that positions stated by only a proportion of the body of the faithful must ultimately be tested by the whole. That means that churches have to receive ecumenically what they had no direct part in producing. By definition that must end separation. So we have a profoundly important paradox. The separated traditions are to be respected and perhaps remain distinct. But they are also to be humble and open to change, so that they cease to be separated. The crucial difference here is between 'distinct' and 'separate'.

All this means that the reception-processes needed to bring together and maintain in unity a future united Church are different in some respects from the reception-processes of the past, because of this duality of 'receiving from one another' and 'receiving together'. This compounds the ancient difficulties of balancing the 'official' processes of reception in councils and synods with the complexities of formation of the consensus of all the faithful. Max Thurian stressed in his preface to the first volume of the responses to the *BEM* text of the World Council of Churches that what was being asked for in this case was a 'receiving' by the still ecclesially separated bodies judging as well as they could whether not only their own faith but the common faith was set out there. He stressed in his definition of this process the second of the two elements in 'ecumenical receiving'. 'The real significance of the "reception" of the Lima document has perhaps not been sufficiently explained. There is no question of "receiving" it in the same way that decisions of the ecumenical councils have formerly been received in the Churches, i.e. as texts recognised as authoritative explanations of the word of God. The Churches are asked to say whether they recognise in the Lima documents "the faith of the Church through the ages".'[6] That amounts to asking whether the reception which has taken place in separation has really after all been part of a common task, which can now be recognised as such, although that was not apparent during the centuries of separation.

Many churches conscientiously tried to do this in their responses to *BEM*. But in the event the first element (that of receiving individually by the still-separated churches) was more prominent. There was a

[5] It is worth quoting again the words of Pope John Paul II (in an address of 30 November 1979, in the context of Orthodox–Roman Catholic rapprochement): 'We must not be afraid to reconsider, on both sides, and in consultation with one another, canonical rules established when awareness of our communion . . . was still dimmed. These rules perhaps no longer correspond to the results of the dialogue of charity.' Stormon, p. 362.
[6] Max Thurian, Preface, *Churches Respond to BEM*, I, p. 9.

general conscious sense that the reception of the texts agreed between churches has to take place in the first instance in each, even if with reference to the whole. The Church of Greece, for example, said that it studied *BEM* 'both from the viewpoint of Orthodox tradition and theology . . . and from the viewpoint of the special process of their "reception" by each one of the WCC's member Churches.'[7] 'Our Church considers itself in duty bound to engage in this reception process, since it proclaims Jesus Christ . . . as "the Lord of the one, holy catholic and apostolic Church", acknowledges itself "called to the constant renewal of its life" and heeds "the views of Christians both of its own and other confessions",' said the North Elbian Evangelical Lutheran Church, citing the preamble to its constitution. It went on to comment that 'divisions have been detrimental to us all', so that 'we all need the mutual help which the ecumenical fellowship affords'.[8] The Old Catholic Church of Switzerland said, 'we expressly welcome the fact that the question is about the "faith of the Church through the ages", as this is a challenge, especially to all those churches which have come into being during the second millennium, to reconsider anew their understanding of the historical continuity of the faith, for instance with the critical question in mind: does this continuity for each denomination only begin at the times of its emergence which itself stands in ahistorical[9] immediacy to the New Testament?'[10]

Some churches felt themselves especially well-placed to undertake this new kind of reception. Old Catholics reflected on the fact that their 'theology' had 'been formed in ecumenical discussions for a long time in spite of all orientation towards the ancient Church'.[11] The Evangelical Church in Baden remarked that 'the first ordinances at the time of the Reformation for the churches in the territory that was later to become Land Baden already showed a desire to "maintain uniformity" with neighbouring churches, and also to be open to a concept of at least "an overall protestant Church" '.[12] 'It is distinctive of the Moravian Church . . . that they have not developed their own doctrinal system,' claimed the European Continental Province of the Moravian Church in its response to *BEM*.[13] 'It broadens our

---

[7] *Churches Respond to BEM*, V, p. 1.   [8] *Churches Respond to BEM*, I, p. 39.
[9] 'Ahistorical' seems to mean here an interruption in historical continuity rather than standing outside history.
[10] *Churches Respond to BEM*, V, p. 8, the Old Catholic Church of Switzerland.
[11] *Churches Respond to BEM*, V, pp. 8–9 , the Old Catholic Church of Switzerland.
[12] *Churches Respond to BEM*, V, p. 33.   [13] *Churches Respond to BEM*, IV, p. 115.

horizons; we learn from the conceptions of other churches,' re this community.[14]

Others have been conscious of the need to balance an over duty to their own traditions against their duty to the whole Church through the ages. 'An approach the Reformation Churches could not adopt without betraying Protestant truth' would be unacceptable to the Swiss Protestant Church Federation.[15] The Evangelical Lutheran Church in Bavaria attempts 'to describe the extent to which understanding and rapprochement are possible today between the various churches *each in its own tradition*' (my italics).[16] This sometimes bred a negative response. Lukas Vischer sums up:

In general the Churches examined the texts first of all to check whether they agreed with their own particular teaching and praxis. They did not, conversely, ask in how far the consensus challenged and corrected the teaching and praxis of that Church. They read the growing agreement . . . in the light of their own convictions. They did not make the effort to look at their own Churches in the light of the growing consensus. If the texts harmonised with the particular tradition, they were applauded.[17] [and] So far the Churches are still far from convinced that the community of Churches can come into being only if they are prepared for reforms.[18]

But there were unexpected bonuses in the form of subtle changes in attitude and new realisations. As early as the Anglican–Orthodox conversations of the 1930s it was possible for one side to consider whether a given text corresponded not only with its own views, but also with those of the other side. 'Are the Terms of Intercommunion drawn up . . . regarded by the Committee of the Lambeth Conference as expressing the mind of the Anglican Church, and, if not, where and in what do they diverge from that mind?'[19] asked the Orthodox. Several Churches responding to *BEM* noted the stimulus they had discovered in talking locally. 'The Lima text has already achieved considerable significance within our Church, since it has caused congregations and various bodies to discuss Baptism, Eucharist and Ministry afresh.'[20] This stimulus was the sharper where it was recognised that this particular process involved trying to think together with others, or at least taking others' views into account.

[14] *Churches Respond to BEM*, IV, p. 123, United German Mennonite Congregations.
[15] *Churches Respond to BEM*, IV, p. 74.   [16] *Churches Respond to BEM*, IV, p. 201.
[17] L. Vischer, 'The reception of consensus in the ecumenical movement', *One in Christ*, 17 (1981), 294–305, p. 300.   [18] Ibid.
[19] Anglican–Orthodox Conversations, *Lambeth Occasional Reports, 1931–8* (London, 1948), p. 96.
[20] *Churches Respond to BEM*, V, p. 94, Evangelical Church of Kurhessen-Waldeck.

Some traditions were especially sensitive to this kind of learning, because they had always made it a principle to be open to something of the sort. 'The question which, as Friends, we are enjoined regularly to ask of ourselves', pointed out the Quakers, 'is "Is your distinctive Quaker witness characterised by humility and a willingness to learn from others?"' [21] 'The bold personal adventure [must be] tempered by humility in the face of individual fallibility and by the necessity for sharing experience with others.' [22]

We might summarise the stages. The Church asked to receive a report asks itself, 'Is this what we believe?'. It asks itself, 'Is this what (all) other Christians believe?' It asks itself, 'Should we revise our beliefs in the light of this, or at least reexpress them so that it is clear that this is what we also believe?' [23] So it is becoming clear that successful reception will require a consciousness of the provisionality of existing ecclesial bodies and an openness to change of heart. [24]

This is a new area in the theology of 'development' because it envisages the possibilities both that right developments may have been taking place in the separated churches which can now be brought together in the Church as a whole, and that in the coming together that development gradually becomes the possession of all the churches together. It must also allow for the possibility that developments which have taken place in separated communities can sometimes stand in need of correction or adjustment to make them

---

[21] *Churches Respond to BEM*, IV, p. 214.   [22] *Churches Respond to BEM*, IV, p. 215.

[23] On willingness to change see earlier, pp. 40ff. 'In receiving the Lima document the Churches are receiving themselves,' noted Nikos Nissiotis shrewdly. 'What is now required of them is a new spirit of convergence in theology and practice, calling for a change in their way of looking at church divisions namely, looking at them now from within a church fellowship . . . Conversion means that each separate confessional family now regards the others with a renewed determination to appreciate them as sharers in the same apostolic tradition.' 'In receiving the Lima document, the confessional families must share a corporate openness which obliges them to take up new stances expressing their awareness of having adopted a radically new way of approaching the problem of church unity entailing a positive appreciation of the faith and practice of others outside their confessional family, firstly, as possible within the one apostolic tradition, secondly, as challenging their own expression of that tradition, and thirdly, as no longer dividing them but as calling them towards a consensus.' But the sharpest lesson has been 'how difficult it is for the churches to undertake an ecumenical conversion of this kind'. *Churches Respond to BEM*, III, p. xii.

[24] 'For the sake of Christian unity conversion is absolutely necessary . . . and this not once but many times. We must be ready to rethink many of our cherished positions in greater obedience to the Word of God.' 'Can we produce unity by negotiating intelligently with other Churches? This cannot be done unless it is the outcome of a reform movement . . . unless reconciliation is the fruit of renewal, the resulting union will be burdened by the combined failings of the uniting Churches.' Editorial, *Journal of Ecumenical Studies*, 1 (1964), p. 106.

acceptable as common, an expression which now has some claim to be thought of as a technical term.

This is close to what Congar describes as re-reception. 'Reception is that process whereby, in the case of the dogmatic teaching of Pope and bishop, the faithful come to find such teaching beneficial and to live by it faithfully. Re-reception means giving defined doctrine a new context, and a better equilibrium, through situating it more squarely within the overall witness of revelation – in the hope that even greater benefits and fruitfulness may come, not least for those who have had difficulty with an earlier formulation.'[25] But ecumenically it must have a new twist, because the 'situating more squarely' is consciously a situating within a common faith shared by all Christians everywhere.

Reception as recognition

When the people of God 'receive' an ecumenical text as expressing their own faith in the 'faith of the Church through the ages'; or are able to recognise in a union of churches that the resulting Church is the Church of the Apostles, they make an act of recognition.[26] In that act, suggests Tillard, there comes into being a 'sphere of mutual understanding within which there can take place the "recognition" of the evangelical authenticity of what the other group has always considered to be its peculiar character . . . also the "recognition" of the limits and even the errors of one's own group in this matter'.

So recognition is inseparable, paradoxically, both from acceptance of the provisionality of what has gone before in the hitherto separated communities, and from the perception that something enduring persists and is sustained in them. That perception of what is permanent common property involves a rediscovery of something already known but, because of old divisions, not hitherto fully 'owned'. To take an example:

We believe that a pattern can be discerned. When Anglicans and Roman Catholics meet to discuss their faith as openly and honestly as possible, they find that attentiveness to the other's articulation of his or her own faith leads to a point of recognition when each discerns their [sic] faith in the other's articulation of their belief. At this stage there develops a deep conviction that

---

[25] Nichols, *Congar*, p. 111 and cf. Y. Congar, *Diversity and Communion*, tr. J. Bowden (London, 1984), p. 171.

[26] G. Tavard speaks of 'the recognisability of faith'. G. Tavard, 'Ecumenical theology and the Catholic Church', *One in Christ*, 25 (1989), 101–13.

at a fundamental level, Anglicans and Roman Catholics *are* in agreement in the living faith once delivered to the Apostles.[27]

'Recognition is very important for ecclesiology. It is not synonymous with conversion but means something else and is very rich,'[28] continues Tillard. The 'something else' would seem to involve the duality we have been picking up from the world-wide responses to *BEM*, a reception which takes place in common with others, and at the same time as a receiving by each church for itself of the special insights of other churches. It has this in common with conversion, that the experience seems characteristically to contain the senses of both 'becoming new' and 'coming home'.

Convergence to consensus

For the most part, the responses to *BEM* saw the distinction between convergence and consensus in terms which made the first no more than a step on the way to the second. *BEM* was described as 'a paper of convergence and not yet of consensus'.[29] 'The *BEM* document does not yet represent full agreement ("consensus") among the churches, but it is the closest they have ever come to an expression of their common faith ("convergence").'[30] 'The synod welcomes the intention of assisting the dialogue between the divided churches by way of convergences identified in these three texts, even though this reveals that the process cannot yet lead to full agreement and retains its preliminary character.'[31] So it was recognised that one was meant to lead to the other. But questions were put about the way this could happen. One church described it as 'a convergence text with the intention of stimulating consensus in the churches'. But it noted, 'The relationship of these concepts to each other is, however, not always clear.'[32] The Ecumenical Patriarchate of Constantinople 'would like to see this term ["convergence"] clarified. What exactly does it mean?' it asks. 'Does [it] imply the first steps towards a more general

---

[27] 'Canadian ARC: remarks on the CDF's "Observations on the Final Report of ARCIC"', April 1983', *One in Christ*, 20 (1984), 257–72, p. 260.
[28] J. M. R. Tillard, 'The ecclesiological implications of bilateral dialogue', *Journal of Ecumenical Studies*, 23 (1986), 412–23, p. 413.
[29] *Churches Respond to BEM*, V, p. 161, Reformed Church in Hungary.
[30] *Churches Respond to BEM*, V, Melanesian Council of Churches.
[31] *Churches Respond to BEM*, V, p. 94, Evangelical Church of Kurhessen-Waldeck.
[32] *Churches Respond to BEM*, IV, p. 100, Netherlands Reformed Church and Reformed Churches in the Netherlands.

"consensus"? or does it merely represent a rapprochement, as great as possible, towards a common goal not fully attainable?'[33] It was also asked where on the continuum from dissent to agreement a given 'convergence' text may be said to lie. To one Lutheran Church *BEM* seemed ' "a statement of convergence", which implies less than agreement yet more than dissent'.[34] There were comments suspicious that more was being claimed than perhaps ought to have been claimed here. The Waldensian and Methodist Churches in Italy contest 'the distinction between "convergence" and "consent" regarding a text that is being presented as a document of reciprocal agreement and acknowledgement'.[35]

Since it was 'only' convergence which was being judged, some thought that leeway could be allowed for inadequacies or even imprecision in *BEM*'s formulations. 'We take into account that they are convergence texts in which the faith of individual denominations does not have to be stated as adequately as would be the case with consensus texts.'[36] This would seem a dangerous concession on a number of counts. It implies that there is a working from the rough to the exact, rather than a continuous striving for exactness. And there is the equally unsatisfactory notion that in a process of convergence not all individual ecclesial bodies need to be fully included until a late stage.

There were comments in the *BEM* responses hostile to the whole conception of a convergence towards consensus. 'The churches of the magisterial and Reformation traditions plumb matters of truth by looking to confessions, asking whether believers believe truly'[37] (rather, it is implied, than by looking to convergence with others). More moderate reservations wanted room to manoeuvre in thinking out the balance between duty to the whole Church, and duty to the separated churches in which responders found themselves. 'The Lima document does not represent the results of a consensus-forming process but is a convergence document ... Within the Swiss Protestant Church Federation we have therefore asked ourselves how far *BEM* prompts us ... to rethink our ideas and how these are put into practice,' and yet at the same time 'to consider in what respects the

[33] *Churches Respond to BEM*, V, p. 3.
[34] *Churches Respond to BEM*, IV, p. 17, Evangelical Church of the Augsburg Confession (Austria).
[35] *Churches Respond to BEM*, I, p. 245.
[36] *Churches Respond to BEM*, V, p. 8, Old Catholic Church of Switzerland.
[37] *Churches Respond to BEM*, IV, p. 107, Church of the Brethren (USA).

BEM text seems to suggest an approach the Reformation Churches could not adopt without betraying Protestant truth'.[38] There were real challenges in all this to the force of the ancient principle that unanimity is a sign of faithfulness to apostolic truth. That was put squarely by the British Quakers. 'Consensus is but a measure of human agreement. The will of God may (uncomfortably) be what nobody . . . wants.'[39] An Anglican province also pointed to the danger of an 'apparent general consensus' being read, 'sometimes because of what is *not* said'.[40]

Agreement

'Lima is not intended to be a formula of agreement, to which all the parties involved can fully subscribe. In this respect it differs from bilateral statements such as the ARCIC Report.'[41] So we have to ask what do we mean by 'agreement'? Clearly half-hearted acceptance[42] is not enough, and cannot be a foundation on which to build up the one Church of Christ. Equally clearly, there must be no slipping back. 'The agreements already reached within the process of reception should not be abandoned again in the future.'[43] But there are definitional and conceptual difficulties to be addressed as soon as we proceed beyond that point. To agree is, at best, to have in common. Anything less is mere toleration of persisting difference.[44]

How much agreement?

(i) At one extreme lies the view that agreement means exact correspondence at all points. That is set out with its implications by Lindbeck:

Agreement must be comprehensively spelled out in detailed doctrinal formulations, and, furthermore, what is actually taught in the churches must conform to these formulations. One cannot be in communion with churches which, even if officially orthodox, nevertheless tolerate error, or are in communion with other churches which are in error.[45]

---

[38] *Churches Respond to BEM*, IV, p. 74, Swiss Protestant Church Federation.
[39] *Churches Respond to BEM*, IV, p. 215, Religious Society of Friends (Quakers) in Great Britain.
[40] *Churches Respond to BEM*, I, p. 55, Anglican Church of the Southern Cone.
[41] *Churches Respond to BEM*, I, p. 61, Church of Ireland.
[42] The occasional device of using a *placet iuxta modum* in Vatican II was agreement of such a sort.
[43] *Churches Respond to BEM*, V, p. 94.
[44] On this problem see Edward Yarnold's article in the Festschrift for Michael Hurley, reprinted in *Responses to ARCIC*, ed. C. Hill and E. Yarnold (London, 1994).
[45] G. A. Lindbeck, 'A Lutheran view of intercommunion with Roman Catholics', *Journal of Ecumenical Studies*, 13 (1976), 242–9, p. 243.

But it is important to set in contrast to this, I think unattractive, picture another mode of expression altogether of the principle that the ideal is to agree about everything. Here there is no talk of identical forms of words, but rather of a fullness of common faith. 'We would all agree that the attainment of Christian unity can never be the result of masking differences or searching for some lowest common denominator acceptable to all.' Indeed 'our efforts will only be fruitful to the extent that we discover and accept together the full authentic heritage of faith given by Christ through his Apostles'.[46] This is evidently a richer and more beautiful vision, but one which it is hard to envisage being realised without the resolution of some of the difficulties addressed by Lindbeck.

(ii) At the other extreme, Lindbeck suggests, is 'a position which assumes "agreement in the gospel" in the absence of evidence to the contrary, and tries hard to see no stumbling-blocks. One should assume, says this view, that Christian churches understand the gospel in compatible ways providing they tolerate or do not denounce each others' positions.'[47] That cannot be satisfactory because it has historically been very rare for this to be the case. Good-natured tolerance is not only not enough. It is unrealistic to look for it. It is papering over cracks.

(iii) The 'intermediate position... deals explicitly with a few issues, viz., those which have historically been disputed'.[48] That does not necessarily mean dealing with them in isolation. It can be the case that there is a clear understanding that other things are in fact common; or some doubt may remain about that. Here,too, we need a gloss. It is possible to see the 'few issues' as a starting-point for discussion of many issues, or the reverse. That is to say, they can be thought to be final not preliminary difficulties. 'What the document does not discuss adequately has to do with the questions: a) what is the minimum requirement about agreement in faith in order that two churches may be in communion with each other, and (b) is there any positive witness in refusing with pain in the heart to be in communion with another church.'[49]

---

[46] Address by Pope John Paul on the occasion of 25 years of Lutheran–Roman Catholic International Dialogue, *Catholic International*, 3 (1992), and Ecumenical Prayer service, Uppsala, 9 June 1989.
[47] G. A. Lindbeck, 'A Lutheran view of intercommunion with Roman Catholics', *Journal of Ecumenical Studies*, 13 (1976), 242–9, p. 243.
[48] G. A. Lindbeck, 'A Lutheran view of intercommunion with Roman Catholics', *Journal of Ecumenical Studies*, 13 (1976), 242–9, p. 243.
[49] *Churches Respond to BEM*, V, p. 5, Malankara Orthodox Syrian Church (India).

'Two methods were being used in an attempt to bring about church union,' commented one observer of the Second Vatican Council. He distinguishes these as the method of addition and the method of subtraction. In the method of addition a standard believed to be a combination of all the necessary elements was set, and then each denomination was asked to add its own views.[50] 'Rome's habit is to proceed not by substraction but by addition.'[51] Others would prefer to subtract. 'Mullins . . . felt that any change in church polity should come by growth, not by mechanical accretion. He questioned the addition method, because he felt it was psychologically defective and that it approached the matter in an unhistoric way.' To his mind, 'The method of subtraction was an attempt to find common agreement and was more desirable. The approach puts to one side the things which cause offence and seeks a common point of view in an effort to arrive at a consensus.'[52] There is a large issue here about the hierarchy of truths, essentials, fundamentals and substantial agreement.[53]

So 'agreement' has been used ecumenically to mean total unanimity, agreement on sticking-points, agreement on all but sticking-points, tolerant agreement to differ; the refusal to use the term at all, points to unfinished business.[54]

Qualifications of agreement

The term 'agreement' has also been used with various qualifiers and modifiers. We meet 'full agreement' ('A full agreement would mean that on all points, apart from secondary details, agreement was complete.')[55] There is 'full dogmatic agreement' ('A solid basis has

---

[50] D. O. R. 'Chronique de la deuxième session du Concile', *Irénikon*, 36 (1963), 507–27, p. 523, and cf. Lambeth Quadrilateral.

[51] D. O. R. 'Chronique de la deuxième session du Concile', *Irénikon*, 36 (1963), 507–27, p. 523.

[52] Jerry M. Stabblefield, 'The ecumenical impact of E. Y. Mullins', *Journal of Ecumenical Studies*, 17 (1980), 94–102, p. 96, Mullins wrote *The Axioms of Religion* (1908).

[53] See H. Chadwick, ' "Substantial agreement": a problem of ecumenism', *Louvain Studies*, 16 (1991), 207–19. See, too, C. Hill, 'The Decree on ecumenism: an Anglican view', *One in Christ*, 26 (1990), 20–31, p. 28 and G. R. Evans, 'Rome's response to ARCIC and the problem of confessional identity', One in Christ, 28 (1992),155–67. 'Our method requires us both to say what we can together and to recognize without ambiguity that which cannot yet be the object of consensus.(90)' *Toward a Common Understanding of the Church, Report of Reformed–Roman Catholic Dialogue 1984–90*, (Vatican, 1990). *Catholic Inernational*, 2. 16, p. 786. I shall not attempt to deal with this issue here, for reasons of space.

[54] 'It is our view that the BEM document is not definitive and has not been worked out in every detail.' *Churches respond to BEM*, IV, p. 41.

[55] 'Differences of expression, of theology or of liturgical practice do not allow one, strictly speaking, to talk of pluralism of doctrine.' J. Tillard, 'Anglican–Roman Catholic dialogue', *One in Christ*, 8 (1972) 242–63, p. 246.

been prepared for further discussions whereby full dogmatic agreement may be affirmed between the Orthodox and the Anglican Communions.')[56]

There is 'substantial agreement': 'Chosen purposely and after much deliberation . . . the expression substantial agreement is not without theological presuppositions. Far from being "a subterfuge of pure verbal scholasticism", this distinction implies a characteristically ecclesiological approach.'[57] 'There is not absolute agreement between us on every point, [but] we have been able to arrive at a very substantial agreement on the very difficult questions which we have discussed.'[58] Bishop Gummerus said: 'there appeared to be substantial agreement between these two documents'. But it is clear that this was not construed as identity of doctrine, because there followed a series of queries and qualifications.

There is 'general agreement'.[59] There is 'fundamental agreement': 'We the Commission appointed by you [the Archbishop of Canterbury; the Archbishop of Latvia; the Bishop of Estonia] to consider the relations of the Church of England and the Churches of Latvia and Estonia with one another, report as follows: we have considered with great care the agreements and differences in the doctrine and customs of the three Churches, and have to report that on the most fundamental points of doctrine there is agreement.'[60]

These all contain qualifiers. There would appear to be an issue here closely related to that of the use of adjectives such as 'full' or prepositional prefixes such as 'inter' to qualify 'communion'.[61] In the latter case it is becoming increasingly clear that no such limiting adjectives are necessary or desirable before 'communion' in a united Church. They deny the very nature of communion itself. I would wish to argue that the same is true in the case of 'agreement'.

There is also perhaps an implied qualification in the notion that agreement must take place piecemeal, so that it is possible to agree on this but not on that. Malines arrived at a: 'considerable measure of agreement with regard to the following subjects: 1. That Holy Baptism constitutes the means of entry to the Church of Christ, and

---

[56] Romanian Orthodox–Church of England Conversations, 1935, *Lambeth Occasional Reports, 1931–8* (London, 1948), p. 201.

[57] J. Tillard, 'Anglican–Roman Catholic dialogue', *One in Christ*, 8 (1972) 242–63, p. 246. See, too, my article in *One in Christ* (1992).

[58] Anglican–Orthodox Conversations, *Lambeth Occasional Reports, 1931–8* (London, 1948), p. 81.

[59] *Churches Respond to BEM*, IV, p. 7, Mar Thoma Syrian Church of Malabar.

[60] Evangelical Lutheran Churches of Latvia and Estonia in conversation with the Church of England, 1936–8, *Lambeth Occasional Reports, 1931–8* (London, 1948), p. 211.

[61] See my *The Church and the Churches*.

that all validly baptized persons belong, in virtue of their baptism, to the Body of the Church ... 4. That Holy Scripture requires the interpretation of the Church before it can be accepted as the ultimate standard of faith and doctrine.'[62]

The belief that if we understood we would agree

It is plain that the goal is not clear. At the opening of the Bonn Conference of 1875 Döllinger made a speech in which he said that 'the mutual estrangement between the Eastern and Western Churches was largely the result of ignorance'.[63] But he himself came to see that that did not necessarily mean that removing ignorance could be relied upon to result in agreement. Indeed, not long afterwards, Plummer relates, 'Dr. Döllinger remarked on the extreme difficulty of getting the Orientals to assent to propositions taken out of their own Fathers, when these ran counter to the usual Oriental view' ... 'A body of quotations had been collected, which he believed to an *uninfluenced* mind would be irresistible, as abundantly showing that the Greek Fathers themselves spoke of a Procession from both the Father and the Son.'[64] But the uninfluenced mind was not to be had. So arriving at agreement is not simply a process of learning and understanding.

WHOSE RESPONSIBILITY IS IT TO RECEIVE?

In what we have said so far we have been assuming that the reception-processes which have to take place ecumenically are essentially to do with the 'receiving' of ecumenical reports. That is of course by no means the whole story. But the reports are markers of that process and they have prompted responses which we should not otherwise have had, and work in the churches which would not otherwise have been undertaken. So they and their penumbra of reception provide us with working material.

George Tavard calls the texts produced by the bilateral dialogues 'a new kind of theological literature'. He argues that 'they confront

---

[62] Lord Halifax, *Notes on the Conversations at Malines, 1921–5. Points of Agreement* (London, 1928), p. 5.
[63] Alfred Plummer, *Conversations with Dr Döllinger, 1870–90*, ed. R. Boudens (Louvain, 1985), p. 127, August 1875.
[64] Alfred Plummer, *Conversations with Dr Döllinger, 1870–90*, ed. R. Boudens (Louvain, 1985), p. 130, August 1875.

the Churches with a perspective that can only lead to reform, to profound modifications of habits of thought and of work, of ways of life and of faith, whose long status quo has often given the impression of immutability'.[65] They are new not only in purpose and in their implications but also in their form. Normally short and without much in the way of apparatus or footnotes, they seek to make their case in language for the general reader which will also satisfy the expert. In this they have not yet always succeeded, but it is an important aspect of their conception that they have tried.

Reception does not begin with the publication of a report or agreed statement. It goes on during its framing. Baptist–Reformed conversations speak of 'developing processes . . . spread over a four-year time-span'. Any ecumenical committee could echo that. When it came to finalising the text, 'it was agreed that such obvious signs of theological growth should be allowed to stand'.[66] That has not been done in most cases, though where a series of reports is published, such as Methodist–Roman Catholic and Anglican–Orthodox, something of this process of reception-on-the-way emerges.

There are revealing instances of self-assessment in connection with reception by the commissions in the introductions to the reports and agreed statements. An example is the stocktaking by the Lutheran–Roman Catholic Commission in their Malta Report. 'The members of the study commission are convinced that within the framework of their theme they have achieved a noteworthy and far-reaching consensus'(8). 'The study commission however is also conscious of the limitations of its work.' These it sees as limitations created in part by restrictions in subject-matter. 'The theme assigned to it imposed limitations on its approach'(9).[67] But more importantly for our purposes here, it was the view of this commission that its work could not be complete without response from the community of the faithful. It speaks of 'supplementing'. It thus clearly understands the responsibility for reception to lie with the whole Church. 'The limitations . . . can be partially offset by submitting the present report to as broad as possible a discussion among the churches. The work of international ecumenical commissions should be supplemented by work on regional levels'(12).

Unified and 'official' reception, even if it can be achieved in every church, is not enough. Reception is more than that, and infinitely

---

[65] G. Tavard, 'For a theology of dialogue', *One in Christ*, 15 (1979), pp. 11–12.
[66] B–R; *Growth*, p. 135.   [67] L–RC, Malta (1972); *Growth*, p. 170.

subtler and more complex as a process.[68] The question is how the varied levels of knowledge and understanding among the people in the Church can find expression.

This recognition that the whole people of God have somehow to form a common mind is perceptible with greater or lesser clarity in the *BEM* responses. There is certainly an anguished consciousness of the practical difficulties.

'It was open to all who so desired to participate,' commented the Swiss Protestant Church Federation in its response to *BEM*.[69] But it was found that the summary of the comments made in the process of general participation was quite unwieldy: 'because of its scope [it] simply could not be properly debated within the confines of the Assembly'.[70] The Evangelical Lutheran Church in Bavaria consulted 'the grass-roots parish chapters and councils, ecumenical circles and groups, church organisations, theological faculties and individuals'.[71] The Evangelical Church of the Augsburg Confession in the (then) Socialist Republic of Romania described a 'long and arduous reception process. The convergence texts were sent to pastors and other church staff and workers. The Lima document and the theological and ecclesiological questions connected with it were frequently discussed in clergy conferences and retreats.' Academics were consulted and the 'professional council of the German-speaking Evangelical branch of the Protestant Theological Institute' produced a commentary which was widely distributed and discussed in the church.[72] Avoiding this problem, by contrast, the Baptist Union of Sweden explained that its 'response has been worked out by five persons and has been approved by the executive board of the Union'.[73]

A rather more detailed example may be helpful in illustrating the problems which arise when this stage of asking for local and general response is arrived at. In the course of the discussion of the ARCIC II text *Salvation and the Church* in Church of England dioceses each diocese was invited to send an account of its response-process to the General Synod,[74] as a contribution to the debate there. Many of these

---

[68] 'Reception is at work in the reading of Scripture, in the process of receiving and transmitting doctrine that constitutes the tradition, and in the response of the people to magisterial decisions.' G. Tavard, 'Catholic reflection on the Porvoo Statement', *Midstream* (1994), 356.
[69] *Churches Respond to BEM*, IV, p. 76.   [70] *Churches Respond to BEM*, IV, p. 76.
[71] *Churches Respond to BEM*, IV, p. 22.   [72] *Churches Respond to BEM*, IV, p. 80.
[73] *Churches Respond to BEM*, IV, p. 201.
[74] The Synod of the two Anglican provinces of Canterbury and York which make up the Church of England.

accounts included descriptions of the debates in which lay people as well as clergy had taken part, and of small discussion-groups which had studied the text together, often ecumenically with Christians of other communions. In these responses a good deal of ecclesiological awareness was embedded. There was talk of the need to 'begin to grow together in Christ' ecclesially (Lincoln), and (Exeter) the assertion that 'the need to "belong together" is now felt very strongly'. Manchester spoke of 'mutual acceptance' in 'diverse insights into God's love'. Bradford said that it felt its people's faith should be the faith of the one holy Catholic Church rather than of the 'Church of England'. There were expressions of a sense of the Church in eternity, in calls to look to the Kingdom for the context for understanding the Church (Portsmouth); and it was asked in what ways the Church can be a sign to the world (Rochester). There was also a strong sense of the local reality of 'the church in each place' in the stress on the importance of discussion of issues locally as well as internationally (Rochester). There were questions about the 'ecclesiological model' being assumed in the Report.[75] There was a sense (Lichfield) that a fuller definition of the Church was wanted. But almost everywhere there was a felt need for a fuller theological grounding, which could be seen as equipment to help the people of God make up their common mind responsibly and securely.

These varied experiences show that if reception by the whole people of God is to mean everyone having a say and being listened to, the process is going to take a great deal of time and involve a complex educational process.

Education and reception

A number of communions have traditionally been reluctant to set faith at risk by encouraging the free distribution of theological material to readers who will not, because they lack the technical knowledge, understand its background. Such ecclesial bodies would sound a note of caution about the role of detailed study of texts by the whole people of God . . . 'It might be dangerous to let . . . the majority of the faithful . . . read Protestant authors assiduously, because they have no specialized training,' suggested one Roman Catholic author in 1960.[76] The long-term answer to this perhaps lies in striving to

---

[75] Text prepared by Faith and Order Advisory Group of the General Synod, 1192.
[76] G. H. Tavard, *Two Centuries of Ecumenism* (London, 1960), p. vii.

make the whole body of the faithful theologically literate. But that is a very long-term desideratum, and it will never be possible to achieve it for all Christians everywhere, and in the meantime reception has gone on in the Church through the ages without it. So we must be able to see reception as ultimately possible independently of the formal and outwardly visible educational process. The Holy Spirit has demonstrably had other ways of keeping the faith secure.

But that does not mean that the fullest and broadest possible understanding of the faith by the faithful does not matter. One way of getting round the problem has been to see guardianship of the faith as lodged with the Church's leaders. These exercise a teaching office and also hold the responsibility for making 'official' statements of the faith. In the episcopal churches the episcopate has traditionally had a special responsibility for guardianship of the faith. This has been marked in churches – especially the Roman Catholic Church – which have been highly centralised and tended to keep a tight rein on orthodoxy by the control both of the utterances of theologians and of the freedom of the mass of the faithful to believe what they wish undisciplined and unreined-in.

So 'one of the chief anxieties concerns the value to be accorded to the insights of the faithful in the face of certain statements or attitudes of the ecclesial authorities'[77] who have expertise and to whom responsibility for guardianship of the faith is accorded. It remains a problem within the separated churches, and a correspondingly much greater one ecumenically, to know how to weigh, or even to identify, the *sensus fidelium*, in this new, more complex and testing environment:

The *sensus fidelium* implies infinitely more, at least in the eyes of Roman Catholic tradition, than just a force of balance or positive criticism towards hierarchical decisions . . . It is also the bearer of a conviction on which the *magisterium* itself must draw when it feels the need to affirm the content of the faith in the most authoritative manner at its disposal.[78]

That is clearly articulated in both Orthodox and Anglican tradition, too, with the difference that one would have to substitute 'official teaching' for the relatively recent Roman Catholic technical term *magisterium*.

---

[77] J. M. R. Tillard, 'Sensus Fidelium', *One in Christ*, 11 (1975), 2–29, p. 2.
[78] J. M. R. Tillard, 'Sensus Fidelium', *One in Christ*, 11 (1975), 2–29, p. 5. In the working texts published by ARCIC in 1971, the distinction was explored between the 'assent' of the faithful and its 'consent', which is not seen by Vatican II as constitutive of the truth of the 'defined doctrine'. Text as cited in *The Clergy Review*, p. 129.

Both 'popular faith' and 'educated faith', those at the grass-roots[79] and theologians, may confront the ecclesiastical authorities with questions or objections or offer fresh insights from angles of view which their own differing circumstances make possible:

There is a tension between official attitudes and the spontaneous awareness of the body of the faithful, and likewise a tension between the demands of 'educated faith' and the needs of 'popular faith'.[80]

Since Vatican II the model has begun to change in the Roman

[79] Grass-roots and ivory tower, is an aspect of 'double belonging' along with mixed marriage, see R. Beaupère, 'Double belonging', *One in Christ*, 18 (1982), 31–43.

[80] J. M. R. Tillard, 'Sensus Fidelium', *One in Christ*, 11 (1975), 2–29, p. 4. There is a tension between official attitudes and those of the theologians which can be particularly sharp because it is happening at an intellectually sophisticated level. One device here has been to teach students 'to distinguish between revealed truths, which all require the same assent of faith, and theological doctrines. Hence they should be taught to distinguish between "the deposit of faith itself, of the truths that are contained in our venerable doctrine", and the way in which they are enunciated.' They have to learn to distinguish too 'between the truth to be enunciated and the various ways of perceiving and more clearly illustrating it'(24) and 'between apostolic tradition and merely ecclesiastical traditions'(25).

'Already from the time of their philosophical training, students should be put in a frame of mind to recognize that different ways of stating things in theology too are legitimate and reasonable, because of the diversity of methods of ways by which theologians understand and express divine revelation.' On this theme in the Roman Catholic *Ecumenical Directory*, Part II, ii, see John Coventry, 'Ecumenism in higher education', *One in Christ*, 7 (1971), 54–6, p. 55. These two constraints are intimately interrelated in practice. 'Over the course of the nineteenth century, the "sacred" character of rational recollection definitely entered into a crisis; therefore devices such as mandates, authorizations, and the *nihil obstat* appeared obsolete and, instead of being helpful, were actually a hindrance. The confessing communities have the right to reappropriate the faith even in the sense of becoming agents - under the Word of God - of the evangelical proclamation of the formulations which make it intelligible and communicable.' G. Alberigo, 'The authority of the Church: the documents of Vatican I and Vatican II', *Journal of Ecumenical Studies*, 19 (1982), p. 143. 'Theologians were presented as hybrid creatures, endowed with authority but nonetheless subservient to the magisterium, limited to the tasks of commentary and deduction, and bound to the magisterium as the immediate standard of truth for each theologian... The only admissible response to authority was obedience.' G. Alberigo, 'The authority of the Church: the documents of Vatican I and Vatican II', *Journal of Ecumenical Studies*, 19 (1982), 119–45, p. 133. This was in accord with the stand implied in Denzinger's publication in 1854 of an *Enchiridion* which implicitly gave equal status as sources to all its contents, creeds, definitions, doctrinal declarations. Pius IX's papal letter *Tuas libenter* of 21 December 1863 stressed the 'particular and original right of Church authority to watch over and direct theological doctrine' and rejected the view that 'faith and respect need be rendered only to dogmas expressly defined by the Church'. Thus the requirement of obedient believing 'extended to the theological truth taught by the ordinary magisterium of the Church throughout the world and to the doctrinal decisions of Roman congregations'. 'By a moderately formal act the scope of obligatory doctrinal decisions was excessively broadened, while the field of theological research and debate was drastically reduced.' 'Equally as serious was the position which assigned theology the task of supporting and illustrating the conformity of the teaching of the Church's magisterium with the sources of revelation.' G. Alberigo, 'The authority of the Church: the documents of Vatican I and Vatican II', *Journal of Ecumenical Studies*, 19 (1982), 119–45, pp. 123–4.

Catholic Church. The Church's teaching authority is beginning to be seen as working within the Church, rather than as exercised over it. [81] In the new climate, there comes to be a place for letting the whole people of God into the process by which the Church articulates its faith, by consulting as well as teaching them. 'The often painful and perplexing experience of the last fifteen years has shown how the ecclesiastical *magisterium*, struggling to be within and not above the Church, must employ mercy in place of the rod (*virga*) for condemnations and must have confidence in the indefectibility which the Spirit continually transmits to the people of God,'[82] suggests Alberigo. 'It is necessary for the theological effort to be supported by genuine eagerness on the part of the official leadership of the Church and the faithful themselves.'[83] 'We need a forum to report learnings and experiences... which appeals to and actively solicits readers at all levels,' argues another commentator.[84]

[81] So official condemnations of theologians intended to silence them become in many cases inappropriate, although they continue and there have indeed been notable cases recently. It has been suggested that the Congregation for the Doctrine of the Faith should 'eliminate from its procedures "hearings" and the like, substituting for them dialogues that either would be issue-oriented, or if it is deemed important to focus on the work of a particular theologian, would bring together not only the theologian in question and the consultors of the Congregation of the Doctrine of the Faith, but also a world-wide selection of the best pertinent theological scholars of varying methodologies and approaches.' L. Swidler, 'Demo-Kratia or Consensus Fidelium', *Journal of Ecumenical Studies*, 19 (1982). Suenens commented, 'Honesty demands that I also say something of the theological oppression that has put a stop to some projects of research, an oppression emanating from those who consider themselves as having the monopoly of orthodoxy (which is to them synonymous with that fixed and scholastic philosophy which they tried – generally, however in vain, to impose at the Council)... We all know the prolonged sufferings of our finest theologians, held suspect, if not positively condemned, in the name of that theology: Rahner, Congar, Murrat, de Lubac; to say nothing of those men who were the heroes of my young days: Cardinal Mercier... Dom Lambert Beauduin, whose heresy was ecumenism; and Père Lebbe.' Arthur B. Crabtree, Editorial, *Journal of Ecumenical Studies*, 8 (1971), p. 629, citing Suenens' *Dossier*. An extreme example of one theologian's experience of the implications is given by P. Schoonenberg. He was required in a correspondence with the Congregation for the Doctrine of the Faith to agree to Section V of *Mysterium Ecclesiae*, including a commentary which said: '1. For the theologian, dogmatic propositions, which are fixed in the tradition by a definition of the Church, have the value of indisputable first principles which direct the theologian's thought... 2. The theologian is not permitted to appeal to Holy Scripture, against the dogmatic propositions which the Church has derived from it under the guidance of the Spirit of truth... (John 16.13)... 3... a definition by the Church is itself an adequate divine guarantee of such a proposition's truth.' P. Schoonenberg, 'The theologian's calling, freedom and constraint', *Journal of Ecumenical Studies*, 19 (1982), 92–118, p.110. *Mysterium Fidei*, Paul VI, 1965, 57 (1965), 7533–73. *Journal of Ecumenical Studies* 19 (1982) is a special issue on theologians and the *magisterium*.

[82] G. Alberigo, *Journal of Ecumenical Studies*, 19 (1982), p.143.

[83] Avery Dulles, *The Catholic Virginian* (6 June 1975).

[84] J. McMakin, 'Needed: an ecumenism of effort toward Christian unity', *Journal of Ecumenical Studies*, 13 (1976), 99–102, p.101.

Inseparable from this development is another, which reflects contemporary preoccupations in philosophy and the social sciences. 'Theology is in a phase of transition as to those who do theology (clergy–laity, men–women) as well as its method and object.'[85] 'Theology is . . . becoming more varied according to cultural conditions and ecclesial attitudes in different areas.'[86] In both these respects theological decision-making is coming increasingly and overtly into the hands of the whole people of God. But that cannot happen without causing a crisis of authority because it marks a shift for many churches from a mere implicit and assumed *consensus fidelium*, to one in which direct identifiable contributions from anyone involved in the process, whether in an official position or not, can be explicitly and thoroughly taken into consideration.

That does not resolve the problem of the way in which the 'theological layman' is actually to make his or her contribution in making a response to *BEM*. Churches encountered this problem more directly than many of them had done before. 'The insights of the theological layman' frequently 'contribute just as much to the process of opinion-leading . . . as those of a theological specialist . . . But the texts presuppose a knowledge of a theological world of thought which is to a large extent foreign to the members of our congregations . . . Very seldom have we been successful in picking up the convergence statement on the level that in our view is desirable. But even if we could manage to translate it into a simpler language, we could need more time for our response. That is why this answer has been prepared only by theologians,'[87] said the German Mennonite Congregations in their response to *BEM*. Others could echo that experience. There are problems about the information-gap and problems about getting people involved.[88]

In certain circumstances an awareness of a lack of learning or sophistication may be expressed 'officially' on the part of a particular church. One such humble consciousness was expressed in the *BEM* responses by a church which nevertheless had the ecclesiological insight to know that its contribution mattered. 'We did not feel that

---

[85] G. Alberigo, *Journal of Ecumenical Studies*, 19 (1982), p.143.
[86] G. Alberigo, *Journal of Ecumenical Studies*, 19 (1982), p.143.
[87] *Churches Respond to BEM*, IV, p.124, United German Mennonite Congregations.
[88] 'Information about [bilateral] conversations is not easy to secure, and few alternative means of communication have been developed to keep the participating churches informed of progress made towards "trans-confessional understanding".' J. R. Nelson, 'What hope for ecumenism?', *Journal of Ecumenical Studies*, 8 (1971), 913–20, p.917.

we have to contribute to the learnings and teachings of churches of much greater age. Just the same I feel . . . that you might like to hear from us.'[89] The Protestant Church in Sabah (Malaysia) which sent in this modest response was twenty years old at the time. 'We appreciate this document as it gives us insight in the various understandings of churches, helps us to see our neighbouring churches in a new light and indicates that although those different views exist and will remain for some time, there is nothing theologically relevant which should keep us from working towards unity and unites witness in our state.'[90]

There are many difficulties, then, about the working of the intellectual and spiritual processes in reception. It remains an unresolved question whether the faithful can make an act of recognition without being taught or told enough about the ecumenically produced text or the proposed union of churches to be able to form a judgement, or whether the process of recognition is essentially intuitive, and prompted directly by the Holy Spirit at a deeper level.

In practice it seems to involve both. 'Popular faith has solid roots'[91] which are nourished in a soil prepared both by teaching and by the action of grace in a way which makes it impossible to separate the two. Made up as it is of popular and educated faith and the official teachings of the Church, 'the *sensus fidelium* is rooted precisely in this lived margin, this space of truth that emerges between the received Word and what it becomes through the power of the Spirit for the believer who tries to conform himself to it',[92] argues Tillard. To put it like that is to make or postulate a space in which this taking possession anew together of what each community has always had, can take place, and that must be a spiritual space, a space of time to take possession of the experience of being together.

That ought to involve the recognition that there is much that we do not yet know.[93] 'We do not yet know how to answer fully this question that we are led to face' (about baptismal difference) says

---

[89] *Churches Respond to BEM*, IV , p.133, The Protestant Church in Sabah (Malaysia).
[90] *Churches Respond to BEM*, IV , p.133 The Protestant Church in Sabah (Malaysia).
[91] J. M. R. Tillard, 'Sensus Fidelium', *One in Christ*, 11 (1975), 2–29, p.3.
[92] J. M. R. Tillard, 'Sensus Fidelium', *One in Christ* ,11 (1975), 2–29, p.15.
[93] A hint of that is clear in comments in the nineteenth century in terms which still apply today. 'After various proposals and counter-proposals and some rather unpleasant disputation, it became evident that the Greeks were not united among themselves . . . At last the following expression was *all but unanimously* [my italics] adopted: "without sacrifice of *any* true doctrine expressed in the present Western form".' Alfred Plummer, *Conversations with Dr Döllinger, 1870–90*, pp.105–6, Note 1, 1874.

the Baptism–Reformed conversation.[94] The willingness to say 'we do not know yet' must be an essential component of the reception-process.

THE MACHINERY OF OFFICIAL RESPONSES

With all these provisos, then, about shared responsibility and provisionality in reception-processes in the community as a whole, we need now to look at the mechanics.

In the strictest interpretation of the Rumanian invitation, the purpose of the Anglican Delegation was to elucidate the statements interchanged between the Orthodox delegation of 1930 and the Anglican Bishops with whom it conferred, in order that the Rumanian Commission might be able to advise the Holy Synod of Rumania as to whether it should declare that subject to the agreement of all the sister autokephalous Churches, it is prepared to accept Anglican Ordinations.[95]

ARCIC speaks . . . of the 'reception' of decision and rules out a quasi-democratic understanding by explicitly saying that 'it would be incorrect to suggest that in controversies of faith no conciliar or papal definition possesses a right to attentive sympathy and acceptance until it has been examined by every individual Christian and subjected to the scrutiny of his private judgement'.[96]

These two stylistically very different statements of the mechanics illustrate the problem of achieving a mutually agreed mechanism for reception at an official level.

It has been usefully pointed out that 'canonically, "to receive" is the highest form of Church reaction while parliamentarily "to receive" is precisely the lowest'.[97] When, for example, the Church of England's General Synod is asked to 'receive' a text, the model is usually parliamentary. That is to say, no commitment is implied, merely that there is no strong objection *prima facie* to taking it into the Church's processes of consideration, and starting to think about it. Real 'reception', as we have seen, is something else altogether. It is a making one's own as a church, and an enshrining in one's church's life, where approriate, by legislation, and always in the recognition that this is part of a process in which all Christians everywhere are sharing.

---

[94] B–R; *Growth*, p.143.
[95] *Lambeth Occasional Reports, 1931–8* (London, 1948), p.201, and see ibid., Appendix A, for the statements in question.   [96] Ibid., p.136.
[97] W. Lazareth, 'Baptism, Eucharist and Ministry update', *Journal of Ecumenical Studies*, 21 (1984), 10–21, p.11.

The special difficulties of doing for one's own church what is properly the action of a united Church are now very apparent. Christopher Hill describes, giving the case of the Roman Catholic Church, a problem which arises ecumenically in all combinations of churches seeking to agree something together: 'how the Roman Catholic Church could agree ecumenically in faith with another Christian body without the imposition of definitions arrived at in absentia but with assurance that the essential content of the faith is not denied'.[98] The Congregation for the Doctrine of the Faith in the Roman Catholic Church will ensure that 'any document is scrutinized for consonance with current official teaching'.[99] For Anglicans the problem is the *sources* of the dogmas as defined in their *status as binding* on all Christians rather than the *truths* the dogmas are intended to convey.[100]

Here we see encapsulated the problem we have already been considering, that each church must, at least initially, make its separate response to any agreement, and at that point will often draw back into its old entrenched positions rather than move forward in glad affirmation of a new expression of the faith shared with other churches. The strong positive response to the ecumenical reports and agreed statements before the 1988 Lambeth Conference of the bishops of the Anglican Communion was made in the secure knowledge that the Resolutions of the Conference are not binding on the member provinces. This is all a long way from the real 'double-belonging' to one's own and the universal Church to which Christians are called.

The root of the problem is that no church can have authority to make rules for another but only with another; and we do not yet have the machinery to make common rules of decision-making together.[101] One side will often ask the other how it makes decisions.[102]

Arbitrating authorities

Some have argued that the way forward must involve finding a single common authority which everyone can accept.

---

[98] C. Hill, *The Times* correspondence column, 26 October 1991, the 'Ratzinger principle' (C. Hill' s words).

[99] C. Hill, 'Rome's response to ARCIC', *The Tablet*, 7 December 1991, pp. 1525–7.

[100] Ibid.

[101] 'Organizational procedures for making policy choices and settling conflicts between parties are vitally important in the present separated churches and even more so in the Great Church of the future.' J. Corridan, 'Authority and freedom in the coming ecumenical Church', *Journal of Ecumenical Studies*, 12 (1975), 315–34, p.316.

[102] Anglican–Orthodox Conversations, *Lambeth Occasional Reports, 1931–8* (London, 1948), p.88.

In order to be properly evaluated on both sides all points of agreement and disagreement must be examined and judged in the light of a supreme authority accepted by both parties. Only [then] will the two Churches be able to decide whether those agreements manifest their common faith in the same Lord or only conceal a basic disunity.[103]

This is the comment of a Lutheran who wants to take Scripture as that authority. But not every communion would look to the same source for such an authority. Anglicans and Orthodox found that to be a problem forty years ago.

The Orthodox said in effect: . . . 'The Tradition is a concrete fact. Here it is, in its totality. Do you Anglicans accept it, or do you reject it? The Tradition is for the Orthodox one indivisible whole: the entire life of the Church in its fullness of belief and custom down the ages . . . ' Faced with this challenge, the typically Anglican reply is: 'We would not regard veneration of icons or Mariology as inadmissible, provided that in determining what is necessary to salvation, we confine ourselves to Holy Scripture.' But this reply only throws into relief the contrast between the Anglican appeal to what is deemed necessary to salvation and the Orthodox appeal to the one indivisible organism of Tradition, to tamper with any part of which is to spoil the whole, in the sort of way that a single splodge on a picture can mar its beauty.[104]

At the other extreme we find the argument that it is best to aim at something which will arouse neither resistance nor indignation, and can be accepted without demur because it asks so little. Avery Dulles suggests as much.

Directives, to be practical, would have to be rather simple, and could not include all the nuances that academic theologians would wish to introduce. It would be impractical, for instance, to make distinctions among the various Protestant denominations, although the differences between them are important. Thus we may have to live with general rules that are inapplicable to particular cases. That is why directives, rather than laws, are to be sought.[105]

But neither of these is really acceptable ecumenically. One smacks of force, the other of compromise. If there is true agreement, there is no need for an arbitrating authority. There will, however, be a need for internal machinery to enable each ecclesial community to 'know its own mind'. Not only does this not exist universally; it does not even exist in all churches individually at present:

[103] Note by the Lutheran Chairman, A–L Pullach; *Growth*, p.32.
[104] Michael Ramsey in a comment on the 1956 Moscow Conference, quoted by Kallistos Ware in A–O, Moscow, pp.58–9.
[105] Avery Dulles, 'Catholic Response', *Journal of Ecumenical Studies*, 13 (1976), p.249.

Some of our... communions have absolutely no governing canonical guidance for dealing authoritatively with doctrinal materials admittedly co-authored by theologians representing other communions which are still officially anathematized or condemned as either heretical or schismatic... others have absolutely no magisterial apparatus for officially determining what is, or what is not, the authentic faith of the Church 'once for all delivered to the saints,' to say nothing of having any *episkope* authority able to make such official declarations with binding authority for the beliefs of the faithful.[106]

In the responses made by deanery and diocesan synods of the Church of England to the ARCIC II text *Salvation and the Church* there were several comments to the effect that perhaps it was not the task of such local meetings 'to discuss theology' (Derby) and a sense of their incompetence to do so ('We cannot vote on what we cannot understand', Derby). Reservations were expressed about the effectiveness of formal synodical debate as an instrument of decision-making (Exeter), and it was suggested that the diocesan synod is too large a body for it to be useful for it to discuss theological problems (St Edmundsbury and Ipswich). These anxieties do not necessarily reflect the view that it is not the responsibility of the whole people of God to accept or reject a formulation of the faith. But they do suggest that at a local level the people may well feel inadequate to the task of forming a judgement, and also that the machinery of decision-making available to them is not best suited to the task. The Anglican pattern is not itself the same all over the world, and in other communions the degree and mode of participation of the whole people of God in acts of formal reception varies a great deal. It is not everywhere clear that it is their responsibility to become involved in these *formal* acts of their churches, as distinct from their playing a part in the process of reception as a whole.

The churches' machineries vary. The Anglican pattern has not been the same everywhere, but it has consistently tended to involve synodical debate at diocesan and provincial level.[107] In discussing *BEM* and *The Final Report* of ARCIC I the Church of England's General Synod Faith and Order Advisory Group produced a study-guide *Towards a response to BEM and ARCIC* as a help to local study. At the level of making a diocesan response to ARCIC II's *Salvation and the Church* the Church of England devised a variety of

---

[106] W. Lazareth, 'Baptism, Eucharist and Ministry update', *Journal of Ecumenical Studies*, 21 (1984), 10–21, p.11. [107] This was a major theme of the 1867 Lambeth Conference.

strategies. A number of further study-guides were produced locally. Some dioceses held full debates in the diocesan synod. Some invited outside speakers, including Roman Catholic bishops and theologians, members of ARCIC and of the Church of England's central theological committees. Some held reconstructions in the form of dramatic presentations to explain the way the historic divisions discussed by the statement had arisen (Lichfield and Portsmouth). Some allowed deaneries to make their responses to the diocesan synod, or if they wished, directly to the Church of England's then Board for Mission and Unity, which was to collate the responses for the consideration of the General Synod. The most common pattern was to have a talk by a presenter, or more than one presenter, followed by debate and then a vote. Collectively, and at the highest level, Anglicans can do no more than make Resolutions at Lambeth Conferences in favour of ecumenical reports and agreed statements, as was done warmly and almost unanimously for a series of such texts in 1988. But these Resolutions can have no binding force in the provinces because the Lambeth Conference is not a council of the Church.

The Roman Catholic Church's method has been to publish interim observations by the Congregation for the Doctrine of the Faith and an official Response. In the case of *The Final Report* of ARCIC I this Response took ten years and bears the marks of unresolved conflict between the Church's dicasteries.[108] By contrast with this highly centralised and official way of going about things, the worldwide responses to *BEM* collected by the World Council of Churches came mostly from local level.[109] So there are, at a superficial level, strong crude contrasts between the official machineries of the churches which mean that they cannot all deem themselves to have 'decided' in the same way, or at the same point.

Complicating the problem of official machinery is the fact that reception should ideally involve studying ecumenical documents ecumenically, that is, the churches studying them together. That may

---

[108] C. Hill in *Catholic International*, 3 (1992), also Weakland, ibid. Corridan sees the canon lawyer as 'structural theologian' or 'ecumenical engineer'. J. Corridan, 'Authority and freedom in the coming ecumenical church', *Journal of Ecumenical studies*, 12 (1975), 315–34, p.316. 'One often receives different and contradictory vibrations from . . . the three interested dicasteries in Rome - the Secretariat of State, the Council for Promoting Christian Unity and the Congregation for Oriental Churches . . . the Orthodox could be rightly confused and frustrated by such divisions.' R. G. Weakland, Archbishop of Milwaukee, 'Orthodox–Catholic relations', *Catholic International*, 3 (April 1992), p.392.

[109] See examples throughout this chapter and elsewhere drawn from *Churches Respond to BEM*.

be possible locally, and has indeed begun to happen in some parts of the world. But it cannot be done at the level of official recognition while there is no machinery which will allow churches to decide together.

Too many reports to absorb

It is not always plain to readers what the reports are for. 'A satisfactory starting-point for interchurch conversation,' says the Mar Thoma Syrian Church of Malabar conservatively of *BEM*. But, it warns, 'we are eager that it should not be made a confession of faith and order'.[110] The Evangelical Lutheran Church in Bavaria suggests eirenically but cautiously that such texts 'contain guidance to help the churches overcome the differences which divide them'.[111] This difficulty about understanding their purpose is greatly compounded when report after report is published and sent for 'reception' to the churches. It is often a significant problem that there are felt to be too many reports to absorb. Their multiplicity can lead to confusion about their distinctive and collective contributions. Bilateral reports and agreed statements must ultimately be received by churches not directly involved in framing them, but that is a process which has scarcely begun. Then there is the problem of fatigue.[112] The Church of England made a vigorous approach to the problem of receiving *BEM* and *The Final Report* of ARCIC I at the same time.[113] Taking more than one report at a time proved a useful method here. But there has been less energy for mounting and organising the study throughout the community of reports published since, and this is perhaps likely to be an experience shared by other churches.

ELUCIDATION AND FEEDBACK

A complex move in the reception-process is to respond to the responses to ecumenical reports by way of elucidation. Elucidation should be a process of communication. It should involve really listening to people and seriously trying to meet their difficulties. But it is not always easy to make it plain that that has been done. It is hard

[110] *Churches Respond to BEM*, IV, p.13, Mar Thoma Syrian Church of Malabar.
[111] *Churches Respond to BEM*, IV, p.20, Evangelical Lutheran Church in Bavaria.
[112] On 'consensus fatigue', see Harding Meyer, 'The ecumenical dialogues: situation-problems-perspectives', *Pro Ecclesia*, 3 (1994), 24–36, p.30.
[113] Faith and Order Advisory Group. *Towards a Church of England Response to BEM and ARCIC* (London, 1986).

to know 'how the twin processes of evaluation and reception operating during the lifetime of ARCIC I actually influenced the published text of the Final Report',[114] commented one sympathiser with ARCIC's work. If there is a lapse of time, and the membership of a commission has changed, one may be asking for elucidation from a commission whose membership is not the same as that which framed the original text.

In principle response might make it necessary to rewrite the original text. ARCIC I made a policy decision not to modify the original texts of the Eucharist, Ministry and Authority statements, but to publish its Elucidations separately as appendices.[115] ARCIC II has continued along this road with its *Clarifications*.[116] These Elucidations deal in detail with points which proved still to be sensitive and where the text had not sufficiently allowed for continuing anxieties. They certainly involved a good deal of honest heart-searching. ('The commission has been accused of an over-emphasis . . . '(ARCIC AI, Elucidation, 4).) But they are strictly clarificatory. It has been suggested that ARCIC's elucidations have rather the character of Augustine's *Retractationes* in not being retractions at all, but geared on the whole to supporting what had been said in the text as published at first. They have thus often been seen as 'justifications' rather than 'elucidations'.[117] The decision to let the original text stand was not everywhere approved of. The Roman Catholic Congregation for the Doctrine of the Faith objected in connection with *The Final Report* of ARCIC I that there had been a 'failure to revise the original statements' in the light of criticisms, because the Elucidations had not been integrated.

More positively, some have felt that 'to review the progress made since the Second Vatican Council, and to see this reflected in *The Final Report* is in many ways more encouraging than a simple

---

[114] Roger Greenacre, General Synod Debate, *Proceedings*, Vol. 20, no. 1, (1989), pp. 125–6.

[115] Much as Anselm did in the case of Gaunilo's comments on his *Proslogion* argument.

[116] (London, 1994). These concentrate on the points raised in the Vatican *Response* to *The Final Report* of ARCIC I in the areas of Eucharist and Ministry. The Vatican has been able to respond positively to these, in a letter published with the document.

[117] 'The points selected for response indicate the sensitive areas of these statements, as revealed by various critical reactions.' G. Tavard, 'The bilateral dialogues: speaking together', *One in Christ*, 16 (1980), 30–43, p. 40. 'By and large, the Salisbury Elucidations do not add anything of substance to the findings of Windsor and Canterbury. They reiterate the conviction of the Commission that its methodology was correct, and that the scope of the two agreed statements really amounts to an agreement at the level of faith concerning the Eucharist and the ministry.' G. Tavard, 'The bilateral dialogues: speaking together', *One in Christ*, 16 (1980), 30–43. p. 40.

statement of the present position in our agreement. *The Final Report* allows us to see how far we have come, and, discerning the trajectory, to believe that we are accurately aimed at unity in truth.'[118] The *Clarifications* are even more controversial.[119] For one thing, they are published as a text of ARCIC II, a different body of people, although in fact the drafting sub-committee consisted of members of ARCIC I. For another, they have been accused of having concentrated on satisfying one side's anxieties more than those of the other, because the spokesman-authority for one side (the Vatican) had expressed more anxieties than that of the other (the Lambeth Conference). ARC/USA led the way in trying to meet the concerns of Rome on Rome's own terms.[120] The *Clarifications* have accordingly drawn hostile comment from the Anglican constituencies still most uncertain of Rome.

This mixed appraisal in the public arena so far of the methodology of using 'elucidations' raises the question of its value. 'One could wonder if answering critics is the best method of dealing with the problem of arriving at a universal consensus.' The result is certainly likely to be 'piecemeal answers'... 'I am not aware that other bi-lateral groups have tried to start a dialogue with their critics,' notes Tavard.[121] The *BEM* text of course has done so as a multilateral dialogue, though there is no plan for Elucidations of that.

It seems to be helpful to distinguish at least between requests

(i) for clarification of certain words or concepts examined in the existing text of a report. That was the particular concern of the ARCIC Elucidations. ('We have been asked to clarify the meaning of... an expression we did not use'(ARCIC *AI*, Elucidation, 5).) It also appears as a concern in the *BEM* responses. We do not 'set a condition for the acceptance of the texts' [by making criticisms]. 'Rather we want to clarify what is very important for our church and how it understands certain statements of the texts,'[122] reassured the Old Catholic Church of Switzerland;

(ii) for reassurance that the issues in question have been fully resolved and ought not now to be church-dividing;

---

[118] 'Canadian ARC: remarks on the CDF's "Observations on the Final report of ARCIC", April 1983', *One in Christ*, 20 (1984), 257–8.
[119] *Clarifications – On Eucharist and Ministry* (ACC and Pontifical Council for Promoting Christian Unity, 1994).
[120] This will be conveniently accessible in J. Robert Wright's article in the *Festschrift* for Jean Tillard (Louvain, 1995).
[121] G. Tavard, 'The bilateral dialogues: speaking together', *One in Christ*, 16 (1980), 30–43. p. 40
[122] *Churches Respond to BEM*, V, pp. 8–9, Old Catholic Church of Switzerland.

(iii) for fuller treatment of a number of themes touched on only in passing. That may include requests for more information, either on matters unfamiliar to Christians from one tradition or on matters apparently at variance with the theology of the Report. For example 'Concern has been voiced that the Commission's treatment of regional primacy is inadequate'(7).[123] Anglicans have commonly asked for more on penance and indulgences after reading ARCIC II's *Salvation and the Church*. Some churches responded to *BEM* in a similar way. The Netherlands Reformed Church and Reformed Churches in the Netherlands wanted coverage of an unexamined agenda, concerning 'the pope and his cardinals, female ministry, the ministry of those who are not theologically trained and do not work full time'.[124]

NEGATIVE RECEPTION

Unexpected things can happen in reception. There can be apparent setbacks. We saw at the beginning of this study that it is becoming a common experience that at the moment of greatest hope in ecumenical conversations something sticks. Communions find it relatively easy to arrive at mutual respect and goodwill, but hard to get beyond that. To take a typical instance, from Baptist–Reformed conversations, 'From these positions we can arrive at a mutual respect for the intentions of our varied practices, even though we cannot yet reach a common mind as to the right way of fulfilling our discipleship together in today's situation of mission.'[125] Aware that 'verbal agreements have not been enough to create unity', the Anglican–Reformed dialogue made a list of things keeping the two communions apart. In an effort to 'identify the factors' sustaining separation, 'which are still, apparently, stronger than the theological agreements which have been reached in some places,'[126] they found the following. (i) 'Our two communions define themselves in different ways'; (ii) 'the accent falls differently' in each over the balance of word and sacrament in the life of the Church; (iii) 'the role of the bishop in Anglican piety and churchmanship has no exact parallel in Reformed experience' and 'perhaps it is at this point that one of the deepest emotional barriers to union lies'; (iv) Anglican 'bonds between church and state are still important obstacles to full mutual acceptance';

[123] ARCIC *AI*, Elucidation; Growth, p. 102.
[124] *Churches Respond to BEM*, IV, p. 100, Netherlands Reformed Church and Reformed Churches in the Netherlands.   [125] B–R; *Growth*, p. 139.
[126] A–R, *God's Reign and Our Unity*, 6, p. 4.

(v) 'More subtle, but not less important, are the bonds which tie our two communions to the national feeling and the folk religion of the people to whom we minister.'[127] Then there are obstacles on the broader front which also operate between Anglicans and Reformed: (i) the fear that union means loss of identity; (ii) 'the widespread and well-grounded fear of large organisations'; (iii) 'a false understanding of the Church and of God's calling to the Church'.[128] These are all, whether mechanical or more profound, differences which are clung to because of a need to retain a familiar identity, and thus reactions of fear of change.

Similar concerns are expressed by many churches in their response-process. 'A widespread unease that the model of visible unity assumed and the nature of consensus sought make inadequate allowance for a diversity which is arguably compatible with living in communion one with another'[129] was expressed by the Baptist Union of Great Britain and Ireland in its response to *BEM*. This is, as it were, the negative face of reception. It is saying no. But it is still reception. Most marked everywhere is suspicion of the other side and concomitant fear of loss of one's own church's identity.

There are other reasons for negativity. One is sheer apathy, or battle-weariness or disillusionment, resulting in a short- or long-term lack of engagement with the reception-process. 'Very few circuits and only one synod responded to the invitation to comment on the Lima text,' admitted the Methodist Church of South Africa. Of those who did, 'Several respondents simply expressed satisfaction or referred to the complexity of the language for lay people... It is significant that comment was very limited; that it related exclusively to baptism; and that it concentrated on criticisms and did not evince any readiness to learn.'[130] There is sometimes a strong sense of difference of priority. A prior commitment outweighs any future call. 'We have to ask ourselves to what extent our church, which is committed to the Reformation, can accept this statement.'[131] More refreshingly, an honest and attractive admission of anxiety is expressed. 'We feel fearful. What if we should be called to relinquish that very inheritance which constitutes God's

[127] A–R, *God's Reign and Our Unity*, 7–11, pp. 4–8.
[128] A–R, *God's Reign and Our Unity*, 12–14, pp. 8–10.
[129] *Churches Respond to BEM*, I, p. 77, Baptist Union of Great Britain and Ireland.
[130] *Churches Respond to BEM*, II, p. 237, Methodist Church of Southern Africa.
[131] *Churches Respond to BEM*, IV, p. 17, Evangelical Church of the Augsburg Confession (Austria).

gift and promise to us? We know their communions also have such anxiety.'[132]

This drawing back can be a spur to apologetics and self-definition. The Seventh-Day Adventists saw *BEM* as challenging them with a 'general call to decision concerning non-Adventist communions'.[133] They promised, 'We will apply ourselves to provide clear and convincing explanations of our positions and practices for the people of good will outside our Church who are confused and disturbed by Adventist belief and behaviour.'[134]

It can also prompt challenges, even a major methodological challenge which seems to undermine the whole enterprise. 'The Army's traditional approach to the subjects dealt with differs significantly from the hypothesis on which the present study rests,'[135] points out the Salvation Army. In fact it would begin from the premiss that there is no problem at all, at least not in the form in which ecumenism has been addressing it. 'Salvationist reviewers are troubled by the apparent inference that we start divided and must see how we can achieve unity. The basis of the Salvation Army's cordial relationships with other denominations is its belief that we are already "one in Christ Jesus."'[136] That is a position others share. 'The unity of the Church does not have to be brought about, it is there already,'[137] says the Evangelical Church of the Augsburg Confession in Austria.

A different kind of methodological challenge came from the Church of Greece in its response to *BEM*. This church suspects the World Council of Churches is itself trying to behave like a church (although it has in fact never done so). 'The procedure followed by the WCC in sending the texts in question to the member churches for the promotion of the idea of their "reception" . . . is a novel initiative of the WCC and is outside the framework specified by the Constitution's articles for the carrying out of the multilateral dialogue within this inter-christian organisation. The WCC is simply the framework within which its member churches independently carry on this dialogue.' The committee 'considers the novel methodology being introduced . . . as a process ecclesiologically and theologically unnecessary' (because no review of *BEM* is planned). 'The WCC by such an

[132] *Churches Respond to BEM*, IV, Church of the Brethren (USA).
[133] *Churches Respond to BEM*, II, p. 347.   [134] *Churches Respond to BEM*, II, p. 348.
[135] *Churches Respond to BEM*, IV, p. 231, The Salvation Army.
[136] *Churches Respond to BEM*, IV, p. 233, The Salvation Army.
[137] *Churches Respond to BEM*, IV, p. 17, Evangelical Church of the Augsburg Confession (Austria).

initiative aims . . . to turn itself into the main and dynamic dialogue partner of its member churches, which shall be obliged to carry on dialogue not only with one another within the framework of the WCC, but with the WCC itself.'[138] There is something in this which needs discussing. A dialogue of that sort would be inappropriate, certainly. But part of a conversation's purpose is to air things, to allow them to be heard. And the minds which hear, understand and frame their own views more fully as a result. That is the positive side.

Defensive moves such as justificatory self-definition and challenge to the foundations of the ecumenical enterprise have a counterpart in expression of hurt and disappointment. These are often precipitated by an unexpected reversal which creates a crisis when things had seemed to be going well in the reception process. This is a noticeable recent phenomenon because close success in reaching agreement has more than once now led to stand-off. In the Anglican–Orthodox Athens statement of 1978 it is acknowledged that the ordination of women to the priesthood within the Anglican Communion 'has brought our dialogue to a point of acute crisis'. The Anglican members say (13) 'The present crisis in our conversations with the Orthodox has forced all of us to reconsider the way in which, in our Communion, decisions are made on matters of such fundamental importance. How far in such questions should consensus precede action . . . What method of decision and debate are appropriate in such matters?' It proved possible to find good in this particular crisis. 'We have found a real willingness to listen to one another, to respect one another's viewpoints and to hear what those we disagree with are saying. This has brought the discussion on this subject to a welcome level of serious theological exchange which has helped us to find a common language of discourse'(14).[139] But the new barrier was not itself shifted by this. A similar problem arises between Anglicans and Roman Catholics over the ordination of women. ARCIC I on ministry was a document completed in real hope that the 'null and void' of 1896 could be got over and Anglican Orders recognised. But the advent of women priests and bishops in various provinces of the Anglican Communion made that a practical impossibility, although it did not in itself radically alter the theology of ministry put forward in the ARCIC text.

---

[138] *Churches Respond to BEM*, V, p. 2, Church of Greece.
[139] A–O, Athens Statement, 1978; *Growth*, pp. 53–4.

The problem of the non-responders

'It is well known in the inner circles of the World Council of Churches e.g., that very few member churches ever return a substantial response, or *any* response at all to the reports of the assemblies, the Faith and Order Conferences, and studies on various questions which are central to Christian faith.' Such reports, prepared after years of work by highly respected scholars, are usually forwarded to the more than 240 member churches for 'study and action'. 'No doubt the reports do have some sympathetic reception by some; but for the most part, the churches are too diffident about their conciliar participation, or too preoccupied with their own affairs, to benefit by these studies and to communicate responses for ongoing consideration.'[140] This statement has to be weighed against the multi-volume *Churches respond to BEM* which shows that endless trouble is often taken over a long period of patient effort. Nevertheless, it is true enough that apathy and bewilderment and numerous other factors work against active responding in many churches, because what is being asked is unfamiliar, and, again, the machinery for doing anything about it is often lacking.

Continuing openness

For all these reasons, we should not be trying to close questions in a hurry in the reception-process.[141] Open questions may allow the continuance of variation at least in rite. Karl Rahner suggests that 'dogmatically it may be a completely open question whether the materia used in the Eucharist can be only bread made from wheat. Holding that this dogmatic question is open need not require the Church to change anything in its concrete practice.'[142] It is also possible for what seemed closed questions to be reopened. Rahner comments that the discussion of Vatican II on Scripture and tradition 'made what since Trent had been a traditional teaching now an open question'.[143]

That raises the question whether reopening of an issue so as to make

---

[140] J. R. Nelson, 'What hope for ecumenism?', *Journal of Ecumenical Studies*, 8 (1971), 913–20, p. 917.
[141] *Growth*, p. 460.
[142] K. Rahner, 'Open questions in dogma considered by the institutional church as definitively answered', *Journal of Ecumenical Studies*, 15 (1978), 211–27, p. 212.
[143] K. Rahner, 'Open questions in dogma considered by the institutional church as definitively answered', *Journal of Ecumenical Studies*, 15 (1978), 211–27, p. 213.

it no longer a divisive matter can act retrospectively so as to undo old divisions. Rahner touches on that, too, but without real optimism. 'A Catholic theologian may maintain that today there are no theological opinions that with certainty can be pointed to as absolutely binding on Catholics or Protestants of such a nature as to require or to legitimate a separation of churches . . . One could, of course, object that if today there are no differences of opinion that legitimate a separation of churches, they could not have existed in the past either, which is quite improbable.'[144] 'It would be useful . . . to explain why it is and how it happens that frequently an opinion can be formed within the Church's faith-consciousness (though not in a manner that engages its absolute act of faith) that a specific teaching is seen as the clear and definitive answer to a specific question, when in fact such is not the case at all.'[145]

THE TIME-SCALE

Small though they are as elements in the reception-process, responses to reports and agreed statements can take a long time to achieve. A Resolution of the (Anglican) Church of England General Synod of January 1989 stated 'that this Synod invites the dioceses and deaneries to study the Agreed Statement [of ARCIC II] on *Salvation and the Church* and to send any preliminary comments to the Secretary of the Board for Mission and Unity not later than 31 December, 1989'. This proved unrealistic and in due course September 1991 was decided upon instead. Lambeth Conferences can 'resolve' only at their ten-yearly meetings. Rome's *Response* to ARCIC took ten years. Similar unavoidable delays in the operation of the machinery have been experienced throughout the *BEM* process.[146]

At the same time we have to recognise that reception is not merely a matter of machinery, but of the human need for waiting-time and time for adjustment. Several churches responding to *BEM* commented in this way. 'We do not expect any quick results, but by its response our church wishes to make a contribution such that the outcome will in every respect be to the advantage of the Church of God.'[147] 'We are

---

[144] K. Rahner, 'Open questions in dogma considered by the institutional church as definitively answered', *Journal of Ecumenical Studies*, 15 (1978), 211–27, p. 225.

[145] K. Rahner, 'Open questions in dogma considered by the institutional church as definitively answered', *Journal of Ecumenical Studies*, 15 (1978), 211–27, p. 213.

[146] *Churches Respond to BEM* has been published over a period of years as responses have come in.

[147] *Churches Respond to BEM*, VI, p. 43, Slovak Evangelical Church of the Augsburg Confession in the CSSR.

conscious that the road still lies ahead and that it is a long one.'[148] 'In our experience a discipline of expectant waiting under the directing Spirit of God is necessary in the search for this unity. This process may on occasion be a protracted one.'[149] 'Reception refers to all phases of the process whereby a church appropriates the fruits of ecumenical conversation as integral to its own life and faith. It is a process that may take years, and only comes to fruition by the power of the Holy Spirit.'[150] 'The Lima texts...attempt to point out convergences without hastily claiming agreement.'[151]

The 'living' and the 'recollected' processes stand in a complex relationship. What was evident to one commentator looking back on Vatican II could be echoed by many who have worked on commissions.

Even more crucial, in ecumenical terms, is the question as to how the conciliar texts were to be read and understood by succeeding generations, when the principals and 'eye-witnesses' would have passed from the scene, and when tacit assumptions about intended meanings, so nearly 'self-evident' at the time, would have been forgotten? Already, what seemed then to be 'progressive developments' to so many (including the immobilists), may now be read with more conservative overtones. What seemed to us as minor concessions in the interest of the widest possible consensus now appear to some as 'proofs' that Vatican II changed little or nothing, after all. But they should be remembered, so as to temper all claims to absolute certitude about '*the* literal meaning' of this ambiguous passage or that.[152]

Conclusion

The stumbling-blocks to ecumenical reception are broadly of two sorts. Behind those delays and resistances in the reception-process which come from fear of loss of ecclesial identity lies the ecclesiological problematic of churches claiming to be uniquely the Church.[153]

My denomination must grow less in my eyes if I am to grow more towards Christ. I am willing that my denomination shall be forgotten if thereby may be hastened the unity of the Church of our Lord. That denomination is most

[148] *Churches Respond to BEM*, IV, p. 119, Waldensian Evangelical Church of the River Plate (Uruguay).
[149] 'We...do not necessarily mean unanimity, but a clearly recognised "sense of the meeting"' *Churches Respond to BEM*, IV, p. 215, Religious Society of Friends (Quakers) in Great Britain.
[150] *Churches Respond to BEM*, IV, p. 105, Church of the Brethren (USA).
[151] *Churches Respond to BEM*, IV, p. 20, Evangelical Church of the Augsburg Confession (Austria).
[152] A. C. Outler, 'Strangers within the gates', Stacpoole, pp. 174–5.
[153] See some discussion of this in my *The Church and the Churches* (Cambridge, 1994).

prophetic that is willing to disappear for Christ's sake – to go to its disappearance as deliberately as Christ went to his crucifixion.[154]

That is noble, but it does not directly address the question where *is* the Church when that happens? We should perhaps want to say that one answer is that the Church is where its mind is at one.

The second sort has to do with pace. Reception cannot be rushed:

Schism and heresy are the fruit of impatience and violence. Reunion will be the fruit of long enduring patience and much gentleness and humility . . . reunion will come from . . . disinterestedness.[155]

Sufficient agreement on the restoration of the outward sign of unity (sacramental communion) suggests another answer to the question where the Church *is*.

[154] Peter Ainslie, Disciples of Christ, *Faith and Order, Proceedings of the World Conference, Lausanne, August 3–21, 1927* (London, 1927), p. 343.
[155] Congar, *Dialogue between Christians*, p. 174.

Conclusion

The changing scene

Material for ecumenical reception is being published all the time. The appearance of the 'scene' constantly changes, under the pressures which have taken us from a sense of wonder at the novelty of agreements which had seemed impossible to a bewilderment at the task of absorbing a veritable stream of such agreements. 'Bewilderment' is perhaps the wrong word, because their very multitude is prompting fresh critical appraisal. I will take two examples where this seems to have negative elements.

The first is the two Anglican–Lutheran 'local agreements', the *Concordat* arrived at between the Lutherans and the Episcopalians in the United States of America (LED) and the Porvoo Common Statement of the conversations between the British and Irish Anglican Churches and the Nordic and Baltic Lutheran Churches (1992). They are 'local' in that they respond to the special circumstances of the participating churches in the geographical areas they cover. But they deal with Church-dividing issues which are far from local, notably that of the way in which a mutually recognised ministry is to be arrived at. The two texts propose different solutions to the problem of the episcopate. The *Concordat* proposes a common ministry under parallel jurisdictions as an interim way forward; it suggests the temporary suspension of the Anglican requirement that all ministers should be episcopally ordained. The Porvoo statement attempts a different route, dealing as it does with a group of Lutheran churches some of which, for historical reasons, preserved the 'historic episcopate' while others did not. Its thrust is the attempt to argue that mutual recognition of churches as being in the apostolic succession as communities has theological priority over the laying on of hands in historic succession(53). These are both theologically creative routes.

But one goes the way of adjustment of the machinery, the other of taking a leap of faith. There has been a response to these two texts not only within the areas where they were framed[1] but between the two. From a 'methodological' point of view it is the second which is striking. Those involved in the framing of either text have a commitment to its solution which makes it hard for them to welcome that put forward in the other. But most importantly it is noticed, as it were, after the event, that the two commissions failed to work together as fully as they might, to exchange drafts systematically as they went along, and thus to keep completely in touch with one another's thinking. This is understandable under the pressures of time and above all in the excitement of making progress internally. But it contains a serious lesson about the importance of thinking 'universally' as well as 'locally' in all ecumenical conversations, because if both texts gained acceptance in their respective areas, the result would be the setting-up of new tensions between the linked churches thus created.

The second example is that of the *Clarifications* published by ARCIC II in 1993 in reply to the *Response* of the Vatican to *The Final Report* of ARCIC I. The point of departure of bilateral dialogue is the equality of the participants and the willingness on both sides to come together freely to talk, in openness to the outcome. That always becomes a reality for those actually involved in the conversations. It is harder to make it a reality for the participating churches as a whole. The ARCIC I Elucidations differ crucially from the new *Clarifications* in that whereas the first are a response to a variety of relatively informal preliminary reactions, the second are a reply to a formal *Response* by only one of the participating churches. It could be argued with hindsight that when ARCIC I's *Final Report* was referred to the Anglican and Roman Catholic Communions respectively (as was structurally the only way, for no common formal decision-making is possible within the existing machinery), it should have been done on a basis which assumed that 'we' were responding to what 'we' seemed to have agreed in the persons of the Commission's members. The reference to the two communions quite separately has created a situation in which Rome's *Response* sometimes seems to forget that *The Final Report* was not the work of Anglicans but of Anglicans and Roman Catholics together. It can be asked how helpful it was to make

---

[1] For example, in the correspondence in *The Tablet* between Christopher Hill and J. W. Hunwicke of December 1994 and January 1995.

the implicit explicit in terms of questions set up by one side only and with such narrow reference to their own particular confessional statements. In other words, adversariality has become a factor, with all its concomitant loadings of trade-off and sell-out. There is a danger that ARCIC will be seen to have departed from its rule of seeking to carry everyone with it by saying nothing with which all cannot feel at ease. There is also a problem of accessibility in the relatively technical character of the discussion.[2] This may alienate those who complain that ecumenical reports are not written for the whole body of the faithful. It is important to be both exact and easily understandable, and ARCIC I tried hard to be both. A further methodological 'slippage' seems to have occurred in the modes of 'getting behind' the old divisions employed here, as compared with those of ARCIC I.

These three things matter in a document published in a way which makes it a companion-piece to *The Final Report* and the Elucidations. They would look different in relation to a piece simply sent to the Vatican in response to its *Response*. There is a real difficulty here. The *Clarifications* simultaneously 'answers a letter' and 'publishes a correspondence'. It is important that the correspondence should be open. But it is likely to be difficult for many readers to understand the special character of what has been attempted here unless it is explained.

ARCIC I's text has gone further than any other down the line of 'continuing conversation in print'. The decision was made at an early stage not to revise but to 'elucidate' in a separate document. The *Clarifications* continue that policy. Cardinal Cassidy's letter asks for one further point to be tidied up. There will certainly be calls from other quarters for further comment.

But even for some of its critics the *Clarifications* seem paradoxically to have strengthened the real solid impact *The Final Report* has had. 'That report was a significant learning experience for many readers,' says Timothy Bradshaw, 'I can remember being struck by the transcending of reified notions of atonement and eucharistic offering in favour of the action of the living Christ in and through his Church.'[3]

A comprehensive review of the positive and the negative methodological lessons of the reception-process so far was attempted by the Sixth Forum on Bilateral Dialogues held at Bossey in Switzerland in October 1994. It was emphasised in the resulting *Report* that 'the

---

[2] On, for example, p. 7 of the *Clarifications* (1994).   [3] In an informal communication.

process of reception requires trust'(13). The negative elements in the two examples above arise in part from a sudden uncertainty about that trust. In particular they reflect concerns for fairness and consistency ('Some churches have felt that the churches with which they are in dialogue are saying contradictory things to different churches,' comments the Forum (III. I)); and for what might be called 'symmetry' or balance. Some 'asymmetry' is inevitable. 'For churches such as the Orthodox and Roman Catholics it is impossible to be in communion with churches that are in communion with others not in communion with them' (Forum, III.7). Disturbances like this of the confidence in which trust flourishes are the most worrying phenomenon of the modern process. But I think they do not need to worry us in the long term. There is a deeper security which it is reasonable to feel.

This is warmly expressed in the papal Encyclical *Ut unum sint* of May 1995, which marked a milestone stage in the commitment of the Roman Catholic Church to the ecumenical movement, at a time when it is especially important that that commitment be firm and clear. It made a powerful assertion of the centrality of the ecumenical endeavour; unity is taken to be of the *esse* of the Church. 'God wills the Church, because he wills unity, and unity is an expression of the whole depth of his *agape*'(9). There is a recognition that it will not necessarily come easily to all Christians to make an ecumenical commitment. They have to have their eyes opened, so that they can realise why it is not enough to live out the Christian life in separated communities. The new text sees this clearly as requiring a 'dialogue of conversion', in which not only must 'each individual . . . recognise his own faults, confess his sins and place himself in the hands of the One who is our intercessor before the Father, Jesus Christ', but also each community must do the same(82).

There is another aspect of the need for conversion. Conversion involves humility and repentance, the recognition that there have been wrongs, that 'people of both sides were to blame'(11). The problem of 'longstanding misgivings inherited from the past, and of mutual misunderstandings and prejudices' is acknowledged, and also the fact that 'complacency, indifference and insufficient knowledge of one another often make this situation worse'(2). The Encyclical calls for 'mutual forgiveness and reconciliation' within which it can become possible for separated communities 'to re-examine together their painful past and the hurt which that past regrettably continues to provoke even today'. The theme of 'purification of memories', which has been strong in Orthodox–Roman Catholic dialogue, is mentioned here(2).

What difference has ecumenical theology made?

Ecumenism is of its essence a group or community affair. As Jean Tillard puts it, 'We agree to be challenged by the other group and perhaps to be called to a change.'[4] This asks a great deal. Recently churches finding themselves thus challenged have been tending to shrink from the risks. Winning them to the confidence to venture is perhaps the most urgent ecumenical need. Pope Paul VI, at the second session of the Second Vatican Council, made the 'move' which all communities have to be able to make at the outset of this process, in acknowledging that there may have been fault on both sides. 'If we are in any way to blame for our separation we humbly beg God's forgiveness and ask pardon too of our brethren who feel themselves to have been injured by us.'[5] The process also demands a consciousness that the requirement of humility and repentance is not a once-and-for-all but a continuing imperative. Chapter II of the Vatican II Decree of Ecumenism says as much. There is a call to continual reformation in the context of ecumenical dialogue.

The hard nut to crack is proving to be agreement on the goal of unity. It is possible to argue that the Church is already invisibly united in Christ and that is enough. Or it may be said that the visible unity of mutual acceptance of baptism can be sufficient. But if the goal of unity is a Church which is able to act visibly as one Body, with a common ministry all can recognise and above all room for all to share in a common Eucharist, the structural difficulties bulk large. They show up uncomfortably again and again the fact that ecclesiology has been from the time of Paul and the Johannine Epistles, partly an ideal description of the Church – certainly one which can hope for full realisation only eschatologically. But that is no reason for not getting as close as possible to it now.

Solid progress has undoubtedly been made. It is now three decades since the opening of the Vatican Council which brought the Roman

---

[4] Jean Tillard, 'The ecclesiological implications of bilateral dialogue', *Journal of Ecumenical Studies*, 23 (1986), 4.

[5] Quoted by C. Hill, 'The Decree of Ecumenism: an Anglican view', *One in Christ*, 26 (1990), 20–31, p. 21. He adds 'The renewal of the Churches will go hand in hand with agreement on new expressions of truth and this will entail a certain sacrifice of imperfect and partisan formulations.'

Catholic Church wholeheartedly into the ecumenical movement and transformed the worldwide ecumenical scene. In those decades a great many conversations between churches have been visibly if only as yet partially successful. There is now a tidy stack of published reports and agreed statements to show for ecumenical efforts.

The real achievements are those which have altered assumptions and viewpoints. After Malines there was a sense of irreversible engagement, and it could be said that 'never again can representatives on either side approach the subject of Reunion in the spirit of cold and critical detachment which prevailed before the Malines Conversation took place'.[6] The fundamentals of ecumenical attitude laid down in earlier decades are solid still: 'To be ecumenical is to be open, unafraid to acknowledge differences and confess deficiencies, to be convinced that Christians belong together, at least in dialogue, rather than remaining alienated.'[7] The continuing encounter has been educative and has made it impossible to go on in old separate ways. 'Ecumenical . . . dialogue has forced theologians to be more cautious in the use of terms[8] . . ., to be more open to the insights of other traditions, and to rethink the presuppositions out of which one theologizes,' argues one commentator.[9]

As a result, we have genuinely stopped being suspicious of one another, for the most part. With a few exceptions, Christians no longer caricature one another as children of Antichrist, which was a way of expressing ultimate alienation from each other. It is more and more accepted that Christians share one faith. 'It is now inconceivable to promote the mission of the Church, particularly a Church resolved to renew itself and its spiritual resources, without that church becoming irreversibly involved in the pursuit of Christian unity.'[10] 'People are now talking to us as they do normally among themselves.'[11]

In this changed atmosphere, there can be a powerful drive to unity even before disagreements are resolved and formal schemes for unity

---

[6] Lord Halifax, *Notes on the Conversations at Malines, 1921–5. Points of Agreement* (London, 1928), p. 4.
[7] There must be no exploitation of inter-religious discussion for partisan advantage. Elwyn A. Smith, Editorial, *Journal of Ecumenical Studies*, 4 (1967), p. 300.
[8] 'Transubstantiation' is given as an example.
[9] He adds 'other causative factors, such as the rise of historical consciousness, the development of philosophical pluralism, the confrontation of the Church with the third world' as having contributed to these changes. Kenan B. Osborne, 'Contemporary understanding of the Eucharist', *Journal of Ecumenical Studies*, 13 (1976), 192–201, p. 195.
[10] Alan Clark, 'The growing point of unity', *One in Christ*, 15 (1979), 2–10, p. 3.
[11] M. Richards, 'Twenty-five years of Anglican–Roman Catholic dialogue – where do we go from here?', *One in Christ*, 18 (1992), 126–35, p. 127.

can be framed and implemented. Many have found that 'the experience of "being brethren" has been of such intensity that it has been and remains extremely difficult to direct and control'.[12] If all this has been happening, why do attempts at reunion made in good faith and with prayer often not succeed?[13] Congar was already asking the question in a climate of experience which had not yet shown how insistently it was to arise. Disappointments can seem to put ultimate success seriously in doubt. (With 'hopes dashed . . . the ecumenical movement appears to many to have lost its momentum and there is serious concern whether it can recover its lost momentum'.[14] Another commentator speaks of the 'frustration being experienced by many people who very enthusiastically joined in the movement towards Christian unity and who fail now to see realised the practical results for which they had so ardently hoped'.[15]) And they will make it necessary to ask whether we are ourselves to blame in any way. 'Current contempt . . . and rejection . . . should prompt those of us who feel a strong ecumenical commitment to ask whether we have made some theological or functional *faux pas* which seems to be leading, after early sensational accomplishments, to a sense of frustration and irrelevance.'[16] The prompting to ask 'what are we doing wrong?' is valuable all the way through the ecumenical exercise, not least because it encourages us to think hard about how we are doing it. And the harder it gets the more necessary that becomes.

I do not think present problems arise because ecumenical methodology has been wrong, but because the task is larger and more complex than it seemed at first, and allowance has to be made for the persistence of patterns of separation. We have failed to realise how long the natural time-scale must be. Let me quote again:

Schism and heresy are the fruit of impatience and violence. Reunion will be the fruit of long enduring patience.[17]

We have been slow to learn that failures as well as successes can mark progress. That has meant learning the hard way that hope is a

---

[12] Alan Clark, 'The growing point of unity', *One in Christ*, 15 (1979), 2–10, p. 5.
[13] Congar, *Divided Christendom*, p. 40.
[14] J. C. Murray, 'Ecumenism: the next step', *One in Christ*, 25 (1989), 162–8, p. 163.
[15] Edward Cassidy, 'The uphill ecumenical journey', *Catholic International* 2 (July 1991), p. 653.
[16] J. Miguez Bonino, 'Christian unity in search of locality', *Journal of Ecumenical Studies*, 6 (1969), 185–99.
[17] Congar adds 'absolute loyalty and' here, by which of course he does not mean partiality. Indeed he continues, 'and much gentleness and humility . . . reunion will come from . . . disinterestedness'. Congar, *Dialogue between Christians*, p. 174.

necessary virtue in the enterprise along with love and faith, and the acceptance that to some degree ecumenical methodology has to work blind, in trust that God will bring out of what has been happening solutions we cannot yet see. Fear, resentment and hopelessness are the three ecumenical vices which have to be conquered if we are to get anywhere. 'A great deal of truth is told in discussions and articles that lay bare the veritable abyss that separates human beings from each other. When such truth is set forward in the hope, however implicit, of finding one another, it is done ecumenically; when it is inspired by the conviction that separation is inevitable, final and even right, it is not ecumenical.'[18] 'In the ecumenical confrontation our claims and counter-claims will be challenged, disavowed, even contemptuously rejected as arrogant and incredible.'[19]

To speak in such terms is in itself to move into an applied theology, where the questions are not only, 'Is this true?' but also 'Does this bring unity about?'[20] I have been arguing in this study that we must above all be conscious of what we are doing and aware of the common pitfalls. It may be useful to summarise in conclusion the main lessons we can begin to learn from the study of recent practical experiments in a methodology of ecumenical theology. At the outset of its involvement in ecumenical endeavour, it has been natural for each existing church to take the view, at least to some degree, that it is itself the true Church, and that the best plan will be for other Christians to see this and join it. That was a pronounced feature of Roman Catholic thinking throughout the twentieth century until Vatican II.[21] Before Vatican II, in 1961, Heinrich Fries stated a key principle not easy to keep exactly in position in minds conditioned by centuries of suspicion to mistrust Rome's intentions. 'The reunion of divided Christianity in one Church, which will be Catholic, does not therefore simply mean submission to Rome or unconditional surrender. It

---

[18] Elwyn A. Smith, Editorial, *Journal of Ecumenical Studies*, 4 (1967), p. 300.
[19] G. Stephanopoulos, 'Denominational loyalties and ecumenical commitment: a personal view', *Journal of Ecumenical Studies*, 17 (1980), 626–46, p. 642.
[20] The issues of theory and practice, and of the claims of the imperative to seek unity against other calls on the Church, were explored at the beginning of this study. 'It seems to many, inside and outside the Church, that the struggle for Christian unity in its present form is irrelevant to the immediate crisis of our times. The Church, they say, should seek its unity through solidarity with those forces in modern life, such as the struggle for racial equality, which are drawing men more closely together, and should give up its concern with patching up its own internal disputes.' Report of Section 1 to the Uppsala Assembly of the WCC, quoted by James R. Kelly, 'Attitudes towards ecumenism: an empirical investigation', *Journal of Ecumenical Studies*, 9 (1972), 341–51, p. 342.   [21] See pp. 40ff.

means regaining the full and undivided faith that believes the Church as the one work of Jesus Christ, not the Church of the Pope, but Jesus Christ's Church.'[22] This is in fact a substantial move away from a 'return to Rome' stance, but that is not absolutely clear. The lurking fear that the success of the ecumenical endeavour will reveal itself to have been after all nothing but a path back to submission to one of the existing churches is incompatible with the confidence in equality on which all ecumenical trust must rest. But it is a powerful and lingering fear. The rule that unity cannot involve submission of any church to another, or its swallowing up into it, is now ecumenically well established. But while the exact relation of a future united Church to any existing church (and all existing churches in general) remains unclear, that fear will remain, and with it a sense of the 'otherness' of Christians who belong to the feared community. We find Orthodoxy envisaging a united Church which will result from the coming over of others to Orthodoxy.[23]

Over against the unsatisfactory model of 'submission', we have to set various other patterns of assumption which can help or hinder. It has been suggested that in the 1930s Europeans had a sense of a unity once given and now sundered (and therefore needing repair), and Americans a sense of a given pluralism requiring (perhaps) construction of an (eschatological) unity.[24] Whether that really applies so broadly or not, it can certainly be argued that there are two possible and opposed starting-points. The one experiences the Church as a natural unity now fragmented; the other as a natural diversity whose unity can be real but will remain invisible, or can be realised only in the life to come. Both pose ecumenical problems. The first suggests lasting grounds for resentment about the breakages. The second that we need not strive too hard to mend differences in this world. Both are to some degree implicitly adversarial. I have been arguing that both, if

---

[22] 'Die Einheit der Kirche nach katholischer Auffassung', *Oberrheinisches Pastoralblatt*, 62 (1961), p. 168.

[23] In 1968 at the World Council of Churches meeting at Uppsala 'the Orthodox participants held firmly to the bi-polar ecumenical principles which are essential to a sound ecumenism: one principle is that Christian unity is rooted and expressed primarily in the one Apostolic faith and that disunity derives ultimately from a departure [from] or distortion of the unalterable sources of Revelation; the other principle is that the goal of the ecumenical movement is the unity of all Christians in the living *Una Sancta* which has never been lost but which *exists substantially in* the historic Orthodox communion.' R. G. Stephanopoulos, 'Reflections on Orthodox ecumenical directions after Uppsala', *Journal of Ecumenical Studies*, 9 (1972), p. 302. Cf. the 'subsistit in' of Vatican II.

[24] D. Bonhoeffer, *No Rusty Swords: Letters, Lectures and Notes 1928–36* (New York, 1963), pp. 86–118.

turned round to face the other way, are ecumenically necessary. The Church is both a natural unity and a natural diversity. But these are complementary not rival aspects of its being.

Let me take up once more another quotation from the end of the last chapter:

> My denomination must grow less in my eyes if I am to grow more towards Christ. I am willing that my denomination shall be forgotten if thereby may be hastened the unity of the Church of our Lord. That denomination is most prophetic that is willing to disappear for Christ's sake – to go to its disappearance as deliberately as Christ went to his crucifixion.[25]

The lesson here is that we must learn much more thoroughly what it means to accept the ecclesial equality of other churches. The implications are full of paradoxes. We have to abandon adversariality for convergence. We have to be ready both to change, and to respect others as they are. We have to see that we may have been wrong and acknowledge that others have been right. We have to trust one another and to take risks with our own ecclesial identities. We have to be open to the Holy Spirit's prompting, which may take us anywhere, and at the same time work patiently on the existing structures so as to learn how to share them. The most testing problem here is the lack of any authority common to the churches which would enable them to decide and to act together. The discrepancy between real and ideal is a continuing challenge to accept the reality while pressing forward towards the ideal.

These are the essential preliminaries to the learning to do theology together which is the distinguishing feature of ecumenical theology, together with the search for a wholeness to replace one-sidedness, to make the talking round the common table a meeting at the Lord's Table.

---

[25] Peter Ainslie, Disciples of Christ, *Faith and Order, Proceedings of the World Conference, Lausanne, August 3–21, 1927* (London, 1927), p. 343.

Index